African American Cultural Theory and Heritage
Series Editor: William C. Banfield

D0782724

Art, by definition, says, this is beautiful and this is valuable. Black arts expressions depict Black people as beautiful and their story as valuable.

—Nelle Painter, *Creating Black Americans*

It is the philosophy of Negro music that is important, and this philosophy is only partially the result of the sociological disposition of the Negro in America. . . . [B]ut all these attitudes are continuous parts of the historical and cultural biography of the Negro as it existed and developed since there was a Negro in America, and a music that could be associated with him that did not exist anywhere in the world. The notes mean something; and the something is regardless of its stylistic considerations, part of the black psyche as it dictates the various forms of Negro culture.

—Amiri Baraka, *Black Music*

For us, the questions should be . . . what in our backgrounds is worth preserving or abandoning. . . . [Folklore] offers the first drawings of any group's character. . . . It describes those rites, manners, customs, and so forth, which insure the good life, or destroy it; and it describes those boundaries of feeling, thought, and action which that particular group has found to be the limitation of the human condition. It projects this wisdom in symbols which express the group's will to survive; it embodies those values by which the group lives and dies. . . . [These symbols] represent the group's attempt to humanize the world.

—Ralph Ellison, "The Art of Fiction"

It remains for the Negro intellectual to create his own philosophy and to bring the facts of the cultural history in focus with the cultural practices of the present. In advanced societies, it is not race politicians or the rights leaders who create the new ideas and the new images of life and man. That role belongs to the artists and intellectuals of each generation.

—Harold Cruse, *The Crisis of the Negro Intellectual*

The young Black writers of the Black ghetto have set out in search of a Black aesthetic, a system of isolating and evaluating the artistic works of Black people which reflect the special character and imperatives of Black experience.

—Hoyt W. Fuller, "Towards a Black Aesthetic," *The Black Aesthetic*

If this country can't find its way to a human path . . . conduct a deeper sense of life . . . all of us are going down the same drain. Humbly now with no vaulting dream of achieving a vast unity . . . I wanted to try to build a bridge of words between me and the world outside . . . hurl words into darkness and wait for an echo, and if an echo sounded . . . I would send other words to tell, to march, to fight, to create a sense of the hunger for life that gnaws in us all, to keep alive in our hearts a sense of the inescapable human.

—Richard Wright, *Black Boy*

The Good Lord in the spirit had to send something down to the peoples, to help ease the worried mind, and this is where the music comes in, working what you trying to do, what you strivin' for to help give you a vision of a brighter day, wherever ahead, to get your mind off of what you were dealing with right now. They used this song, talking about the woman being so mean, "she take all my money."

They are talking about the boss man. They had to give the message under cover, 'cause you can't come out and say it or they's find you up in the tree hanging the next morning. The blues is just survival, "it's a healer," as John Lee Hooker would say.

—An interviewed bluesman, from *Martin Scorsese Presents the Blues/A Musical Journey*

Black music can be seen as a function, and to some extent, a cause of a peculiarly Black ontology. Thus the investigation of Black music is also the investigation of the Black mind, the Black social orientation and primarily, the Black culture. . . . The first Black solo musician on the scene was the blues singer. . . . These musicians composed their own songs, based for the first time on secular problems of the Black individual. . . . The musician is the document . . . the information itself. The impact of stored information is transmitted not through records or archives, but through the human response of life. And that response is ongoing, in the air, everywhere, an alternative constantly available to those who have ears to hear.

—Ben Sidran, *Black Talk*

On the basis of what we have done in the past, and the basis of how we do it, I'm calling on my people to reach back one more time and come out with a mojo, and the brer rabbit. What we need now is a new way to be Black, a new way to apply all that we've learned from the past. . . . But as time goes by, we will pick up the beat. We will catch the keynote, then we'll put our instruments to our lips and add to a symphony and I'm sure our addition will change the whole thing for the better. I can't wait to be as Black in the 21st century as I was in the 20th.

—Ossie Davis, *Unstoppable: Conversations with Melvin Van Peebles, Gordon Parks, and Ossie Davis*

What are these songs, and what do they mean? I know these songs are the articulate message of the slave to the world.

—W. E. B. Du Bois, *The Souls of Black Folk*

I think the main thing a musician would like to do is to give a picture to the listener of the many wonderful things he knows of and senses in the universe. That's what music is to me.

—John Coltrane, in Ken Burns's *Jazz*

From the days of chattel slavery until today, the concept of travel has been inseparably linked in the minds of our people with the concept of freedom. Hence the symbol of a railroad train occurs frequently in our folklore in spirituals and gospel songs, in blues and ballads, and the train is usually bound for glory and headed for the promised land. And there are boats too, like the old ship of Zion, and the Old Ark that will take us over the waters to freedom and salvation.

—Paul Robeson, *Here I Stand*

It is clear to me from looking for an African world view that music exists because it does something. It never is the art for art's sake kind of phenomenon. If it doesn't make it rain, if it doesn't infuse herbs with a healing spirit, then what good is a song? Quincy Jones asks, "What good is a song if it doesn't inspire, if it has no message to bring? If a song doesn't take you higher, higher, higher, what good is it to sing?" Because of how music is so integrated to every aspect of life activity for African people, I started asking how that applies for black people. It applies totally. We can see how our music has evolved and at every point that our history has taken another turn, our music has taken another turn. That to me is evidence of music's functionality. Then when you start to look at what the music says and how it was created and how it is used, it is totally clear that we have never dropped that aspect of who we are as African people.

—Dr. Ysaye Barnwell, quoted in William Banfield, *Black Notes: Essays of a Musician Writing in a Post-Album Age*

Cultural Codes

Makings of a Black Music Philosophy:
An Interpretive History from Spirituals to Hip Hop

William C. Banfield

African American Cultural Theory and Heritage

THE SCARECROW PRESS INC.
Lanham • Toronto • Plymouth, UK
2010

Published by Scarecrow Press, Inc.
A wholly owned subsidary of The Rowman & Littlefield Publishing Group, Inc.
4501 Forbes Boulevard, Suite 200, Lanham, Maryland 20706
http://www.scarecrowpress.com

Estover Road, Plymouth PL6 7PY, United Kingdom

British Library Cataloguing in Publication Information Available

Library of Congress Cataloging-in-Publication Data
Banfield, William C., 1961–
 Cultural codes : makings of a Black music philosophy : an interpretive history from
spirituals to hip hop / William C. Banfield.
   p. cm. — (African American cultural theory and heritage)
 Includes bibliographical references and index.
 ISBN 978-0-8108-7286-8 (pbk. : alk. paper) — ISBN 978-0-8108-7287-5 (ebook)
 1. African Americans—Music—History and criticism. 2. Popular music—United
States—History and criticism. I. Title.
 ML3479.B364 2010
 780.89'96073—dc22   2009036698

∞ ™ The paper used in this publication meets the minimum requirements of
American National Standard for Information Sciences—Permanence of Paper
for Printed Library Materials, ANSI/NISO Z39.48-1992.

Printed in the United States of America

Contents

Preface

One of my mentors, the late great scholar and teacher Harold Cruse, told me, "You've got to deal with it [our art, Black music culture] and explain it . . . you have to attempt to explain its implications. . . . We need you!"

I have tried to live up to Cruse's charge ever since. No matter how far my own creative work tries to forge ahead, it will always be coupled with that charge. My own ideas and hopes for art and expression are intertwined with my attempts to define Black music culture as a universal expression. In my second book, *Black Notes: Essays of a Musician Writing in a Post-Album Age*, I focused on the shift from what was "old school" in music to what I call a "post-album age," where musical practices in the popular marketplace are today. Arguing for a foundational cultural theory, the book also issued a "Hold on, wait a minute!" call. In that book, I included a mixed bag of my articles, newspaper columns, radio show transcripts, and interviews of leading artists, as well as essays and poems. This book differs. Here, I offer a focused examination of the historical development of Black music artistry. My goal is to discover and to articulate a useable philosophy tied to how music is made, shaped, and functions. No culture over time has existed without a belief system to underpin and sustain it. No art can survive without an understanding of and dedication to the values and vision of its creators. It's time then to engage in conversations about our cultural codes, a philosophy.

I believe this kind of exploration keeps us grounded in a rich musical past and answers the dilemmas we face today about what we value. Such a view guides our discussions as we create and make choices about where we are headed. What is being done to address our codes of creativity? Art is a critical part of our social consciousness, and culture is about how we live in the world. This book is about creative Black artistry and its impact on shaping modern culture and society. The focus is on the artistry of music. I will share ideas about Black music culture from three angles: history, education, and the creative work of musicians. I use art and music interchangeably as creative ideas, codes that inform much and deeply.

I hope you enjoy these ideas.

> Even though few recognized it, such artists as Ellington and Louis Armstrong were the stewards of our vaunted American optimism and guardians against the creeping irrationality which ever plagues our form of society. They created great entertainment, but for them (ironically) and for us (unconsciously) their music was a rejection of . . . chaos. . . . [Ellington was one of the] masters of that which is most enduring in the human enterprise; the power of man to define himself against the ravages of time through artistic style.
>
> —Ralph Ellison, "Homage to Duke Ellington,"
> *Washington, D.C.*, *Sunday Star*, April 27, 1969

> James Baldwin said it best in a 1962 interview. "Artists are here to shake people up, to disturb the peace." He was talking about the need to shake people up, to make them aware of the burning issues of American society, especially of those of race and class. But I want to push Baldwin a bit further here by arguing that we are called upon to be artists. As students, teachers, composers, performers, observers of nature, as citizens of the larger world, we all have to be dedicated to disturbing the false peace of complacency, of the status quo, of looking for and listening for only this expected, predictable surfaces of music and life.
>
> —Walter Harp

Acknowledgments

Special thanks to Dr. Camille Colatosti for her editing and help with the completion of this huge undertaking.

Thanks, Ed. Thanks, Stephen!

For all musicians, and for all students and lovers of this great artistry and incredible history and culture.

Lord, what must I do to become clear? Clarity is a form of salvation.

PART I

A CULTURAL CHARGE

Sunday Morning Jubilee. *Acrylic on canvas by Emily Russell*

CHAPTER ONE

Black Notes and Cultural Codes: Makings of a Black Music Philosophy

My parallel is always the music, because all the strategies of the art are there. . . . Music makes you hungry for more of it. . . . It slaps and it embraces; music is the mirror that gives me necessary clarity. . . . The literature ought to do the same thing.

—Toni Morrison, quoted in Paul Gilroy, *Small Acts*[1]

Aim

How does a culture stand, define itself, and be? And how does it see and sustain itself and keep on moving?

Artistic vision embodied in a work of art has the power to lift us to quintessential expressions, questions, and spirit. Art celebrates and ennobles viewers/hearers to move toward an order of the soul and society, and to sustain the ideas for such living. Art does this as it projects and propels images, ideas, and questions that both delight and make demands of us. We need the artists; we depend on their pictures and perceptions of the world. Without them, market forces take over, unchecked. Today's cultural codes, as they play out in the marketplace, warrant support for and instruct us in a value system that is based on sensory gratification, getting "things," entertainment, automation, commodification, and fixation on speed or "on-demand delivery." An aesthetic vision that helps us understand art today, while primarily defining and sustaining great artistic work, is critical to clear our consciousness and illuminate a better way.

Such thinking is about articulating the codes for what defines and sustains. In addition to the importance of social, political, educational, and economic strategies, American culture could not exist without a consistent, coherent, and connected plan of expression from artists. Now, more than ever, we need vision, song, consistent groove, and expression from the artistic community. In the history of Black ideas, no movement has been successful without the imprint of the consciousness and soul led by artists. An exploration of the history of Black music conceptions is critical to the exploration and definition of a Black music aesthetic.

In play here is the work of James Brown, Paul Robeson, and Bessie Smith, in the African griot traditions; the intellectual sophistication of the Harlem Renaissance, with the work of Langston Hughes and Zora Neale Hurston; the radical social/aesthetic politics of the Black Arts movement and others that followed. All of these gave us maps on a journey through art, identity, culture, and lives of Black people, and these were essential to defining human existence in modern culture.

As I mentioned in the preface, this book addresses very specific ideas about traditions of Black music culture as these relate to what the music expresses and its importance: the makings of a Black music philosophy. The potential of a useable philosophy can be tied to how music is made, shaped, and functions. Such a philosophy, it is hoped, will inform interpretive listening, cultural critique, teaching, scholarship, and most importantly how we understand these cultural codes. No culture over time has survived without a belief system to underpin and sustain it. No art can survive without an underpinning of and dedication to the values envisioned by its creators. It's time, then, to engage in conversations about our cultural codes. Artists, speak up and out about what *we* are, what *we* see, how *we* sound and feel, what *we* can hear, and how *we* are moved. Black music culture is an art form of ideas and ideals which are spiritual, cultural, intellectual, and aesthetic. It is also a form of social-political human language. This music exemplifies being human, creative, and steeped in the multiple meanings of freedom.

A philosophy should help us interpret and live in our world. Arts are an outgrowth of philosophical contemplation. In other words, a philosophy of art helps us realize and understand experiences of human creative expression. Such contemplation cannot be understood by a single interpretation, but surely art is always connected to tenets of collected beliefs representing heard, felt, and lived experiences. The philosophy that I am presenting merges Black culture studies and Black music studies. It is that long pass of mobilization, cultural creation, and consciousness through artistic ideas that ground lives, protect and project being, and sustain culture and identity.

Let's be clear. There is a danger here. Some might perceive that I am suggesting restrictive, prescriptive frameworks that direct or define art agendas. But this danger is insignificant compared to the way that, over the last fifteen years or more, Black popular music in particular has been commodified by the commercial monster. Examining an aesthetic, engaging in dialogues to explore artistic philosophy and illuminate Black music's rich valued history, is timely and needed—now more than ever.

My entire premise rests upon an understanding and a conviction that an interpretation of our society can be viewed through the lens of the work of creative artists. Peeling back the layers of that meaning within the contexts of a developing modernity reveals an infinite amount of information about the reciprocal relationship between music and society.

The impact of Black popular music and artistry on modern life is unparalleled. My goal is to map and measure the meanings of the songs and history of the people. Music is my meaning—full measure.

The Journey

As a Black musician, I repeatedly ask myself, what is happening to Black music? What is happening in American culture and society? Market forces disrupt the value streams that sustain us and tear at the possibilities of how people see themselves. How and why is this happening? For those who create, teach, produce, and advocate for the importance, beauty, and necessity of artistic expression, our histories and our walks within culture, the ideas about our musical-cultural narrative are essential.

People who look to artistic expression and culture see the world according to what music and culture suggest about our living conditions. New ideas are always needed, and a revisit of our rich past moving swiftly to inform our present is critical. In this moment, the meaning of one's art is not simply driven as a response to current politics, missing spirituality, or social chaos. Music is always the sounding of humans' experience in real living time. Your music is your voice, what your heart hopes and what your mind has responded to—expressed in tones, rhythms, and accents.

The question an artist raises at different crossroads in life is, "What is the meaning of my art now as I live, participating in the world in which I am living?" Few artists throughout time have missed an opportunity to address this question. I am one who as well believes in the power of creative artistry to inspire hope, greatness, and a spirit that changes people and ideologies, and critiques and challenges. At this moment, I believe in the humanity of music. I have come to this after years of being a musician and realizing that, at the end of the day, what matters most to people about music is that they are moved, transformed even by the experience of it. This politics of artistic action, implicit in the values of Black artistry, has never been absent from Black music. Voice, cadence, riffing, blues form, improvisation, collective improvisation, rhythm, flow, free expression, free styling, groove, pocket—all of these are musical words that define a Black aesthetic, performative and living.

It is clear to me for reasons that will be examined in this book that we need to revisit the cultural codes that critically define what our music, our art, could become. Music has become such "bigger business," inextricably attached to the entertainment and media industries. This drives and determines cultural shifts and mindsets that are now solely defined by commercial profit. So much of the thinking that moves the world is determined by greed and profit, at all costs. This affects the total cultural environment. This is not new, of course, but the "choking techniques" are different now than in the past, and more and more of us have become strangled and suffocated.

Criteria for a Black aesthetic and philosophy should address meaning and define the values, reception, interpretation, and function of our art. But these criteria must address performance as well. How do artists effectively and meaningfully capture, construct, and represent these values and codes, and then artistically perform them? What will be the shape of our music to come? It is also important to discuss why it is necessary to address such questions.

Every generation of artists carried, created, and cultivated important values that produced its life and culture. Music has been for Black people an expression of various sets of ideas (spirituals, blues, jazz, gospel, rock and roll, r&b, reggae, soul, and hip hop). Musical ideas allow people to formulate worlds of meanings. These inform and inspire people about the kind of living they are doing in the world. It is important that singers, instrumentalists, composers, poets, even producers—all artists—be informed about the effect and potential of their work in the public market.

As a musician and educator interested in the work of musical artists, I see music as a body of expressive ideas that is both produced for and influenced by social and human needs. I see music as art that grows from cultural experiences, experiences heard in notes and sounds, experiences that help us understand the life that we are living. Music comforts, confronts, and accompanies us in our social reality.

Given the profound relationship that everyday people have with music in its many forms, wouldn't it be great if they knew about the origin and history of the music that they listen to and identify with? If artists and the people—consumers of music, the listening audience—were involved in a reciprocal dialogue about what matters in this sounding, this would result in a worthwhile philosophy, a useable quest for truths.

Commercial culture actually disrupts and corrupts artistic value codes. Market gain, superficial posing, and mass production run counter to interpersonal skills, sensitivity, individuality, deep expression, and originality. Today, the contemporary macrocultural dislodging of key codes about music is troubling. Younger musicians must consider a range of pressing questions about how their music is defined by the pervasiveness of market forces, image representation, oversaturation of sexuality in lyrics, improper downloading of artists' work, advertising lockdown on the media machine, the influence and legitimacy of media network boosts like *American Idol*, branding (from clothes to watches to foods and other products), and the seductive lure of this culture's materialistic gadgetism. All of these forces in our culture impact the creative world of an artist.

A Historical Picture: The Birth of the Codes

One of the leading artistic strands in our history is Black music culture. Beginning with the spirituals, Black music specifically is the only modern music/culture tradition created by slaves, former slaves, and their grandchildren and great-grandchildren. Spirituals provided language that defined the experience and expression of freedom. Musicians were saying, "I'm a slave, in bondage and humiliated, but I'm going to use my voice in song to free my soul, liberate me, and ensure a hope in my destiny." That language became a powerful performing music, which became the grand root form of much music to follow. Musicians consciously developed performance techniques and conventions to actualize the sound of this form, and it was culturally coded.

The figure of the West African griot is another critical component of that singer, storyteller, values carrier, tradition setter, genealogist, performer, and artist who defined many of the frameworks by which a community participated in ritual. This is huge and formidable. Black artists throughout the diaspora defined their performance approaches, and they set the patterns on one kind of freedom, a spiritual-based music. The spirituals transformed into a more mobile form used by roaming singer/poets looking for the right to live free, and that music, the blues, accompanied that quest. These Black music traditions expanded, combined with music from other cultural and regional traditions, and mobilized, growing into a larger tradition that included ragtime, gospel, swing, bebop, rhythm and blues, rock and roll, free jazz, Afro-Caribbean artistry, reggae, soul, and hip hop. All represent Black creative freedom, expression, and innovations, which were disseminated, culturalized, interpreted, and then consumed as popular culture. This music is tied to ways of thinking, looking, being, and working in the world creatively. This is the ideas stream we swim in when we talk about music culture, codes, and their implications. These concerns extend to newer forms of traditional jazz, gospel, blues, concert, and roots music expressions. Black music culture is a great example of a mix of multiple influences which extend toward and flow through continents. This global resonance has become a fertile place for many to find common ground. This music empowers people to demand voice and agency.

Black music exemplifies an incredible quest of the human spirit. A creative act, a performance practice, can inspire people and lift them toward freedom on several levels. To groove, swing, and funk means to be able to live grounded and free. It was only after James Brown's death that I began really to remember what his song "Say It Loud—I'm Black and I'm Proud" meant to me as a youth. I lived in the feeling of that music's meaning. Music liberates when you are especially submerged in doubt due to the lack of worth assigned to you in this world. The music/culture can again point you toward the way out of that negativity, that blue cloud. It can do this because it was created to connect to your human worth, your value as a living being. That's why you feel it, that's why the music matters, because it connects and operates within the "inner domain," the inwardness of your human mind-soul-spirit makeup.

All of these ideas have been served by and within the history of Black expressiveness, and have been created within a social and cultural history that is inextricably bound up in these meanings. "Let freedom ring" and "It don't mean a thing, if it ain't got that swing" become examples of the meaning of the Black beat in the world. Political speech and song lyric together belong to the expressive culture that so powerfully connects numerous discussions about the totality of the human condition: universal, transcendent, multicultural, global—this is a music of engagement, an inclusive, participatory art.

Many statements in Black music—like "Before I'll be a slave, I'll be buried in my grave," "What did I do to be so Black and blue?" and "Don't push me 'cause I'm close to the edge, I'm trying not to lose my head"—speak more about how we pose the questions of life than about anything within the music. As composer-aesthetician George Lewis wrote, "For bebop musicians, the music had more to do with the assertion of self-determination with regards to their role as artists." According to Lewis, "it created new possibilities for the construction of an African American improvisitive musicality that could define itself as explicitly experimental, a direct challenge to the social order applied to Blacks in the 1940's."[2]

Because of its West African cultural roots, steeped in function, meaning, spirituality, craft, and skillful execution, the music rarely operates in ways outside of all these meanings—even if the creators, participants, consumers, educational system, and cultural apparatus of the recording industry miss it. These traditions are a great example of what it means to sing a song that changes the way people live in the world. My primary interest in Black music culture is how this music continues to be a model, example, and map, fully equipped with a history, peoples, movements of ideas, and establishment of styles, as well as an aesthetic, intellectual, and poetic enterprise that stands out as monumental in human culture. This is the larger focus of this book.

The practical application for a musician is that the music we make is grounded solidly in foundational culture. It's grounded in focused, expressive work that can imbue artists with a sense of integrity that shapes the way they think, perform, appreciate, and share their gifts. The connections between music-making and music-meaning, and an understanding of how those meanings touch and affect people's lives, have to do with the connections among artists, performers, composers, and historical contexts.

This book's focus on cultural codes provides a connective coherence among the meaning, relevance, practice, and culture of Black music and education in contemporary society. In this tradition, human expression provided a reality, a song, a dance, and a polemic that transfixed its performers and transformed the rest of the world, due primarily to its depth of conviction and meaning. All of these expressions throughout the African and Black diaspora—from Cuba to New Orleans, from Jamaica to Detroit, from Mississippi to London, and back again to Brazil—focus on the human reality to aspire and fight for the freedom to be spiritual, intellectual, artistic, and socially-politically mechanized for meaning and being in the world.

Cultural Codes

"Cultural Codes" are defined here as sets of principles, representations, practices, and conventions understood to be embraced by an artistic community. These are cultural, ideological inscriptions of meanings conceived, created and constructed, and then projected by performances which suggest that certain ways of being, thinking, looking, and styling are normative, preferable, and validated. They are reflective of ideas, and they project powerful images and imaginings that are sustaining and impressionable. Because these codes set patterns of particular paradigms for how people think, behave, and then as well define their roles, their rationale, worldviews, and value systems, some critical questions at this time come into play:

- Who is writing the codes?
- What is contained in the codes?
- Who carries the codes?
- How are the codes disseminated?

These information blocks, the cultural codes, are consciously, and sometimes unconsciously, constructed. The construction, deconstruction, evaluation, and critique of culture are essential. Paramount are the musician, the artistry and the music, the culture, and our dialogue about meanings, practices, and the impact on life.

One could argue that the main engines that should drive a Black music philosophy are:

- The social, cultural, aesthetic, performance history of the music.
- The unique artistry and musical movements.
- The social themes: freedom, equality, identity, finding "voice," empowerment, and cultural preservation.
- Cultural image construction, cultural rituals, and the public dissemination of expressions of Black culture.

It is hoped that this framework may be suggestive and provide helpful themes for the exploration of Black music culture, a "school of thought" where musicians and artists' ideas are at the center. It is also hoped that people are illuminated and moved by these reflections, expressions—these codes.

CHAPTER TWO

A New Black Music Arts Aesthetic

The driving posture of this project rests largely on the ideas of establishing a philosophy that underlines the sustenance, relevance, existence, and continuation of Black music. As we begin to examine a history of ideas that provide the foundation for a Black arts aesthetic, it is important as an overall view to begin with where we are today. No generation of dancers, singers, musicians, or other artists ever left out of the equation a definition of being an artist or adhering to a shared definition of an aesthetic.

There is a most alarming shift in our current cultural debates: for the first time in African American history, our codes of Black culture are being set and argued pervasively by a business-constructed identity. Consequently, too many of today's youth are being sold an identity, a posturing poisoned by attitudes and behavioral codes constructed by business people who pose as "artists" or by industry producers selling this prison culture gangsterism and anti-establishment, anti-education, pseudo socially conscious ranting that is paraded as having "meaning."

In the past, artists, intellectuals, and educators took on the direct responsibility of making sure young people were educated as they performed, created, argued, and persuaded that art was for the good of the soul. Our "rap poets" in the public youth movements not only run laughingly from once believed ideas about Black beauty, but also constantly muse about their right to be brutal and belligerent. This has become a recognizable pattern of behavior and associations. As Bakari Kitwana writes in *The Hip Hop Generation: Young Blacks and the Crisis in African American Culture,*

> Understanding the new crises in African American culture that have come about in my generation's [born between 1965–1984] lifetime (high rates of suicide and imprisonment, police brutality, the generation gap, the war of the sexes, Blacks selling Black self-hatred as entertainment, among others), I often wonder what life will be like for the generation of African Americans that follows. What will be our contribution to the centuries-long African American struggle for liberation, and how do we redefine the struggle for our time? Our generation of African Americans must come to grips with the damage we do to ourselves in popular culture (rap lyrics and 'hood films) and in everyday life (inadequate parenting, resentment filled interpersonal relationships, and inferior educational performance), which stands counter to traditional ideas of Blackness.[1]

In this most profound and real statement, we can see that a new youth culture has emerged and is culturally, socially, and aesthetically defined. Kitwana poses the question here, how will history judge this time, and our work and life in it? Is our work suggestive in a young generation of artistry of new worlds of expression, and can this work point toward progressive future paths?

The Black intelligentsia in literature and cultural studies (Henry Louis Gates Jr., Cornel West, bell hooks, Michael Eric Dyson, among others) have done an extraordinary job carving out a resonating place for the role of literature and Afro-American Studies. Their books, CDs, documentaries, academic programs, and radio and television appearances have made Gates, West, and others public intellectuals and recognizable figures. Their important work has helped shape the image of the Black thinker. *Race Matters*, by Cornel West, has defined the discourse about race in America.

Yet, why is there no contemporary music text that rises to mind, one that everybody would know of and refer to, that excites serious debate and engagement about why Black music and art matter? Black music academics have failed to provide the competitive and imaginative texts that engage the aesthetic and cultural issues that we face. VH1 and MTV "old school" specials help, but these are like museum visits, in which television viewers curiously examine old burned-out relics from the past. These specials do not foster a real appreciation and knowledge of music. Nor should they. That kind of analysis needs to be undertaken by academics, by music historians, by experts in the field of Black music culture. It's crystal clear: we have to consciously move ahead and rewrite our cultural codes as they relate to Black music.

As Harold Cruse famously advocated in his chapter "Cultural Leadership and Cultural Democracy": "In advanced societies, it is not the race politicians or the 'rights' leaders who create the ideas and the new images of life and man. That role belongs to the artists and the intellectuals of each generation."[2] Paul Gilroy, in *The Black Atlantic*, argues further, calling music the gift that provided "an enhanced mode of communication beyond the power of words."[3] In this same writing, he quotes Edourd Glissant, who states, "It is nothing new to declare that for us, music, gesture, dance are forms of communication, just as important as speech." This is how we managed to emerge from the plantation: aesthetic form in our culture must be shaped from these oral structures.

Hip hop, as one form of contemporary Black aesthetic expression, must factor into this equation as we define the Black music aesthetic today. There are certainly enough arguments aligning hip hop as Black music. There is no doubt that each generation owns the right to define its aesthetic values. I am not taking an anti-youth stance nor attacking hip hop aesthetics, and besides, much of the work of defining a hip hop generation mainstream aesthetic has been done. Hip hop is not only a musical form but a mindset that occupies the thinking among many in the global community. But I want to point out what is missing from the discussion. Lacking is a philosophy that connects hip hop to the past, that guides the traditional line of Black art from the center looking out and around, historically and projecting beyond, informed by the now.

This book stands as both an examination and exploration of constructing current art stances that serve concrete and universal application. This work is about Black music cultural expression and history, and about the role and function of creative expression, the arts, connecting as well to the larger understanding of artistic expression and engagement. This creates another cycle of conversations that perhaps suggest philosophical threads necessary to challenge art/music made as corporate commodities constructed by a selfish, greedy, and profit-driven commercial mechanism.

As Cornel West has stated, "Artists ask the courageous question, what does it mean to be human? Artists wrestle with the cultivation of what it could be to be alive. So, what kind of human being are you trying to be as you are being an artist, and coming up with a sophisticated form and expression of music?"[4]

Defining Your Terms: What Do People Today Believe In?

Arts represent the who-ness of experiences in the world. How do people make meaningful statements about their culture, making and marking their progress through living? How do people value their history, and use history to help them understand what they believe in and why? How are these values represented through artistic expressions? These among a host of others are important questions poised in history that are most profound and engaging, and they may be as well foundational in pointing to a philosophy that guides the meaning of art today. A Black aesthetic in this discussion is defined as a philosophy of Black beauty and being in music, art, and literature. What is the thinking behind this creative work? The aesthetic defines art's shape, ideology, what it feels like to be "in it." The aesthetic is concerned with appreciation, discrimination, value, the historical-cultural line of conception, the common practices and conventions, as well as what is believed to be "the good," how the art is formed craftfully and performed, how the art is recreated and taught. An aesthetic helps to guide how to be in and informed by the meanings and the relevance of creative work. Related in importance is how the artists define and respond to culture.

Culture is defined by the social institutions created as well as the intellectual and artistic manifestations that characterize a group or society woven into a web of meanings, values, and significance. An examination of a culture and a philosophy, then, studies the products and processes of culture, human work, and thought within a given society and in a given time. Culture is inclusive of ethnicity, nationhood, creative enterprises and practices (e.g., jazz music), creative sites such as a museum, human rituals (church service, football game, jazz club jam), artifacts (songs, a doll, a magazine). Culture is also behavioral tendencies; laws, rules, and ideologies that govern us; stories, mythologies, and legends that give expression to beliefs, aspirations, and perceptions. All of these then serve to explain cultural/social phenomena or the origins of people.

What then are the central debates in Black culture? For example, how are the issues of identity formation, power, values, spirituality, definitions of America, definitions of womanhood/manhood, race, class, gender, and ethnicity dealt with, explored, expressed? How are these themes presented, and then worked out, in our daily life practice? How are they heard in our historical narratives, media, popular culture and TV, politics, and policy? How are those central themes then contained and accounted for in a song, poem, play, movie?

What is the role of art (e.g., music, sculpture, literature/poetry, dance) in shaping and carrying ideas about our culture and values? Who are some of the central figures who have shaped this identity, and how do these constructed icons send messages about what our citizenry and identity is?

Music provides an appropriate framing for many of these themes: individual, cultural, and collective identity, gender exploration, voice and agency, narrative of human experience, contesting of power, construction of symbols, and advocacy of a utopian or better society.

Music is an expression that carries social and cultural consciousness. Folk and vernacular expressions carry the national, ethnic "soul" and common story narratives of people—the folks. Spirituals represent freedom, spiritual and religious expression of the African American slave experience. The blues represent uninhibited sincerity, Black folk narratives illumining the dark clouds of real anxiety and complexity, then laughing at it, philosophizing about it, while singing a resolution in a flexible creative form that's useable and artistic. Jazz represents American urbanization of popular music, highly developed, an expressive Black folk art form, individuality, innovation and free expression through the mechanism of improvisation, a Black refined way of music-izing. Protest and soul movements in music represent social consciousness of the civil rights era. Rock and rap represent youth culture and rebellion against perceived and real human restrictions and oppression expressed musically. American popular music—in particular blues, jazz, Afro-Cuban, Afro-Latin, rock, and folk—best exemplify a melding of cultural influences, and impulses. They are authentic American narratives and myths, expressions, rituals, and values, supported by American music industry and popular culture practices.

We can perhaps go further in a functional angle to see that music is:

1. A transport into various dimensions of the soul and psyche, tapping into how we feel about our present, past, future, and memory.
2. A form of social protest.
3. A vehicle of moral reasoning and expression of religious or faith stances.
4. A vehicle of identity formation.
5. A cultural ritual, and a celebration in community.
6. An artistic, aesthetic expression, representation of an agreed upon excellence.
7. A cultural commodity, by itself and in partnership with film, dance, literature, and visual arts.

Hop Ain't Hip without the Music

What happened to our music in popular culture markets? Apart from who the current artists are and what the music means and carries, the critical question is, what is the music in today's "music"? What happened to Black popular music? Black mainstream commercial music (blues, jazz, gospel, r&b, reggae, urban contemporary, Afro-Caribbean pop) used to be music made and performed by musicians. It is sad to say that the generations coming up as consumers in the public marketplace were not brought up on a music culture that is centered in music made by musicians for the purpose of being music. Post-1990, we have been living in what I have termed a post-album age.

To define what Black music is and when its codes of definition were initially set, you have to look closely at music history, culture, and artistry (see part III). For many musicians who grew up in the public school system in decades past, these codes, standards for music and excellence, were set and disseminated by trained, serious, and dedicated music teachers. Artistry requires focus, dedication, integrity, and commitment, all of which need to be strongly cultivated. A musician has a skill to perform or create on a musical instrument; the musician's work—organized through pitches, harmonies, forms, and songs—expresses humanity and creative gifting. We have to ask, today, what do people hear in the music marketplace when they are responding to what they like and value musically?

Criterion for Growing an Aesthetic

> Culture is the basis of all ideas, images and actions. To move is to move culturally, i.e., by a set of ideas given to you by your culture.
>
> —Maulana Karenga, *Introduction to Black Studies*

The evidence of a culture using its collective, creative, and intellectual capital throughout time to mark triumphs and struggles within the living narrative is something to note and cherish. Equally compelling is an attempt to read culture as one clear interpretative map of where the impulses of meaning came from and out of, pointing to what could lie ahead in terms of cultural forecasts, new expressive forms, and new dynamics which guard against downward spirals. As a place to start, using our educational and cultural analytical tools to measure some lived outcomes is one way to make sense of what is witnessed every day in communities. As Maulana Karenga in his *Introduction to Black Studies* points out, "From its inception, Black Studies has had both an academic and social thrust and mission." There has always been as well, from W. E. B. Du Bois onward, a real attempt to merge the consciousness of contemporary living by real people with thinking and developments that were intellectual in design and focus. Given the breadth and importance of such ideas, a Black arts philosophy in music should:

1. Grow out of the mind and work of artists in creative response to the collective reflections and needs of a culture.
2. Be made known in the culture through media, writings, festivals, gallery openings, a happening that is a public witness to these expressions.
3. Express as excitement a commitment that is always a brew driven by passionate beliefs, a conviction to ideas, values, and the art which embodies ideals expressed artistically.
4. Be based on musical (artistic) skills and the desire to use those skills to express one's art.
5. Have an understanding and appreciation for form, and execution of it. This is indicative of a serious focused mind where creative expression and excellence are valued.
6. Be interested in the development and continuation of sound, image, movement, and ideas of what are being made. (This may seem obvious, but in a commodified megaculture, so many of our definitions are shaped by product, and produced on demand quickly.)
7. Be active in listening to and studying art forms.
8. Be active in enjoying the "doing" of music/art, hearing it, seeing it, and dancing it, having pride in it. You've got to believe in it and have a passion for it to sustain it. A Black aesthetic should be grounded, invested in the future development and continued activities for the education in culture, cultural production, and preservation.
9. Have a knowledge and be active in continuing the path of virtuosity as seen in Art Tatum, Oscar Peterson, Charlie Parker, Dorothy Donegan, Ray Charles, Nat King Cole, John Coltrane, Donny Hathaway, Jimi Hendrix, Aretha Franklin, Stanley Clarke, Stevie Wonder, Patrice Rushen, Prince, Kenny Kirkland, Stanley Jordan, Me'shell Ndegéocello, Wynton Marsalis, Joshua Redman.
10. Extend these definitions, expressions, and applications to the Black community, public, and society at large so that people, too, are affected, moved, and reflectively defined by such ideas, outlooks, and expressions. Black arts must always be for the betterment and uplift of people and the society we live and participate in.

Looking toward the Artists

Writing in his *Traditions of Studying Urban Youth Culture*, Greg Dimitriadis notes,

> Grounded aesthetics is the way young people subvert dominant music and fashion industries by using their products in new and different ways. The omnipresent cultural media of the electronics age provide a wide range of symbolic resources for, and are a powerful stimulant of, the symbolic work and creativity of young people. . . . But whilst the media invite certain interpretations, young people have not only learnt the codes, to reshape forms, interrelate the media through their own grounded aesthetics. They add to and develop new meanings from given ones.[5]

There are a few figures most recently that strike at exemplifying what is meant by artists who represent and work within "grounded aesthetics" that mirror attention to craft and social commitments where attitude, meaning, and music/art combine. All of this points to firmly held beliefs that support the art, style, rhetoric, and ultimately artistic performance codes of artists like Jean-Michel Basquiat (1960–1988), Wynton Marsalis (b. 1961), Kurt Cobain (1967–1994), Erykah Badu (b. 1971). Their sounds and representations ignited other artists and the generation of their times: Basquiat—out of the consciousness of the late 1970s and early 1980s bohemian New York, hip hop, and graffiti arts; Marsalis—the burgeoning aesthetic renaissance in jazz in the early 1980s; Cobain's redefinition of rock in the 1990s; and Badu as one of the leading lights of the new soul movement of the 1990s. All represent conscious expressions which defined ideas about the meaning of their arts, their society, and a loyal audience base.

Basquiat, more than the others, cuts across music, meanings, and shapes with an aesthetic that significantly defined his voice. His artistry is something of a mix of avant-garde graffiti hip hop meets Jackson Pollock, shaped by Picasso, flavored significantly with the tragic inner pain and twisted imagery of Frida Kahlo, and brushes of the bold cartooned poignancy of a Romare Bearden. Basquiat played in a band named Gray. He may be one of the last Black image artists who represents the merging of a populist aesthetic, bubbling with the youth dynamics of social protests, yet resonating as both iconic and anti-commercial simultaneously. Basquiat's work connects to other aesthetic movements of rage and rebellion from 1950s bohemia, to Warhol's pop art, to punk, grunge, and hip hop. His aesthetic claimed urban landscapes, clothes and fashions, arrested originality, and individual voice, yet it was Afrocentric and anti-establishment. His SAMO moniker and philosophy held, "SAMO as new art form. . . . SAMO as an end to mind wash religion, nowhere politics, and bogus philosophy. . . . SAMO as an escape clause. SAMO as an expression spiritual love. . . . SAMO as an end to confining art terms. Riding around in daddy's convertible trust fund company."[6]

It is hard to say whether Basquiat, with such a short life, represented a youthful adherence to older socialist, bohemian rhetoric or a fully worked out aesthetic philosophy. But what is clear is that the expression of his art work mirrors in design an attention to his craft as an artist, linked within themes, commitment, and a consistency that resonate throughout his dynamic work as a painter of striking originality.

If original voice, looks, sound, and the convicted meaning in artists' work defines art with impact, I find the tracing of the griot throughout the development of Black music performing history to be the most compelling and helpful image for artists to understand Black music. If we look back to the opening of the twentieth century, we see that several major shifts took place: American popular culture rose in prominence and was used to define American identity; artists nurtured and carried that new sentiment—identity; and improvisation was the new expressive staple, a soloist's art of invention, individuality, expressiveness, and lively rhythm. By the mid-1920s, all of these attributes were defined by the young griot, Louis Armstrong.

Many passionately wrote about these changes in music culture, and their writings were widely disseminated to readers to recognize the importance and value of these cultural shifts. J. Kinnard, in 1845, put it this way:

> Who are our true rulers? The Negro poets to be sure. Do they not set the fashion, and give laws to the public taste? Let one of them in the swamps of the Carolinas compose a new song, and it no sooner reaches the ear of a white amateur, than it is written down, amended (that is almost spoilt), printed, then put upon a course of rapid dissemination. Meanwhile, the poor author digs away with his hoe, utterly ignorant of his greatness.[7]

In 1893, Antonin Dvořák noted the influence of Black music on all music: "The future of this country must be founded on what are called the Negro melodies. They are American and your composers must turn to them."[8] In 1919, Irving Berlin noted, "Ragtime represents the snap and speed of American life." In 1918, Ernst-Alexandre Ansermet stated, "I am inclined to think that the strongest manifestation of the racial genius lies in the Blues." And he noted, "Their form is gripping, abrupt, harsh with a brusque and pitiless ending like that of Bach's Second Brandenburg concerto." Praising Sidney

Bechet, he added, "he follows his 'own way' . . . perhaps his 'own way' is the highway along which the whole world will swing tomorrow."[9]

In 1939, Leonard Bernstein argued in his Harvard thesis for a new and vital American nationalism, claiming the Negro had created a new music. As he wrote,

> Negro Jazz, Negro Music, Negro Art, Negro melodic peculiarities, Negro scale variants, Negro poignancy, special Negro flavor, Negro timbre, Negro singing voice, Negro character, Negro species of melodic syncopation, Negro rhythmic patterns, Negro tone color, Negro manner, Negro harmonies and the Negro scale. The greatest single racial influence upon American music as a whole has been the Negro.[10]

"These people, these Negroes" were having a significant imprint on the development of modern musical culture. Because of this impact, this art imprint, people began to listen to and to think about music in new ways. The cultural force that ushered in this new way of hearing in the world was Black music. And, as Gerald Early stated, "If Black people had done nothing else, but the creation of the blues . . . it would have made them a *seminally* important people in the shaping of the modern world."[11]

These ideas shaped human destiny. The longest lasting cultural force next to love is music. To be involved in creating music in this way is an awesome thing.

Wrestling with a Black Aesthetic in Contemporary Living

> "Brothers and sisters, my text this morning is the 'Blackness of Black-ness.'" And a congregation of voices answered: "That blackness is most black, brother, most black . . . there was blackness . . . Preach it . . . Amen, brother . . . Black will git you . . . Preach it, dear brother. Good God a-mighty! Old Aunt Nelly! Black will make you . . . or black will un-make you. . . . Ain't it the truth, Lawd?"
>
> —Ralph Ellison, *Invisible Man*

Art and education are ennobling tools to help people attain clarity. Certainly, now is needed an artistic thinking, being, and action which pulls together artists, educators, and community leaders of this generation, including those old enough to "know." Today's prevailing early millennium commercial Black aesthetic seems to be a prescription delivered not by artists but by Hollywood culture for cash and commerce. It is based on and defined by popular market forces and not artistic expression. No art approach that is based solely on commercialism can serve nor survive. Today, it is necessary to talk pointedly among artists about a well-defined, purposeful aesthetic that draws deeply from the past, forcibly from the present, and actively projecting a future. If Black expression is to maintain its roots in artistic excellence, then there needs to be a pulse-taking, an assessment and a critique. In *The Jazz Trope*, Alfonso Hawkins powerfully states:

> The encoding of the African American music expression inspired the vision with which the slave could look "beyond the horizon" into the promise and the possibility of freedom. That same consciousness linked post reconstruction blacks through their "slave gifts of musical manifestation," seeking to overcome the psychic piecemeal of racial tolerance. It is in this climate that true democracy is tested . . . the American plight and journey circumventing restriction, because music is a healing force and universal language that connects human feeling, suffering, aspiration and the desire to be free. . . . I attempt to show how historically the music has maintained African American spirit to rise in the face of doubt and reservation. It was the unsuspecting notion that talking about or singing the blues is the answer to its antithesis. The encoded message behind the spiritual gave divine prayers to a mortal reality. And jazz, an active assertion of will, grit and endeavor . . . blindly assertive, looks for creative, non-traditional means of living and devising ways how to live.[12]

To the generational question of who defines all this now, Samuel Floyd states, "The Harlem Renaissance was a youth movement, despite the ages of the leaders such as W. E. B. Du Bois and James Weldon Johnson. Most of the writers, artists and musicians were in their twenties during the Harlem Renaissance."[13] Today's youth, our most popular artists and musicians, need not simply move to be famous or to make money, but to lead us. We may need to encourage leadership by facilitating an understanding of the artistic codes that have shaped them, and that they, too, are shaping.

CHAPTER THREE

A History of Aesthetic Definitions

The earlier presentation of criteria and the concerns for what should drive and guide cultural codes, a Black aesthetic, have not grown absent from nor outside of a flowering of these kinds of ideas in our history. There are five critical musical periods that define a map for a Black music/art aesthetic: the Harlem Renaissance, the bebop era, the soul movement, the Black Arts movement, and most recently, hip hop. All of these music periods were defined largely by Black artists who raised key questions about America, the destiny of Black people in America, and how their art connected, consti-tuted, communicated, and contained the work, identity, and lives of Black people. Equally pervasive was this music on the shaping of American cultural values and codes.

While the Harlem Renaissance, the bebop era, the soul movement, and the Black Arts movement are thick with social-political and aesthetic divides, including those that defined Black music according to a "White aesthetic and reasoning" (especially during the Harlem Renaissance), the outward and inward resonance was that this work shone with the meaning of Black life and ideas. These movements have not only provided us with an incredible body of work (music, poetry, writings, scholarship, sculpture, and more); they have also defined a Black aesthetic. While these were multiple disciplinary actions, music provided a consistent and public front, perhaps because music is more accessible and easily marketed to the wider general public than are some other art forms.

It is Black music that flowers most publicly. The soul movement is an example. To some extent, Coltrane, Sun Ra, the Art Ensemble of Chicago, Albert Ayler, Max Roach, Mingus, and others in forward and socially vocal jazz found a space to speak in radio, records, and dialogue with critics. While the Harlem Renaissance created the first true, multivoiced discipline statements, it is somewhat problematic due to the sacrifice of a specifically Black criterion of expression and experience. The often heard commentary that this movement was White-backed and agenda-ed is easy to understand. It took Langston Hughes's helpful essay "The Negro Artist and the Racial Mountain," and the subsequent publication of the short-lived magazine *Fire!!*, to begin to allow that generation to break away and articulate a Black arts agenda.

Most notable were the writers of the Black Arts movement, who—like their Harlem Renaissance predecessors Alain Locke, Zora Neale Hurston, Langston Hughes—created a body of writing that truly reflected an indigenous art politic and Black aesthetic. Hip hop, for all its problems, is the first publicly marketed stance in nearly forty years which reflects Black identity and purpose. And while some argue this is only an old-school strength, this goal of articulating a meaning in contemporary Black life has been at the core of hip hop rhetoric since its inception, just as it was at the core of the slave holler, spirituals, blues, bebop, gospel, soul, funk, and all Black expressions, really. A short view of these movements reveals much about the conscious construction and expression of Black aesthetic philosophy tied to creative expression and social-cultural condition. The first four musical periods—the Harlem Renaissance, bebop, soul, and Black Arts—are discussed in this chapter. Hip hop is examined in chapter 4.

The Harlem Renaissance Remix: New York 1920–1929

> America, seeking a new spiritual expansion and artistic maturity, trying to found an American Literature, a national art and national music implies a Negro-American culture seeking the same satisfaction and objectives.
>
> —Alain Locke, *The New Negro*, 1925

The idea of a collective, identifiable Black aesthetic, as an ideology, a movement, first saw its American manifestation during the Harlem Renaissance. The 1920s were a decade of extraordinary creativity in the arts among African Americans largely focused in Harlem, New York, marking a brilliant time in American history and a defining time for African American identity. W. E. B. Du Bois, the leading intellectual of the day, believed racial progress was to be made through mainstream achievement. In his editorial work with *Crisis Magazine*, the official journal of the National Association for the Advancement of Colored People (NAACP), he promoted "excellence in business, education, and the arts." This period showed an unprecedented thrust in American creativity, cultural activity in the arts of poetry, dance, painting, music, and theater. The primary goal was to express a new social-cultural awakening needed to diffuse racial stagnation imposed by racial hatred of Blacks in White America. This was a search for the face of a new dignity focused on upward mobility and cultural achievement.

The New Negro, edited by Alain Locke in 1925, became the manifesto of the movement. It chronicled Black writers, artists, thinkers, and social commentary; it named the New Negro movement, the Harlem Renaissance, and the New Renaissance. The book's purpose was to "register the transformations of the inner and outer life of the Negro in America that have so significantly taken place." Locke called this a "Spiritual Emancipation, grasping for group expression and self-realization."

Aligning the Harlem Renaissance with the American ideals of uniqueness of voice, freedom, and uplift, Locke envisioned an important American moment and a chance for integration of two worlds: White and Black. More than 200,000 Blacks served in War World I; between 1920 and 1925, nearly 2 million Blacks moved North, fleeing Jim Crow, segregation, and lynching, and searching for economic and cultural betterment. The Black population in major cities like New York and Chicago quadrupled in size. In short, Blacks were no longer in isolation. This generated an economic, social, and cultural energy that supported the idea of a new birth.

The migration North began around 1905, and was really spurred on by the ideology of "race men," those who advocated racial uplift based on making visible the social-cultural-intellectual mobility of Blacks. "Economic nationalism" was exemplified by Philip A. Payton and the Afro-American (AA) Realty Company, a Black-owned business. Payton as well as T. Thomas Fortune, editor of the influential Black newspaper *New York Age*, were connected to Booker T. Washington and his National Negro Business League founded in 1900. The AA Realty Co. bought and leased buildings, and progressively placed Negro families. While they folded, they did initiate a wave of purchases among other Blacks who could afford homes. This created a buzz that Harlem was the new Black mecca, the Negro capital of the world. Harlem became the home of the most pervasive cultural and social institutions for Black people: the NAACP, National Urban League, Marcus Garvey's

Universal Negro Improvement Association, newspapers and journals such as *Crisis, Messenger,* and *Negro Word.*

Three forces were at work: (1) economic nationalism, (2) migration of southern and international Blacks, and (3) a buzz within the artistic-intellectual community that fostered this huge cultural springing. The work could be thought of as modernism, the avant garde, but it was saturated with racial feelings of pride, expression, dignity, upward mobility, socially laying the foundation for a representation of Black people in the modern world, a new definition of Blackness, and the first Black public outcry for the importance of Africa as a cultural home. Locke, in particular, studied African arts and connected Picasso, Georges Braque, and Cubism with African aesthetics. White patronage helped to support the movement. William E. Harmon, a wealthy real estate developer, established the Harmon Foundation to provide Negro Achievement Awards. Charlotte Osgood Mason as well as publishers Knopf, Macmillan, Harcourt, Brace, and Harper House published literary works.

The era produced dozens of young progressive artists, writers, musicians, and thinkers who defined the period: Augusta Savage, Palmer Hayden, Richmond Barthé, Aaron Douglas, Archibald Motley Jr., W. H. Johnson, Melvin Gray Johnson, Claude McKay, Zora Neale Hurston, Jean Toomer, Arna Bontemps, Langston Hughes, Countee Cullen, Duke Ellington, Louis Armstrong, Eubie Blake, William Grant Still, Marian Anderson, Paul Robeson, among others. This was singly the most concrete and enduring arts movement in American history. Musically, Harlem was home to great Black musicians and popular styles. James P. Johnson, the great stride and ragtime pianist, created the piece "Charleston," which became a national dance fad. Thomas "Fats" Waller, Eubie Blake, Lucky Roberts, Willie "The Lion" Smith all became "total orchestra" pianists, playing clubs and "rent parties" and creating a style known as stride piano of Harlem. Harlem's Cotton Club was where Duke Ellington got a regular radio hookup and became a national star. He also appeared in films, including the 1935 short feature *Symphony in Black*, the first time a Black artist was presented in the mainstream media as a thinking artist and not merely an entertainer. In total, we had the formation of what was termed "the New Negro." Black people, having come to New York, created this new community. It was cosmopolitism and international. It simultaneously participated with and recreated parts of a larger American culture. This was linked to the conscious creation and backing of a Black intelligentsia whose major concerns were racial and cultural uplift, and the creation of art: the codes of cultural conception. From this came the establishment of a largely held Black American aesthetic steeped in social-cultural awareness, if not cultural criticism; it was a mobilization of ideas, criteria, and standards of excellence as well as definitions of beauty—a true American arts movement that shaped everything that was to come after.

Bebop and Being: The Formation of Music with Political Mind

> The Music proclaimed our identity; it made every statement we truly wanted to make. . . . The role of music goes hand in hand with social reformation—the changing of society to make things right. . . . What we were doing at Minton's was playing seriously, creating a new dialogue among ourselves, blending our ideas into a new style of music. Musically we were changing the way that we spoke to reflect the way we felt. . . . Our music had a new accent.
>
> —Dizzy Gillespie, *To Be or Not to Bop*

While all of the periods mentioned provide incredibly rich and foundational ideas for the discussion of Black aesthetics historically, no period better exemplifies the setting of codes directly and consciously by musicians than the classic bebop period (1940–1949). The first commercial recording was available in 1945, and the continuation of hard bop went into the early 1960s. Here are true Black musician codes. These codes are deeply rooted in the blues and in Black cultural and functional roots worked out for Black people (although along came the gaze of White critics, lovers of the music, cultural spies, and thrill seekers) in a Black club context, by musicians again who believed their music was an extension of a Black movement of ideas, values, critique, and worldview. Most importantly the musicians made bebop as "Black music." These bebop performance conventions were experiments shaked, baked, and disseminated into the wider culture. These expressions in music, slang, dress, language, style, approach, philosophy, and worldview, along with a defiant stance, set standards and defined the codes for what the modern Black artist should be. Dizzy Gillespie's famous autobiography was named *To Be or Not to Bop*. The bebop period defined modern urban musicianship and again set the standard of what a modern, progressive Black musician was to be. This music was deeply embedded into the musical and oral consciousness of Black cultural traditions. Musicians held high standards, and the expectation of virtuosity at all levels was the preferred normalcy.

Caution should be considered here not to overly romanticize or mythologize every aspect of this, as it was a difficult time socially for these musicians. This lifestyle, highlighted to cult "code status," led to habitually late hours and drug abuse. Despite this, every generation of musicians since, even rock and rollers, recognize the important contributions the beboppers made to American music. Charlie Parker, Dizzy Gillespie, and Thelonious Monk have become icons of everything artistically productive, ingenious, and revered. If we look at the music, aesthetics, and social-political ideas, we see the centrality of the conscious posturing, creations, and aspirations that defined what this generation of young musicians were writing as their bebop codes.

Sarah Vaughan, Dizzy Gillespie, Charlie Parker, Oscar Pettiford, Kenny Clarke, Thelonious Monk, J. J. Johnson, Art Blakey, Billy Eckstine, Charlie Christian, Budd Powell, and Mary Lou Williams were all great young musicians who discovered and then set the codes for the greatest musicians movement in our history to date. Mary Lou Williams stated it this way: "If we are to make progress in modern music . . . we must be willing and able to open our minds to new ideas and developments." As bebop drummer Kenny Clarke said, "The idea was to wake up, look around you, here's something to do, an integral part of your cultural aspect."

Charlie Parker, one of the architects of the style which blended Kansas City blues with a melodic, harmonic, and rhythmic wizardry not matched since, mused philosophically, "They teach you there's a boundary line in music, but there's no boundary line in art. Music is your own experience, your thoughts, your wisdom. If you don't live it, it won't come out of your horn."[1]

A bit more of a musical discussion here is important, helpful, and needed to outline the musical, inventive aspect of contributions which were so completely transformative and yet embodied the best of Black American forms already in practice in the public marketplace, on records, on the radio, and in dance halls, clubs, and churches. The beboppers gave us these new music codes:

1. They created a new modern language for jazz, a new vocabulary. They are responsible for "modernizing" jazz. (While jazz was already a "Black invention," they went deeper due to their insistence that commercial White musicians were monopolizing a Black form. They made jazz "mo-deeper Black and in-depth.")

2. They introduced the idea of the Black artistic genius in music and the notion of the musician as a "harmonic scientist," an inventor, experimenter, and not just an entertainer.

3. They extended the depth and range of popular music vocabulary. Beboppers brought into the popular imagination that this Black music was art. The beboppers held onto the idea that music was not only for

entertainment. Music was for listening and appreciating the artistry. This helped to create the first listening fan base for a jazz-record-buying public.

4. They created a culture of the "hepster," hip language and dress, and they projected in the musical/social sense a characteristic flare, humor, wit, wise-guy kind of language, laughing at the establishment. Yet in this they were serious, with a wide view of the world.

5. They were the first generation of social critics who publicly spoke out as musicians and artists against racism, fascism, and the restrictive business and corporate model.

6. They transformed and extended the Black improvisational model created largely by New Orleans musicians and perfected by Louis Armstrong. Big-band soloists in the 1930s and 1940s largely based their improvisations on sweet melodies, but the beboppers' solos were based on a conscious reworking and knowledge of the harmonic chord changes that the melodies came out of or rested on the top of. Again, these were improvisation experiments that went deeper to make a better, more sustained Black music art form.

7. They took old jazz standard songs and rewrote them with "hipper" chord changes and titles and altered melodies. They "sampled" the older music in real-life ways and reformulated them with modern beats. For example, Gershwin's "I Got Rhythm" became Charlie "Yard Bird" Parker's "Anthropology"; the jazz standard "How High the Moon" became Parker's "Ornithology"; "Back Home Again in Indiana" became "Donna Lee." In this harmonic aspect of recoding, beboppers composed "dislocated," humorous, and characteristically angular-shaped melodies. They altered the harmonic vocabulary by emphasizing flatted fifths, tritone substitutions, half-step chromatic melodies, and tonalities. They used what are called upper chord extensions, flatted fifth, altered seventh, ninth, eleventh, and thirteenth polychords, and these upper extended harmonies gave the soloists more "running room." This gave the soloists more expressive options and provided a more dense sonority for the "hipper," more inventive melodies and the bebop sound.

The tempos, the speeds, of the bebop songs were faster. This fostered more interest and emphasis on listening to the music as art and not entertainment. The dominant rhythm that set the pattern for the new language was the triplet figure and the two clipped eighth notes (long short). This is one reason they called the music bebop: *da, dadada, da, da, dadada, be-bop.*

8. They redesigned and expanded the function of the interplay and support within the ensemble (piano, bass, drums, horns) by replacing the piano's more full two-handed approach of ragtime or stride—a 1920s Harlem house-party invention—with a jagged left hand they called "comping." This allowed the right hand to take on more of a soloist role, doubling melodies and embellishing melodic materials of the songs. Pianists began to use a sparse ensemble-connected accompaniment. This created more space for the rhythm section to interact, and this changed the function among the ensemble in ways that heightened the interconnectedness of the unit but also allowed greater artistic support individually for the players.

   In bebop, the bass player lays down a more supportive, fuller harmonic rhythm, more moving, connected, and constant eighth notes, highlighting the complex tones as well of the newer harmonies. The role of the drummer changed also, a change largely believed to be introduced by drummer Kenny Clarke. The drummer changed the time-keeping role of the high hat from the New Orleans and swing band format of the 1930s, to "riding" the ride cymbal, the bass drum, and snare accents to react more freely to the group soloists. Bebop drummers used something they called "dropping bombs" with the bass drum to highlight more expressive moments based on the freedom of what musicians play in real time, and not restricted just to providing a steady beat for dancing. This revolutionized the role of the rhythm section as a separate dynamic unit that is artistic, sympathetic, supportive, and reactionary, a call and response unit with the lead solo player and each other. This creates a new musical dynamic within the music, an interrelated, connected, listening dynamic.

9. Socially and culturally, this bebop movement in the 1940s gave Black musicians a new identity as free-thinking artists in society. Bebop became symbolic of a serious, politicized creativity, the emergence of the figure of the modern jazzman as a defiant, alternative thinker in postwar America. This came to be inextricably bound with a larger movement of Black social-political assertiveness and helped to crystallize a visible leadership model that had constructive implications for the civil rights ideas and movements all over the country.

The death of bebop understandably coincides with shifts in Black and national needs, and with some economic and social realities. The move to r&b and pop music styles was better suited to returning servicemen who were focused on love, family, and building the new postwar economy. Bebop maintained a New York cultural-based identity which did not translate to a majority of Black urban centers, where church music, r&b, and blues were embraced. The urbane, slick, New York model gave way to r&b identities and sounds. But bebop music here, too, shaped everything that was to come from it during the decades of the 1950s through 1970s. It is even the grandfather of hip hop phrasing and posturing, as we will see in chapter 4.

Finding Your Soul and the Meaning of the Note

> The soul era, in particular, was a productive period for Black Americans. The music created by Blacks and for Blacks during this era communicated a general philosophy of refusal to accept the undesirable and a determination to create a better future.
>
> —Portia Maultsby, *Soul Music*

Soul music was a movement, a musical style, and an approach to life that incorporated ideology, spirit, and political consciousness. It is a great illustration of music and social-cultural codes combined. The important music period of soul, 1965–1975, represented for Black people and artists cultural and political empowerment, a musical and style category, spirituality and expression, depth and meaning, race pride and civic responsibility. These ideas were articulated in the concepts of soul music and the slang the music generated: soul brother, having soul, soul food, soul hair, singing with soul, and getting down to the soul of the matter. Authenticity, image, and identity were the dominant expressive and creative themes. In this turbulent period in American history, music sought to uphold a social consciousness about race, class, women's rights, police brutality, civil rights, integration, and antiwar protests. Black music and artists were seen as agents for social change, and they paved the way for Black people to enter mainstream American culture. Most importantly, Black American music was no longer a fringe race music but was "charting" on music stations nationwide. By the 1970s, Black artists were on the major rosters at CBS, Warner, Polydor, Columbia, RCA, and Epic.

The civil rights era erupted in America, and for Black people the music was a direct expression of political concerns. The defining elements of the Black music aesthetic, functionality, and meaning come together. Spirituals, blues, gospel, r&b, instrumental facility, training, technique, innovative artistry, international recognition, appreciation, and the power of a relevant social dynamic now defined the aesthetic. The soul music period included artists such as James Brown, Aretha Franklin, Nina Simone, Earth, Wind &

Fire, Al Green, the Staple Singers, Otis Redding, the Supremes, the Jackson Five, and Parliament Funkadelic.

This period of music production most succinctly mirrored what Black people, and America, were thinking and feeling about living in this culture. The music was inextricably bound to the way people were living. The issues, concerns, worldviews, political perspectives, styles, and social customs were embedded and carried by the music. The simultaneous explosion of Black identity and America's acceptance of this presence could be seen, felt, and heard in volume. The American model of hard work, dreams, and cultural productivity was imaged in Black American music culture in the creation of Motown Records. This record label set new image and visual standards in terms of making Black artists visually palatable and acceptable in "mainstream America" and certainly articulated the codes for Black popular culture.

Black Arts Movement Moving Me "Mad"

The young writers of the black ghetto have set out in search of a black aesthetic, a system of isolating and evaluating the artistic works of black people which reflect the special character and imperatives of black experience.

—Hoyt W. Fuller, "Toward a Black Aesthetic"

The Black artist takes this to mean that his primary duty is to speak to the spiritual and cultural needs of Black people. Therefore the main thrust of this new breed of contemporary writers [artists] is to confront the contradictions arising out of the Black man's experience in the racist West. . . . Implicit in this re-evaluation is the need to develop a "Black aesthetic." We advocate a cultural revolution in art and ideas.

—Larry Neal, The Black Arts Movement

The fact that we are Black is our ultimate reality.

—Maulana Karenga

The Black Arts movement, often referred to as the artistic wing of the Black Power movement, was a radical uprising of young Black artists and thinkers. Overlapping in time with the soul movement, the Black Arts movement came together in 1965 and broke apart in 1975–1976. Its leaders raised up the idea of a Black Arts aesthetic movement to address the conditions of

Black people principally living in U.S. cites in the turbulent civil rights years. This movement, unlike soul, was completely driven by artists living largely on the outside of the mainstream, artists who set the agendas and specifically meant to create a political and "movement" art. Yet, in many ways, these artists were more "inside" the lives, consciousness, and concerns of everyday Black people, hoping to survive equally culturally, politically, and socially. For this group, everything began with the arts. No other movement had the simultaneous politically and ideologically driven manifestos, icons, and grassroots support wrapped around its aesthetic as did the Black Arts movement. Black Power, Black nationalism, and even off-to-the-side but critical, the Black Muslims, with the important symbol of Malcolm X, all helped to crystallize, focus, and energize a Black aesthetic, as artists tuned into the thinking of Black radicals and art for the people.

Although ideas among the leaders of the Black Arts movement varied about what Black people needed to survive, the artists were united in their focus and concern, and in believing that they had an obligation to lift up the community. While the artists of the Black Arts movement focused principally on life for Blacks in the United States, they also looked at the Black diaspora, and especially at Blacks in Cuba, the Caribbean, and Africa. This diasporic aspect and definition of "Black" is as critical now as it was then. Even Black artists outside of the Black Arts movement, like Romare Bearden, were influenced by Black Arts. Bearden's collages, for instance, combined street scenes, music images, and the beauty of Black folks—angled, pasted, and painted objects that were repositioned, redefined, and rethought. All this raised questions about value systems, integration. and the meaning of melding into America. An artist as widely accepted as poet Gwendolyn Brooks invited to her home such young Black Arts poets as Haki Madhubuti, Sonia Sanchez, and Nikki Giovanni to discuss the state of Black people and what needed to be addressed and done.

The Black Arts movement in its more radical formation was guided by the theoretical approach and ideas articulated in Addison Gayle's 1971 *The Black Aesthetic.* The writers collected in that volume examined the codes that were growing forcibly out of the 1960s uprising of Black Power and Black nationalism. They focused on art as a concrete expression of sets of political and cultural principles. Their main hope, as seen in the quotations opening this section, was that the literary, musical, and visual works of Black artists should be politically engaged and socially uplifting, that artists' aesthetic and ethical beliefs should be connected. In Hoyt W. Fuller's words, the poetic work stood in for the "collective consciousness of Black people, a part of the real impulse of the Black Power movement and a 'real re-ordering' of the nature and function of both art and the artist."[2]

These ideas further flowered in numerous movements across the country as well as on college campuses. Black Arts groups formed in cities like Detroit, Chicago, and St. Louis, and on the campuses of San Francisco State College, Fisk, Howard, and the University of Michigan among others. The Black Arts movement was further codified in a more cohesive cultural ideology by Maulana Karenga, who defined seven criteria: mythology, history, social organization, political organization, economic origination, creativity, and ethos. All of this was under a larger social umbrella of "Black consciousness," a concern and connectedness about the consequences of people of African descent having to now define their destiny.

Jazz resonated and created a counterindustry movement and a consciousness as well. Archie Shepp created the work *Fire Music*. Musicians formed cooperatives such as the Jazz Composers Guild in New York, the Black Artist Group (BAG), the Association for the Advancement of Creative Musicians (AACM) in Chicago. The Art Ensemble of Chicago, which grew out of the AACM, called its work Great Black Music when forming in 1965. For the first time since the early twentieth century, there was an all-Black-owned recording company, Black Swan Records. Blacks were independently involved in creating, producing, distributing, and booking their own music.

The founding of the AACM was in May 1965. This ensemble, political, and musical group tried to adhere to principles of Black Power while they trained younger musicians. They led clinics, performances, and concerts where musicians upheld the principles and ideas of the AACM. When we get to Anthony Braxton, a member of the AACM, we see a real attempt to experiment. This is the Black intellectual avant garde. Braxton brought Black vernacular culture to the experimental framework. The AACM was reconstituting forms and traditions. What's interesting about the Chicago movement in the 1960s was that it also extended to the social dynamics of Black folks. There was an incredible bursting open of new kinds of expressive modes. Political venues were examined. The establishment was being shot down. And, for artists like Braxton, the "establishment" included institutions of education, politics, and economics as well as musical institutions. That means the symphony orchestra and Western European mechanisms were rejected.

This Chicago music movement looked to Africa. The AACM saw a spirituality in the way African music was organized; they embraced the notion of music as ritual. The artists were not just performing on the concert stage; they were really engaged with the audience. The music and the movement merged; a Black social cause became an American social concern. Black traditional music circles merged with jazz performers who were challenging traditional concert music and, therefore, breaking into new areas.

Ornette Coleman's 1960 album *Free Jazz: A Collective Improvisation* was an attempt to turn jazz on its head again. The artists played exactly what the energy dictated. They focused not on the musical score but on where the music told them to go. This was radical. With this side of concert music, you had aleatoric practices and free associations. You had atonality and serialism. All of these forces began to converge, and the AACM brought all of this together in very wonderful ways. Anthony Braxton became a central composer in that movement.

This whole Chicago movement was also challenging the European notion of a sole composer. Instead, for them, communal music was important because that was central to the kind of social politics that were part of the civil rights and Black Power movements. They also insisted on playing original music and helping to facilitate one another's music.

Amiri Baraka

Amiri Baraka is the towering figure who embodied and emboldened the Black Arts movement during the 1960s. An artist who speaks from the vantage point of the common language of the streets, Baraka is also a studied literary scholar and one of this nation's great poets. A literary, political, and theatrical trendsetter, a publisher and arts movement impresario, he is an overarching artist, mind, public figure, and personality. Baraka is the cultural aesthetician, poet, writer, social and art critic; the revolutionary and controversial author, playwright, and political activist; the cultural icon and the founder of the Black Arts movement.

Known today as the famous poet of Newark, New Jersey, Baraka was born there as Everett LeRoi Jones and was known first as writer LeRoi Jones. He studied philosophy and religion at Rutgers University, Howard University, and Columbia University. In the 1950s, in his young twenties, he moved to Greenwich Village, coming into being with the beat poets movement, Jack Kerouac, and Allen Ginsberg. A 1960 visit to Cuba birthed within him pieces of his socially active life. He commented in his autobiography, "Cuba split me open," having encountered political activists who challenged his complacency. He began to embrace Black nationalism. His musical counterparts were Ornette Coleman, John Coltrane, Cecil Taylor, Sun Ra, musicians who demonstrated that it was possible for Black artists to produce progressive and not merely entertaining art, music that was rooted in transcendent, African

American musical culture. In 1963, he published his seminal book *Blues People*. In that same year came his play *Dutchman*, which won an Obie award. Norman Mailer commented that it was the "best one act play in America," and LeRoi Jones became a national sensation.

Controversy has always followed the poet, and so has action. In 1964, he galvanized a number of colleagues and opened the Black Arts Repertoire Theater School. They produced plays, poetry readings, musical pieces and concerts, and performances for the community. Based on the Baraka model of arts and social engagement, similar schools sprouted up all over the country. In 1965, Baraka declared, "It's nation time." He formally called on artists to take responsibility to move the community forward. This was the definition of Black art; a Black aesthetic was needed and was now in motion; the Black Arts movement was born. In 1967, the year he changed his name to Imamu Amiri Baraka, he published *Black Music*.

Amiri Baraka is the person who gave us the language to speak critically, socially, and contextually about Black music culture in America. He literally and figuratively wrote the book, *Blues People*. We, as musicians, would be indebted to him if this were all he had done, but he has given us so much more. Baraka's towering presence helps us to cement our perspectives on the critical aspects and importance of Black music in art education in this country. Blues is the most dynamic, functional, and theoretical root of all the popular music forms we study here in this work. Further, *Blues People* established in clear form the appreciation and historical development of several aspects of Black America's "paths to citizenship" through Black music: blues, jazz, and other popular music forms.

In *Black Music*, Amiri Baraka writes, "It is the philosophy of [Black] music that is most important, and this philosophy is only partially the result of the sociological disposition of Negroes in America." He tells us, "all of these attitudes are continuous parts of the historical and cultural biography of the Negro as it has existed and developed since there was a Negro in America, and a music that could be associated with him that did not exist anywhere else in the world."[3]

Given these various themes and directions, hip hop music rises easily as a protest movement of young people into the next modern era of the 1980s. With this, we have the continuation of some codes, the creation of some new, and the busting up of others.

CHAPTER FOUR

Hip to the Hop

Yo Hip Hop is a way of life. It ain't a fad, it ain't a trend. Not for those of us who are true to it. It's reflected in our slang, in our walk, and our stance. In our dress and our attitude. Hip Hop has a history, origin and a set of principles. . . . It's our way to release tension, to let out frustration that young people face in the world today. . . . It has evolved to represent what is happening now, the reality of street life. . . . Hip Hop is the lifestyle, the philosophy and even the religion, if I may. It will remain for some of us as the raw essence of life.

—Guru, *Jazzmatazz*

Hip hop, an inescapable Black aesthetic expression and worldview, may well be the opening Black artist statement of the twenty-first century. It has touched every other Black art form, from music to movement, film, language, literature, and visual arts. Its content, context, and incorporation are crucial to the statement, development, and acknowledgment of a Black aesthetic. A more complete history of the movement comes in part III of this book. In this chapter's discussion of a hip hop aesthetic, it may be helpful to think about the history of DJing and to view two very informative works: Byron Hurt's film *Hip Hop: Beyond Beats and Rhymes* and Derrick Darby and Tommie Shelby's book *Hip Hop and Philosophy: Rhyme2 Reason*. Both articulate multiple and probing views into the thinking and performative, conceptual, and social aesthetic of mainstream commercial hip hop culture. They offer analyses which help to begin this important discussion, but both leave unanswered some questions addressed in this book.

The DJ: Stepping into Black Ritual

In every great record there is a great part.

—Grandmaster Flash

There is a needed moment of clarity here regarding the origins of hip hop culture. In conversations I had with a father figure of the hip hop form, the question of understanding the cultural, the communal space, the traditions of Black music practice, style, function, meaning, and historical reverence took on another perspective. DJ Grandmaster Flash, born Joseph Saddler in 1958, stepped into the Black cultural ritual from a different angle. In doing this, the DJ, not the rapper, became critical to the creation of another form of Black music and a new aesthetic. Grandmaster Flash is a living legend, an icon in popular culture. His is an artistic story of innovative expression, discovery, and triumph going against the grain of several traditions. He took DJing to the next level by inventing a theory. From an idea grew first a practice and then a science. In this process, he transformed the common turntable into a musical instrument. Like Armstrong who did not invent improvisation but did make it an art, Flash made DJing a legitimate sound art form—turntabling.

The relevant and sustaining component of every revolution is that it is a youth expression movement which signals, demands, changes, and reorders. It calls on innovation and leadership. There are risks involved in this balance between order and change. Hip hop has come to be a youth art form, especially in the DJ arena that negotiated this change.

It was interesting for me to sit down with Grandmaster Flash and talk with him about how he came to this. He explained that his art started from a curiosity about his father's records. They were "off limits." In order for him to discover the value of the records, he had to sneak into the place where his dad stored them, listen while he was supposed to be at school, then carefully wipe off the fingerprints and place them back, undetected. This "touching the records, discovering the music" was a rebellious experience that would be transformative. As he matured, he realized that he was "irritated" by the way DJs fumbled the beat, disturbed the aesthetic, and mishandled moving from song to song. He sought a musical answer that could be unearthed, using a technique and electronics, by figuring out a simple thing: discovering the links among every recorded song, in any style and any tempo; discovering the drumbeat and complementary beat in every record.

DJs had figured out how to isolate parts of the records, actually the break beat in the record. Flash began to use two turntables spinning simultaneously, so that he could stop the record in real time and link the songs, connecting them smoothly. He stepped into the usage of music. He had to violate a cardinal rule to do this: he had to touch a spinning record and literally stop it, negotiating the smooth connection from song to song. If the people kept dancing, enjoying themselves and being more ecstatic at the interesting seamless ways that the DJ went from song to song, all the better for his technique. That technique—quick theory, cutting, break and clutch—became a tradition and thus was born a critical mechanism of hip hop, DJing. Out of DJing came rappers, dancers, and the hip hop rhetoric and style, with an art work that "represented." From this angle, we can see the meanings of the movement, the rituals, and the arts in context.

As a musician, I have always been in conversation with hip hop, wrestling with the placement and meaning of this new Black aesthetic. The way in which Flash moves from song to song, steps into the hip hop ritual, requires, in some ways, that he bypass the music, the very thing that musicians create. But in looking at hip hop as an effort to connect songs, rather than an effort to break music apart, it becomes easier to move away from the concerns of profanity and to be both critical and protective of the value of the artistic expression.

As Flash explains, "In every great record there is a great part," the beat, the "get down" part. Hip hop DJing steps into this "get down" part, captures that beat moment, and disrupts it. That disruption became the flash point of a movement, style, and genre. Flash was looking for a way to give himself absolute control of the music, to determine how it would fit successfully into the function of DJing for dances. While one can appreciate the innovation, the idea of enlarging and deepening the Black communal ritual of the block party dance or park jammy jam, the problem with this art form is that, from this angle, it has less and less to do with the making of music. That is where this discussion of hip hop begins. Musicians will have a better appreciation for hip hop, and be able to engage in a more critical dialogue about and with it, if we begin to look at it from the DJs' angle. DJs stop the music, isolate the "get down" parts, and elongate them, infusing them with an expressive format on top of the beats. DJing created a new code. While this code included music—albums—music was not the focus of the code's expressive measure or meaning.

This begs a number of questions. When stepping into the Black rituals, what codes do we engage? Can there be a Black music code that is expressive and artistic but does not have music at its center? Is that how we can understand the Black aesthetic codes in hip hop?

Byron's Beats to a Better Bounce

Byron Hurt's powerful 2006 film *Hip Hop: Beyond Beats and Rhymes* is a disturbing examination of a new definition of Black manhood, largely among artists of the hip hop generation, defined in the documentary as anyone born between 1965 and 1995. That is a generational stretch incorporating a staggering amount of creative development and consumption, thirty years of Black expression. In the film, Hurt opens up very sincerely, reflecting on how our definition of ourselves got locked into the media-made "hip hop box," particularly in the self-destructive notions of twenty-first-century Black malehood.

In loving hip hop, Hurt, a former NFL player turned motivational speaker and educator, examines his own conflicted feelings about the music. He focuses on the way manhood is displayed in hip hop culture. He interviews young Black males claiming to be "aspiring artists," who all rhyme about gunplay and violence, hustling, and facing off with other Black males. Refreshingly, many of these artists admit that they would much rather portray more sustaining, positive images in their work, but they also note that "it doesn't sell to be positive." This is the defining rule that shapes choices of those interviewed. Hurt cleverly brings in an array of cultural and social critics, as well as industry commentators and well-known rappers—Busta Rhymes, Mos Def, JadaKiss, Russell Simmons, Chuck D—who all, to varying degrees, bring attention to America's soiled "social imagination of the violent man and the gun as a tool, an extension of male ability to navigate violence," as Michael Eric Dyson states in the film.

Incorporating news segments showing 1960s and 1970s urban renewal projects in many metropolitan areas, Hurt cites the massive destruction of Black communities like the Bronx, which were broken up by highways and urban development, subsequently displacing and disrupting neighborhoods. Hip hop culture, the film argues, was "a reclaiming, a response to larger systematic violence against the Black community."

The film presents an urban identity of violence and equates this to a growing hardness among Black men trying to deny their vulnerability. It suggests that many feel that somehow a break from this edge would dilute a new and necessary definition, a normalcy of Black urban manhood. Several commentators, including cultural critic Mark Anthony Neal, suggest that in Hurt's film the hyper-masculine posturing, "exerting your power," was also a response to the 1990s crack epidemic, and to the proliferation of guns and drug culture exhibited in films like *Boyz n the Hood, Menace II Society, Juice,* and *Poetic Justice.* Further, commentators suggest that forced environments such as prisons and gangs created relevant allegiances for these young, family-less men. Thus, "living the life" of the streets, being confrontational, and the rise in what Chuck D calls "a culture of Black animosity" against other men began to prevail. The film also points out that American badboy-ness was not constructed by the hip hop crisis, that in fact, Hollywood machines this out as entertainment in films like *The Terminator, Rambo,* and numerous gangster movies. "The nation supports a culture of violence," Hurt asserts.

The very critical question of male/female relations in contemporary Black culture at the heart of a community is no more demeaned than in hip hop videos and lyrics. The now too-often repeated terms "bitches" and "ho's" saturated the Nelly video *Tip Drill.* Years later, in the 2007 Don Imus scandal, that shock jock stated Black people use this kind of imagery in their popular music all the time and "created the terminology." As Imus said, "That phrase [nappy-headed ho] didn't originate in the White community. That phrase originated in the Black community. Young Black women all through that society are demeaned and disparaged and disrespected by their own Black men, and they are called that name in Black hip hop music."

The rage that began in the 1970s was commodified into something that sold as common cultural artifacts in the 1990s. In Hurt's film, Carmen Ashurst, the former president of the hip hop mega-label Def Jam, states, "At the time we were able to get a bigger presence in the place . . . the record industry . . . the music became then less and less conscious [concerned about the message]." And, if one follows titles alone, hip hop went, as Chuck D points out, from "Fight the Power" to "Gin and Juice."

One of the more disturbing yet constant themes in Hurt's film is the way in which Black expression products are marketed and consumed by voyeuristic White youth who, through their access and White privilege, take an equally damaging and active role in nondiscriminating purchases, buying 80 percent of the hip hop market. In the film, one White suburbanite states that Black music "appeals to our sense of learning about other cultures and wanting to know more about what we can never experience."

This young woman unwittingly repeats a decades-old practice of Whites denying their accountability and asserting their right to "pass into and purchase" this look at exoticism for the moment. Here one sees the classic pass from Black expression, beautiful or ugly, sold by a greedy hand to the needy White consumer looking for a cool sneak peak. We see the historical line here: F. Scott Fitzgerald's jazz age (1920s), the bohemian beatnik poets' fascination with the beboppers (1940s), the revivalist White interest in rural old-time blues singers (1960s), the disco age rage with Black clubbing (1970s). The partnership of media and commerce at the expense of Black lives and expression ultimately is the issue. Chuck D further nails this when he calls the media/entertainment company BET "the cancer of the Black man in the world." Hurt concludes, "Hip hop is pure Americana. Hip hop is trapped in a box."

Although the Hurt documentary is extremely well done, it, like much hip hop cultural criticism and reporting, leaves out relevant discussion about the music, aesthetics, and expressive cultural life. By focusing on problematic definitions of Black malehood and the "end identity product" of a commercial process, the film is primarily concerned with hip hop's effects. Discussion in the film is primarily among nonmusicians and industry profiteers. The majority of these talking heads for the most part didn't enter the game to "make music" or educate. They are cultural participants who are not concerned about the well-being or development of Black people, nor are they concerned with the work of the artist or the expression function beyond its entertainment value. We have a huge problem here. What are the purposes, goals, and codes of this hip hop expression? Hurt's film offers little insight. As we consider what is wrong with this hip hop picture, it may be this: it ain't a picture at all. It's more like a scarred hole with no bottom, spiraling downward.

While the entrepreneurial component of hip hop has done much to open closed doors in the marketplace, this relatively new power is more seductive than sustaining in its effect on our communities. Hip hop music is not really the problem. It is only a corrupted messenger of the bigger problem of a capitalist modern mega-culture. Arts should sustain us and critique the undesirable elements that pull us down. The best artists provide alternative sources of information, spiritual and social rallying places, which move the life of a community forward. All the talk about hip hop music focuses on detrimental effects of problematic negative language and imagery. This stifles a much needed public discussion about music, art, and the direction and health of Black people today generally.

There is an absence of other players in this critical dialogue about Black people. In Hurt's film, there are no mothers or concerned fathers, no church or political leaders, no youth who say, "no way." It sometimes seems as if hip hop culture is Black America, and that just isn't so. It may seem as if hip hop is the only relevant critical, popular music voice that reflects Black America today, and that isn't so either.

None of this justifies the overwhelming taking on of the current problematic and defeatist definition of Black identity, even though White greedy corporations have punked, pimped, and slicked vulnerable young Black males to do so. Black people have stood against worse attacks. So what has happened? The communities have fallen short and are to be held accountable. The media and industry have poisoned and simultaneously derailed a critical component of Black cultural agency and identity. And in the process, they have potentially ruined a powerful vernacular art form of protest and social/community activism. Socially there is a problem; culturally and aesthetically there is a crisis.

Hip Hop Philosophy: A View

In the book *Hip Hop and Philosophy: Rhyme 2 Reason*, Derrick Darby and Tommie Shelby compiled numerous essays by writers in the field who take on parts of this problem to, in fact, project hip hop culture as a viable view, a philosophy. They make a good case for hip hop's own aesthetic strengths, but their arguments are overplayed and do not sufficiently analyze the negative impact of hip hop, nor the way that it is controlled and manipulated by corporate culture. In a supportive opening essay, cultural critic Cornel West calls hip hop "the most influential cultural phenomena in the entertainment industry on the globe." He argues that Darby and Shelby's collection will enable us to dig deep "into African American life and culture."[1] Calling attention to the philosophical work of hip hop, West argues that the book facilitates an inquiry that:

1. Shows how sophisticated forms operate within the works of cultural production in the free market.
2. Explains how and why gifted Black people choose hip hop as a dominant form of expression.
3. Evaluates artistic excellence or mediocrity.
4. Examines Black cultural expressions and presses them to be revealing of the meaningful topics of race and music.

West then poses the question: Does not the love of wisdom require that we interrogate in a Socratic way the voices and the views that have emerged from the killing fields and gangsterized hoods of the American empire? But, tellingly, he describes hip hop as "a cultural phenomenon in the entertainment industry." He does not refer to it as a musical movement.

One of the most helpful essays in the collection is Richard Shusterman's "Rap Aesthetics: Violence and the Art of Keeping It Real." He writes, "Many of the more thoughtful MC's claim not only to be creative artists but also philosophers; and they see their artistic expression of truth as part and parcel of a political struggle to achieve greater economic, social, political and cultural power for the core hip hop constituency of African-American society." He further defines a philosophy of pragmatism, arguing that hip hop "captures its fans not simply as music but as a whole philosophy of life, an ethos that involves clothes, a style of talk and walk, a political attitude and often a philosophical posture of asking hard questions and critically challenging established views and values."[2]

Another helpful aspect of this collection is its broad and consistent usage of terminology that helps establish expressions, values, and methods of evaluation for hip hop. Some essays are written by artist/performers, and some by cultural critics and scholars, but all are seemingly in accord. The volume helpfully notes that in addition to the classic four hip hop elements—rapping, DJing, dancing, and graffiti—there is a fifth element: knowledge and consciousness. The authors highlight ideas in hip hop: sexuality, violence, language, the politics of pondering the truths about inner-city life, "dropping the needle," understanding the contemporary human urban condition, philosophical probes into the nature of God, mysteries of love, depths of self-consciousness, subtleties of living an "authentic life," the aesthetics of noise, and how to respond to injustice.

Shusterman explores "aesthetic violence," which he describes as "hardcore poetic expression that . . . channels violence onto an aesthetic medium in a field of artistic production and rivalry that manifests in kicking rhymes, rocking beats, dueling over the quest for truth and artistic excellence." For Shusterman and other authors in the collection, the concept of "aesthetic violence" is the ruling and defining code for how to explain and explore much of mainstream contemporary hip hop. I would love to trust that this purposeful view exists in contemporary and forward-moving hip hop, and it does, but truthfully, this is not seen in the majority of mainstream rap products that common folks listen to daily.

Darby and Shelby explore hip hop as a space for aesthetic philosophy, contemplation, and play, and their volume provides a number of helpful commentaries, but the book's analysis is problematic in some ways and limited in others. The book attempts to place philosophical aim at the center of hip hop culture. It is tricky to superimpose a philosophic agenda on a public, folk ritual. We have to start at hip hop's premises, questions, inquires, functions, and usage first.

The book argues that the pursuit of knowledge, in order to develop a higher consciousness, is a goal of hip hop. There are many examples where poetry and music performances truly attempt to deal with higher values. At present, unfortunately, most mainstream popular hip hop artistry is trapped in the folly of confrontational rhetoric, pursuit of pleasure, glorification of sexual conquest, and thuggery. Again, in several instances, the book begins to delineate a definition of aesthetic pragmatism, performance, artistic expression, form, and drive for power. Here we can see how the creators of hip hop lyrics relate to and see the form and forum of hip hop itself as expressing common life discourses. This begins to break into very helpful definitions of function, aesthetic design, experience, and perception. In this sense, some qualities of expression such as "flow," "flipping meaning," "keeping it real," though limiting, provide designs for articulating formative worldviews. The description of limiting here is not meant as a put down, but these expressions are vernacular forms. While some extremely piercing social analyses and critiques are made, most of the lyrics and narratives are little extended beyond "our living, play fields." As I pointed to early on, an aesthetic should address the fuller picture of Black living in the larger world.

The public products in hip hop are not from poets, rarely artists, and almost never musicians. Most rappers, hip hop entertainers, are not concerned with musical value; it's not their domain. Musical and artistic value rarely rise as a primary concern. It is secondary to the words and the rappers' argument.

Darby and Shelby's book problematically mixes the agendas of popular production and philosophical pretense to achieve clarity for arguing hip hop's academic worth. This agenda is superimposed and therefore suspicious, although some of this is very useful because it serves as one inquiry that produces helpful examinations into critical issues. Hip hop is a product, an artifact of our culture, and extremely relevant, because it objectifies experiences in the form of human struggle, reason, inquiry, and expression of the human narrative.

Hip hop culture is adequately defined as a form of style that itself delineates qualities of a preferred performance idea and sets an appreciation for normalcy. And the book does help locate specific "communities of concern," which elevate their needs, identity, and preferences. The community largely expressed is urban Black America. Hip hop locates its activity of experiences and concern here (though the market extends greatly beyond this realm). In some sense, hip hop provides a relevant, if limited, worldview and identity for groups of living folk.

The hip hop definition of Blackness, as I pointed out in my analysis of the Hurt film, is limited. Its formulations of Black art are limited. It is "class exclusionary." It is generational gapped and divided and its anti-educational posturing limits cultural discussion. This dysfunction is tied to age-specific experience and expression and cannot totally serve Black folks. Because hip hop situates itself exclusively as a youth-identity rhetorical form, it will remain in arrested development artistically and will fail to provide an outlook which can serve the problems of the Black community. And it must then remain subservient to commercial market forces.

Hip hop rhetoric in the mainstream lacks prescriptive codes for the failing of racism, Black on Black crime and attack, and worse, it exemplifies and glorifies these as normative. Hip hop has a snag in its consciousness. Who best defines its cultural identity: Common or Snoop? Nelly or KRS-One? Missy Elliott, Queen Latifah, or Lil' Kim? Suge Knight or Chuck D?

Sustained identity in the aesthetic formulation over the years in most cases operates as a part or product of moral and cultural authority. The margins of a system of power are certainly places for art, but hip hop sets little value on the moral or artistic implications of its function. It neither questions the implications nor the consequences of dysfunctional product. It ignores the demise and consequences of young Black people who participate in its expression, ritual, and purchase, as Black music is foundational and fundamentally an expression of Black ideas in the modern world. Every art of protest considers the results as significant to achieving impact, meaning, and significance. "Say It Loud—I'm Black and I'm Proud," "Fight the Power," "Express Yourself," and "Respect," while all commercial products, seem to emote a consciousness about the meaning and effect of song. This is rhyming for a reason.

Hip hop must address its own internal challenges if it is to continue to succeed as a place for sustaining Black life artistically. In examining hip hop in this chapter and the four movements in chapter 3, we can see there has clearly been a precedent set for codes that reflect the thinking of Black artistry and that connect to the ways in which people have lived. From this, how might a history be viewed that incorporates the specific musical movements, and how might a study, a philosophy, be constructed that would be in line with the best thinking and art making? Part II of this book tackles these questions.

PART II

BUILDING A BLACK
MUSIC PHILOSOPHY

Musicians. *Acrylic on canvas by Emily Russell*

CHAPTER FIVE

A Cultural Education

Culture is the basis of all ideas, images and actions. To move is to move culturally, i.e., by a set of ideas given to you by your culture.

—Maulana Karenga, *Introduction to Black Studies*

The Negro writer who seeks to function within his race as a purposeful agent has a serious responsibility. He is being called upon to do no less than create values by which his race is to struggle, live and die . . . create the myths and symbols that inspire a faith in life. It means that in the lives of Negro writers must be found those materials and experiences which will create in them a meaningful and significant picture of the world today. . . . And the time has come to ask questions, to theorize, to speculate, to wonder out of what materials can a human world be built.

—Richard Wright, "Blueprint for Negro Writing"

A philosophy driven by practiced codes, supported by an overarching aesthetic, and created by connected artists is a beautiful thing. Moving from defining an aesthetic of music expression to an overriding education philosophy is helpful at this point. My focus is on the work of musical artists. I see music as a body of expressive ideas that is both produced for and influenced by social and individual needs. I see music as art, and more importantly, I see music as an outgrowth of people's experiences heard in notes and sounds. I'm interested in that narrative told in tones, actions, and ideas as a manifestation of certain meaning in human experience. The meanings, ideas, and

49

sounds we call music are living patterns that tell the story of our lives and experiences.

This kind of theology of music involves looking at how music addresses the life that we are living and how it comforts, confronts, and accompanies our social reality and living conditions. I'm interested as well in examining parallels, changes, and challenges of popular musicians in different eras. Young artists today are faced with defining their creative voice and image in an era where powerful technology and big-money markets rule. How this affects the choices musicians make, how it propels or impairs careers, is important. Ultimately these outcomes determine what we hear in the popular market, and what influences our society.

Despite the hegemony of American mass media, these popular resonances contribute to a youth culture that shares common grooves. Common people—from a wide variety of cultural backgrounds, commitments, and contributions—create a folk music that empowers people to demand inclusivity and a fair voice. Through their varied identities and talents—from spirituals to rural folk songs to social protest music—they have used music to achieve democratic agency. These expressions, products, have reflected artistic innovation and genius. The blues to British rock to Jamaican reggae to Japanese rap all extend to meanings which address where people "live."

In these multivoiced narratives, what are the central debates in modern times? The music has functioned and remained a critical component in determining identity and values which contribute largely to the shape of society. How do we reach a sensibility that is informed by the best of what our music culture offers and that bridges the gaps from old to modern, old school to new school, folk vernacular expression to art to commodity, from suppression to expression and from cultural indifference and hatred to embracing a wider world?

Contemporary music education ought to equip musicians to think about a sense and place of themselves as artists, participating and contributing in culture. I encourage younger artists to think critically about the meaning of their art, from the standpoint of an individual and a critical, creative thinker. Artistic identity is important. Who am I as a creator? This "music culture view" is a journey through a cultural studies lens that explores artistry, identity, history, values, and spiritual-social-political plains. Young aspiring musicians need an arts-centered, humanities curriculum that engages and refines their thinking as well as the development of their "inner core-soul." Contributing to society as citizens, or being socially and politically aware, won't seem so distant from their musical-life experience. The teaching role is really to lead as a tour guide, pulling together an illustrative narrative overview that is reflective of the artistry and social movements that gave rise to music.

Today, a global worldview is absolutely essential to our vitality as artists and citizens. Artists and educators need to be in touch with these impulses, with a multiethnic world and a host of strategies and views found in contemporary culture, artistic creation, production, education, and business. Educational programming must broaden the understanding, definition, and direction of contemporary music culture. From an educational perspective, the music-making is affected by broadening the base in terms of exchanges among cultures from around the globe.

Downbeat

If we consider only the development of popular musical movements in the twentieth century, Black artists are dead center and on the pulse of them all, initiating, innovating and naming the crazes within them: spirituals (unnamed Black poet-musician/singers), the blues (Son House), jazz (Louis Armstrong), swing (Ellington/Basie), gospel (Sister Rosetta Tharpe), as well as the artistry of Dizzy, Parker, Miles, Coltrane, Ornette, Louis Jordan, Aretha, Bob Marley, George Clinton's Funkadelic Fantasy Fusion, Prince, Busta Rhymes, Me'shell Ndegéocello, Bessie Smith, Thelonious Monk, and Stevie Wonder. These are powerful, poetic-philosophical inquiries which are spun out and lived:

- Before I'll be a slave, I'll be buried in my grave (spiritual verse)
- What did I do to be so Black and blue? (Louis Armstrong)
- It don't mean a thing, if it ain't got that swing (Duke Ellington)
- Say it loud, I'm Black and I'm proud (James Brown)
- What's going on? (Marvin Gaye)
- It's a jungle sometimes; it makes me wonder how I keep from going under (Grandmaster Flash)
- I'm not the average girl from your video, I ain't built like a supermodel, but I learned to love myself unconditionally, because I am a queen (India.Arie)

Through this music, every generation has come to see itself mature: the jazz age, Harlem Renaissance, swing, bebop, rock and roll, and hip hop. One of the underlying foci of cultural studies is to consider how expressions came from people who had reason to create, and then to assess the power of those expressions. Taking this as one criterion for the measurement of modernity, Black music movements would come in very high on the meter to measure human accomplishment. As cultural critic and historian Gerald Early has stated, if Black people had created only the blues, "they would go down in history as one of the seminal peoples contributing to the development of the modern world." Turning to Black music/culture studies is not simply a historical inquiry; it is an exploration of a discourse that emphasizes new cultural creation because of the direct impact of African people in the modern world.

This discussion continues to concern itself with a philosophy of music and meaning, as well as a phenomenology of Black music-ing. Black music has given us a lens through which we can view the development of modern American society. Of critical importance is the idea that, in this music tradition, many people saw places where they, too, could and would connect, contribute, change, and share in making it their voice. American music is the story of multiple cultural exchanges and collaborations. Recognized as one of the great art flowerings in human culture, the music has affected social movements and served as a fuse igniting global humanist social protests. What we might call the spiritual-blues mode and rhythm affected modern music conception so completely, it must be the single most influential music since the beginning of modern notions of harmony and rhythm combining. In Black music culture studies, it has become increasingly important to show not only what impact the music had in the world, but how the music made and is making a difference in the lives of the people from whom the music came. From a musician's angle, the idea that this music is doing something that carries, that represents, "my people's voice" is a very different kind of commitment and connection. For these reasons, Black music traditions are influential to modern thought and culture, and their full study provides an invaluable window into human history. Because of its breadth, Black music culture lets us examine the best of artistry, history, social-cultural application, and educational approaches.

Upbeat: A Culturalist Interpretation for Musical Meaning

What I term a "culturalist interpretation" of music may lead to different views, insights on the understanding of performance, appreciation, meaning, and reasons for musical expression from a traditional historical view. The culturalist view I propose focuses on what the music means and how it functions for the people. This interpretation results in, perhaps, a deeper respect for the music and the values out of which the music culture comes. When exploring any questions of interpretation and history, it seems logical to look at what it meant for the people who created and lived the expression first. This is the most difficult and trying issue for educational institutions and "information thrill seekers." If we want to deal with Black music culture—not simply stay on its margins, but seriously and substantively investigate it—we must deal with Black people: the history, the culture, the Black church, the rituals, the literature, the worldview, the value systems—and, of course, the music.

Black musicians from every corner of the world speak from a "Black culturalist view" in discussing the sound, function, performance practices, and meaning of Black music. One can cite specific African retentions, those cultural attributes which mark Black music throughout the diaspora and the social-spiritual values that consistently thread Black culture and experience to a West African sensibility. This includes functionality, participation, communality and spirituality, the role of the musician-griot, melodic conception in blued notes (3-5-7) or glides, phrasing, rhythmic dynamism, cross and polyrhythmic conception, forms of call and response, riffs, soloing, ostinato backbeat grounding patterns, the styling of growls and moans, falsetto, glisses, word fluidity, meaning, flexibility, improvisation, and dance forms, intricately locked with musical performance. Music is always a human expression. Black music is reflective and symbolic of these kinds of twists and changes. Black musicians took musical materials and formed grooves and turnarounds, melodies, songs, and whole traditions of making music that sounded out life experiences. They twisted, remade, and reinvented forms from preexisting song traditions to create new music that resulted from all these views, interpretations, and sayings about what it feels like to be alive. The artistic result, experimentation, was this music in the Black tradition.

When this music gets frozen into a record, or discussed in a theoretical analysis, the understanding and appreciation are only partial. We have to provide a human and cultural dimension to learn the music fully. In Black literary and folk culture, cross-references from spirituals, blues, love songs, humor, stories, rhythms, sayings, myths, and images are all interlocked as a special set of meanings from which the music comes. The music appears because of people's struggles, the dilemmas of living.

Black music is a "jump blues," a shout, a boogie, a gospel vamp to celebrate the joy of being and the recognition of the craft of musical geniuses. Every speech pattern, harmony, improvised solo, rhyme, walk, dance, vocal delivery, and groove/pocket is a particular way of moving musically, and that way was devised by people in response to particular life circumstances. To skip this dimension of the values and meaning of the art is to miss what it means and why it exists. If you teach creative Black music, you teach the American Dream and all its benefits. Black music emboldened the machinery of the human pursuit of that American spirit/dream: freedom, freedom of expression, invention, innovation, empowering agents of change, community.

This discussion ultimately weaves together three groups: the music makers; those who teach music; and the folks on the street who live, love, listen to, and purchase music. Given this line of thinking, how might a view of contemporary forms in popular music culture raise, contrast, or connect to the idea that music in society moves within a humanist design of "spiritual/social purpose"?

A Philosophy of Theology within
Black and Popular Music Practices

Art is not a pastime but a priesthood.

—Jean Cocteau

Music is a movement of views, values, ideas, and creativity among individuals. In talking about the definition of theology, an exploration of musicians' social-cultural movements includes images and ideas constructed within the popular culture marketplace. The range of our emotions, thoughts, and actions can be represented and reflected through art. In his *Theology of Culture*, Paul Tillich defines aspects of a "religious analysis of culture." He writes,

> Religion is the substance of culture, culture is a form of religion . . . in the most intimate movement of the soul, [this] is culturally formed. In order to fulfill his destiny, man must be in possession of creative powers, analogous to those previously attributed to God (In the beginning, God created . . .) and so creativity must become a human quality. . . . Some may have the strength to take anxiety and meaninglessness courageously upon themselves and live creatively, expressing the predicament of the most sensitive people in our time in cultural production. The great works of the visual arts, of music, of poetry, of literature, of architecture, of dance, of philosophy, show in their style both the encounter with non-being, and the strength which can stand this encounter and shape it creatively. This makes the protesting element in contemporary culture theologically significant . . . based on man's encounter with reality . . . used for the needs of daily life, for the expression and communication of our ultimate concern.[1]

Tillich claims that religion is our ultimate concern. He continues, "Anxiety and despair about existence itself induces millions of people to look out for any kind of healing that promises success." Given that our work is to explore culture to understand what it says about the living condition and particularly about a musician's perspective, the examination of these movements, ideas, and artifacts tell us about the conflicts, the yearnings, the aspirations, the dilemmas, and the values in society. When music, lyrics, and creative expression address these concerns, human values, conflicts, and aspirations, it is theologically valid. Humans are a product of culture and a larger creative universe—God, spirit, creativity. How people, culture, the world and musical construction intersect and have meaning to explore existence is also theologically valid. For the humanist, people are spiritually and creatively connected; for the theist, the connection is with "ultimate reality," a search for a "God connection." One can see that the discussion of what artists do for us in society can come from various angles, and this is illustrative of how great is the impact of that work.

I often think, what would happen if all the singing and playing just stopped? How would we interpret the silences of the sounds we were so accustomed to having? If we have come to appreciate music as a spiritual force and language that is able to inspire, empower, and direct ideas and feelings, then it follows that creativity is a unique kind of gifting that, once imparted, has many possibilities.

One theological analysis/lens through which we can see this is the transfer of West African artistic codes of griot musicians who used music as the "framework" through which all life was mediated. That basic music usage and philosophy, from original West African impulses and traditions, was powerfully and practically transformed to a portable American version. This was first heard in the slave hollers, work songs, and spirituals. Then the blues functioned to give expression, exploration, and negotiation while accompanying the singer/performers within life's experiences. So many performers—Muddy Waters, Son House, B. B. King, Charley Patton; then the early rockers, Little Richard, Chuck Berry—got their first musical training from the spiritual and musical influences and the traditions of the Black church.

When the 1954 *Brown v. Board of Education* decision knocked down the doctrine of separate but equal, this ushered in a fuller integration and a reordering of the American social fabric. Music first heard in jazz, swing, then r&b and rock and roll brought this together. Teens, regardless of race or ethnicity, listened and idolized the same stars and music. As one observer noted, "It was a revolution, music did it. We did as much with our music as the Civil Rights Acts and all the marches for breaking the race thing down."

This music awakened in American youth a basic impulse, though largely represented in carnal reaction to rhythms and the themes of dance and romance. Yet this music carried an inner, spirited drive that is consistent with the cultural traditions of Black music. The music also carried with it a human/cultural identity and social commitment to bettering the world, which brought once segregated groups closer to experience common concerns. This common human experience base was a huge force in disarming major social/cultural barriers held in place by the very unholy American laws of racial prejudice and segregation. These musicians' passionate work unearthed a more human spirit, a humanity of common people that allowed America, or better yet, by social pressure, forced America to wake up. Rock and roll as a social/cultural impulse can be seen as the first major music movement to tear at the American social/cultural soul, and this directly impacted the future of our society.

Michael Eric Dyson puts it this way:

> The genius of Black people is, that you ain't seen rap coming. We keep reinventing ourselves through our expressions. The reality is the different styles that young people invent are an attempt to mark their own particular environments with the style they are accustomed to. And style is an attempt to put your stamp on your existence. . . . Black people keep inventing and re-inventing, asserting and re-asserting so that we can mark our own existence through the prism of style and give some sense of the weightiness of our existence. But we should not resist the edifying character of Hip Hop culture as a tool of aesthetic, economic and social expression for young people.[2]

It is useless to try to negate the profound influence and impact of popular music culture, its music, artists, ideology, and spirit. One has to conclude that above the fray of the madness of the opiate of popular cultural forms, media hype, and Hollywood's seductive imagery machines, there is something extremely powerful and meaningful. Its appeal at deeper levels is telling.

All Black music—from spirituals to blues to gospel, big band, bebop, rock, reggae, soul, funk, r&b, and hip hop—is attached to the same family and bears the mark of African functionality, musical, cultural, social, and spiritual roots. This is the very basis of Black culture and Black American music forms.

We are all witnesses to the potential and power of popular culture and its role in shaping who we have become, to a large degree, post-1970. Popular culture in its various shapes is the most influential human-driven agency in contemporary society. While we wait, the church in its various denominational divides hardly moves toward its prophetic self.

Artists in the past have "called up" spiritual, intellectual, and aesthetic power to represent authentic and vivid examples of human need and meaning. They have reflected and projected prophetic musical musings, which have moved us in times to consider who we were and were fast becoming. Given the last hundred years of extraordinary musical/historical movements, artistry, and social revolutions (jazz age, Harlem Renaissance, bebop, social protest and social action, hip hop, MTV, the Internet), how are artists in popular forms continuing in the Black arts prophetic vein and moving us to self-reflective listening and action? And given the stream and spray of influences from contemporary commercial markets and ideologies (what sells), does such moral vision and hope for artistry to speak in this way even make sense in terms of assessing a spiritual value?

Given our contemporary need to be relevant, musical, and commercially viable, does a religious sensibility or a moral commitment strike a dissonant chord in this generation, this society, and these contemporary markets? What effect will such rubs between commercial market needs and a growing necessity for a morally conscious culture have on the artistry of contemporary popular culture?

It makes sense to pose these questions and explore historical examples of how Black musical forms have maintained a balance of artistic integrity while being commercially viable and accountable to the community. Any attempt to discuss a philosophy that grounds itself in relevancy for contemporary people and times must seriously engage popular culture and its hold on common folks' imagination and construction of meaning.

Disconnected Discourses: The Relevance of Theological Inquiry in Popular Cultural Forms

In this day of confusion, we must find the root of the problem in order to solve it. The problem is the lack of truth and communication among man and woman. The word of music is one of the strongest means of communication on the planet. The message is Peace, Love, Wisdom, Understanding and Unity.

—Kenneth Gamble, O'Jays, *Message in the Music*

"A release valve," "cry for help," "CNN for the youth," "rap and rage" are terms we don't normally include in our discussions relative to spiritual reflection or inquiry. Yet each of those terms (used in the media to describe rap music) actually relates very easily to the spiritual ideas of prayer, redemption, gospel, the Word, and revelation. The theological quest for exploring and hearing the work of contemporary artists is both compelling and important.

Sometimes seen as disconnected discourses, the dialogue between theology and popular culture deserves more serious time and attention toward examining, decoding, and interpreting. Theological inquiry of this type is absolutely essential.

The theology of American popular music—the idea of such a thing! Mass media would have us believe that these are two contrasting concepts, that there can't be a religious or spiritual influence in popular music. We can look at this in several ways. First, if we go back to the foundations of music, there are certain directions to consider: the Western European notion of history and philosophy, and also the African notion of being and philosophy. Popular music really is the marriage of those ideologies. If we look at it in terms of the spiritual implications of both traditions, popular music results from a modification of what might be a spiritual quest for the blues or gospel singer, and even, in some cases, for the rock and roll singer as well as the jazz performer.

We know for sure that in the Greeks' notion of this connection, music was able to affect human thought and behavior. There were many concerns because people would hear music and become ecstatic, and there were concerns even then that this thing—music—could not be controlled. That tells us right there that music is about something transcendent, that there is something beyond. That's why music is so powerful. It's very easy to see how artists can understand that their role as creative agents has to do with connections that are beyond the finite toward the infinite. That's where the philosophical definition and understanding of this comes from the West.

When we look at the larger world beyond Europe, to Africa especially, we understand music primarily to be the connection between the individual participating and speaking with things spiritual. In many traditional West African theologies, the overarching concept is "We think; therefore, we are" as opposed to "I think; therefore, I am." In this view, everything "I do" relates to my community and it has no reason, no meaning unless that community is connected to the Theos.

But we have moved away from this tradition in modern Western society; that element is often forgotten. In traditional Anglican or Catholic services, for example, in order to hear the voice of God, one perhaps sits in quiet contemplation. But if we go back to the traditional biblical scriptures, we read, "Make a joyful noise before the Lord." These two ideas always go hand in hand. In short, in American popular music, many songs that became a part of the mainstream grew out of the camp revival meetings where Watts hymns and then later Wesley hymns were used. These hymns were emotional, very connected to the people's passionate evangelical beliefs. Enslaved American

Blacks had their own read on this, and they gave it a kind of stylistic spin, too, and folks took notice. "The African slaves are going on and 'carrying on' in ways which are beyond what these hymns are about."

The commodification of popular music began with these Black folks doing different things with this Western European music, first in supervised religious services, and then on their own time. From this came the spirituals, blues, ragtime, and jazz. So much of early popular music—whether country and western or rock and roll—gets significant portions of its aesthetic spin from these unions. Many artists have maintained that spiritual connection. They say, "What I do is a part of my spirituality." Viewed historically, much popular music becomes relevant for theological discourse. Even when artists are seen yelling out at the Theos in their songs, it is relevant for theological examination.

The Theory

Theological inquiry is the probe through which we ask questions about the nature of things, meaning, content, delivery, and intent. Popular culture and expression are so important and compelling because this is where people express in vibrant, innovative ways their uncompromising willingness to be alive. My own definition of theology is the conscious thinking, asking, probing, and activity which encircle and illuminate the human condition. In that revelation, enlightenment can come. A professor in divinity school defined theology as "anything that illuminates the people and moves them beyond." Maintaining a balance between market forces and artistic and moral integrity is the great rub among artists. The most compelling artists today find themselves swimming in an ocean of market sensibilities which too often seem in conflict with art that moves us along and illuminates our paths.

Within these forms, people celebrate the victories of being human. Contemporary popular music is the place specifically within the framework of Black American cultural mapping where we find the makings of relevant, rich theological "matters." As an ideology and cultural movement, popular music teeters on the edges of "socially defined religiosity," at least in terms of an identifiable cultural system defined by a need to be in touch with a community. Anthony Pinn, in his *Why Lord? Suffering and Evil in Black Theology*, effectively argues for "a hard labor, a strong and aggressive inquiry which must have the capacity to appreciate and respond to the hard facts of African American life."[3]

His nitty-gritty hermeneutics is a deeper understanding of Black religious thought and its various discussions on the matter of the problem of evil. He speaks of a "guiding criterion" as the presentation of Black life, couched in

Black "expressivity and linguistic creativity, a concrete orientation in which the raw natural facts are of importance." Any exploration of cultural activity must happen from the inside, where the participants set the rules for engagement and expression.

The role of culture in providing places where folks find healing and explanations for direction in their lives is paramount. This is what Tricia Rose indicates in terms of the nature and function of hip hop music. She argues that it moves among the folks who yearn for revelation. She writes, "Rap music and hip-hop culture are cultural, political, and commercial forms, and for many young people they are the primary cultural, sonic and linguistic windows on the world." In another place, she writes, "Rap music brings together a tangle of some of the most complex social, cultural and political issues in contemporary American society. Rap's contradictory articulations are not signs of absent intellectual clarity; they are a common feature of community and popular cultural dialogues. Cultural expression that prioritizes black voices from the margins of urban America . . . they speak with the voice of personal experience, taking on the identity of the observer or narrator."[4]

In this search, there is a point of human inquiry and a place of human activity contained in the music. It is at their crossroads that music, culture, social progress, morality, and market demand meet. This core dialectic (sacred/social) has been in Black music performance since the spirituals morphed into the blues with Charley Patton, and race records morphed into gospel music with Thomas Dorsey and Sister Rosetta Tharpe. When these musical forms—which embodied the questions, interests, artistic explorations, and sacred/social aspirations—became marketable, the rub emerged. Early rural blues singers were itinerant preachers, just as were the West African griots who, with song, gave myth, wisdom, family history, insults, jokes, and artistic virtuosity. The lines were continually crossed. As Charley Patton sang about love interests and morals, he rapped and preached over his blues licks, substituting words for runs and runs for words ("you gon' need a lawyer when you come around. . . . King Jesus is his name"). When this product was recorded and became a saleable item, it created the demand and interest in style, song, music, and moral reasoning. These questions from the artist's position are usually inextricably bound together and become a part of the cultural dialogue.

Word and Revelation

One way to perhaps gain further meaning in this cultural dialogue is to rely on unmediated truth, that which is not powered by humanity's authority, petitions, or actions but appears despite people's futile attempt to reach "God." Revelation, our truth, happens when human action, living, and waiting occur and are evident and illuminative because people's lives are changed. This business of changing lives is a reality and why so many people are moved by the music, artistry, and inner motivation. The belief in oneself that artists elicit from their audiences and fans, the general public, is real. Consequently, the role of the artist often is to speak outside of reserved places of religious languages, and this perhaps may not inhibit a revelation of sorts. Truth appears because we took a look there; what drew us was the yell and the scream. One has to ask, what does this form of creative expression—contemporary, popular, and hip hop music—tell us about the human condition that the news, CNN, a preacher, a teacher, a theologian, or market demographic cannot? There is an understanding that music moves people and speaks to certain dimensions of the deeper inward that our rhetoric cannot reach. Popular culture has always provided young people with their platforms.

These are some of the places where there is fire and smoke among contemporary young people. Without artistic and compelling viewpoints, we would simply not hear and would silently watch the fire burn. Contemporary music is not theology, of course, but here are road maps of inquiry and analysis from the ground that provide theological insight, to move people along and help illuminate the way. We need to eradicate the blockages that prevent us from seeing the morality that comes through hip hop and popular culture. Like its cousin forms before it, contemporary musical expressions identify real sore points in our social constructs. The moral implication rests on the response and actions of citizens to hear the clamor and the ring, and to act. Popular culture opens the doors to communication and addresses us as "potential neighbors." In this function, it helps to balance the pull between morality and market interests.

Broader Spiritual Dimensions of Music Practice

Music and the arts rely on inner subjective experiences and are the outgrowth and reflection of the musician's conscious thinking about those realities in relation to the world. As Albert Murray has written, "Artists who use their work to recall experience . . . provide the most adequate frame of reference for coming to terms with contemporary experience."[5]

A model work is Dobie Gray's "Drift Away." This song is an appreciation letter to musicians for what the music does: "Give me the beat, boys, and free my soul; I want to get lost in your rock and roll and drift away. . . . And when my mind is free, you know a melody can move me. And when I'm feeling blue, the guitars coming through to soothe me. Thanks for the joy that you've given me. I want you to know, I believe in your song. Rhythm and rhyme and harmony, you help me along, making me strong."

Bernice Johnson Reagon, founder of Sweet Honey in the Rock, writes:

> I think that I have always found it important to sing. Because once I became involved in the Civil Rights Movement, I found the way I wanted to live. I wanted to live being clear and articulate as an artist about what I thought about the world, my people and the society we are living in and helping to shape. If we are a socially conscious people, and if a point of view, a system of principles and values are going to affect the space we live in, it will be most effective if we "put it out there." We can't talk about living in a time when we're losing ground, and losing young people. You lose ground when you don't hold it.[6]

American popular music owes many of its expressive, structural, and stylistic formulations to great artists creating within a new language and indigenous music forms; these merged together African American sacred and folk traditions. The music has created a value system of our soul, values about what we want and hope for in life, values about our identities, values about our love relationships, values about our ethnic/cultural names, and values about the notion that I am somebody and I have an experience that is worthy.

Neil Postman, in *Amusing Ourselves to Death*, states: "Our conversations about nature and about ourselves are conducted in whatever languages we find it possible and convenient to employ. We do not see nature or intelligence or human motivation or ideology as it is but only as our languages are. And our languages are our media. Our media are our metaphors. Our metaphors create the content of our culture."[7] If this is so, seeing musical expression as a metaphor for a kind of theological probe is helpful, especially if getting to the music allows us to get closer to the people who are screaming or celebrating aspects of life.

The trick has been about transposing our everyday veiled understanding of this activity as entertainment and seeing it unveiled as meaningful. There is a kind of theology which is essentially decoding and interpreting the work of artistry. Part of this is understanding that, in many cultures, music marks thinking, reflection, prayer, and conscious human activity. Music is carried by chosen and trained, spirit-led, and artistically gifted individuals.

Some Brazilian traditional native tribes kidnap the village composers for the worth of their songs. Our own American artists—from Louis Armstrong to Mahalia Jackson, Janet Jackson, and Tupac—all have been given by the public, and then negotiated with by the record industry, a certain space of worship in our lives.

These are our popular priests. It is relatively easy to see this connection and the movement of ideas, emotions, and sensibilities when we consider music that was connected to these three players: the artists, the audiences (society), and the industry (market). I don't think they are always on the same page, but when intention, need, and musical artistry link up, then important impulses resonate and produce an engaged and sensitized society. I believe, as do many artists, that these are driven by singing and performing musicians. Here is the theology of music.

The word *religion* is from the Latin word *religare*, meaning "to tie back together." Music is a public expression, a ritual, a quest to find meaning in community, song, and performance. It is easy to see this in the performers at Woodstock in 1969, when our society had accepted the place and space of musicians, and young people declared their pulpits and saw them as priests. And while some critique can be made of motives, behavior, and suspect ritualistic manifestations, the fact remains that there was a cultural synergy laced with a committed meaning, and we must conclude that this is significant.

Since then, every ten years or so, a generation of young people adopts or creates a musical, cultural, or even spiritual identity, represented though artistry. More important than its being a manifestation against mainstream culture is the fact that this identity is a committed and grounded sort of "faith" that covers young people's "ultimate concerns." This is where we find ourselves again with hip hop. Hip hop culture is connected to a historical musical/cultural development; we can link it to the way Mamie Smith's "Crazy Blues" set the rules of how images and messages got constructed. We have to look beyond the interests of commodity and grapple with the aspects of an ultimate concern that is manifested.

Music artistry gives shape and voice to ideas that everyday people have; at the same time, people experience music as empowering them to articulate what they may not have been able to express. These deeper dimensions, sometimes unspoken but a reality, get at a kind of spiritual, inner experience that music carries. The philosopher Susanne Langer said, "The forms of music are more congruent with human expression than other forms of communication because they speak with . . . a detail that language cannot approach."[8] In her thinking, music is the language of our emotions. Spirit, deeper inner ideas, do not always live in the realm of spoken thought.

Music is the "appropriate framework," as John Miller Chernoff has pointed out, through which identity, values, community expression, and teaching are mediated.[9] The African saying "The spirit will descend with a good song" comes to mind. When the whole community is "feelin' it," dealing with it, in song, when the care and concern of our worth is being realized, the gods give blessing and descend among the people. There is a Negro spiritual that states, "Up above my head, I hear music in the air . . . there must be a God somewhere." This kind of spiritual ritual in the Black public domain is evident in the civil rights period where song, as Bernice Johnson Reagon points out, moved the people to righteous activity and gave them not only music but principles, values, and a way of life that cut across civic, religious, interpersonal, and aesthetic places. This is music theology.

Music in our society, our culture, functions as a form of moving expression that shapes the practices of everyday life. So persuasive is this expression that every generation "logs on" to the program; the artists hold onto the spiritual and deeper dimensions of human relevance, the expressive core values, no matter how diluted they are in the industry. It is nearly impossible to play convincing music without this deeper performance dimension. And this is precisely why people respond so passionately, in almost spiritually instinctive ways. The challenge is to "rescue" artists from the commercial exploits of a solely market-driven music, but this challenge, left unattended, can continue the further demise of these powerful art forms.

The Reality and Rhyme of Roots Music Responses

All music has to be valued and measured against the social, commercial, and cultural backdrop of popular music in our society. All popular music today, deriving largely from an African performative, functional root, encounters many historical creative impulses, styles that have percolated up and have intertwined. The roots music traditions from folk, to bluegrass, to rural blues, while seemingly distant cousins, all grow from people's needs to address life and social inequality. This has always been forcibly and pervasively done with music. The reality of the roots music responses cannot in this discussion of popular music trends—rock to hip hop—go unmentioned. This is because even the soils that nurture hip hop were first prepared by a wide host of singers and social activists who used their voices and song to awaken a nation's social consciousness. As Bruce Springsteen makes clear,

> I try to come in and be that alternative source of information. I always felt that the musician's job . . . was to provide an alternative source of information, a spiritual and social rallying place somewhere you went to have a communal experience. There is a long tradition of artists being involved in the life of the nation. For me, it goes back to Woody Guthrie, James Brown, Curtis

Mayfield, and Bob Dylan. These were all people who were alternative sources of information.[10]

This long, great sharing and connected tradition of roots music is a part of the creative stream of social protest that continues today. That list could begin with the spirituals and would include Bessie Smith, Lead Belly, Woody Guthrie, Pete Seeger, Odetta, Richie Havens, Bob Dylan, Joan Baez, Sweet Honey in the Rock, Tracy Chapman, Ben Harper, John Mayer, and India. Arie. The connection is there, and hip hop continues that line, extending over and embracing Grandmaster Flash and the Furious Five, Chuck D, Public Enemy, Fugees, Arrested Development, Common, Jill Scott, and Talib Kweli. All embrace and reveal the American roots music tradition, in essence.

While on the surface this connection may not be obvious, the comparison is not at all out of place. The most difficult thing to parse out, and yet the most American phenomenon of this roots music, is the clear intermingling, cross-cultural influencing among seemingly countercultural influences: rural Black and rural White folks and how those traditions crossed over into urban terrains. Traditionally, the myth has been that through racial hatred, anxiety, and economic battlegrounds, these two groups had little in common or to share. In music, this is not the case. One could argue that music was precisely the medium through which people connected, and the result is folk, roots, and country music. Johnny Cash said, "Every successful country singer I know has a humble background . . . and the colored blues has been a part of their musical heritage. Every one of them, bar none. Elvis will tell you himself that's where he got his style from, colored blues singers."[11]

Records and radio were the first great technological help of the dissemination and growth of roots music culture and introduced a variety of styles and common stories from a wide diversity of regions and artists. An exploration of these songs tells us about who we have been, are, and hope to become. These are our treasures. Jimmie Rodgers, the Carter Family, Uncle Dave Macon, Fiddlin' John Carsen, Woody Guthrie, Lead Belly, Johnny Cash and June Carter Cash, Sonny Boy Williamson, B. B. King, Chuck Berry, Elvis, Dolly Parton, Natalie Maines and the Dixie Chicks are artists associated with the roots music tradition. They follow public music traditions, beginning with eighteenth-century fiddle contests and continuing in the nineteenth century with the emergence of Swiss yodeling singing groups, and White and Black minstrel singing troupes. Commonalities exist within dance, as well—from barn dances, the cake walk, the charleston, and even the hustle.

Early radio programs helped to codify these cross-cultural, mixed traditions. Scholar John Lomax published *Cowboy Songs and Other Frontier*

Ballads in 1910. In 1920, Mamie Smith, a Black blues singer, recorded "Crazy Blues" on Okeh Records. This became a national hit, providing a blueprint for jazz, r&b, and rap. During this same period, several popular radio show formats, including the Grand Ole Opry, were born. Soon country records were produced and sold. While jazz and blues held firm as the preferred music reflecting modern urban culture, roots music stayed connected with the life of people of the rural farm territories and frontier communities.

Blues and rural protest folk forms are the basis of Woody Guthrie, Bob Dylan, and the later folk protest traditions. Interestingly enough, those folk traditions were connected to a kind of urban intellectualism from the work of Alan Lomax, son of John Lomax. Populist and people's movements raised again the democratic idea that collected voices could give agency to their needs and ideas. In 1933, with the aid of the Library of Congress, John and Alan Lomax began to document folk music and found the Black folk singer Lead Belly. The Lomaxes connected Lead Belly to intellectual and socialist movements. Connections between blues and folk are heard, too, in Billie Holiday's rendition of "Strange Fruit." Writers speak of the profound sense of loss in the 1930s, a loss of faith in the American Dream. The music that emerged was folk.

The creative tradition that includes Lead Belly, Woody Guthrie, Billie Holiday, and Bob Dylan shows American folk music's interesting mix of topical songs, European ballads, Black rural southern blues, and the idea of the common person protesting the state. This latter connects directly to the Rolling Stones' youth anthem "(I Can't Get No) Satisfaction" and Public Enemy's "Burn, Hollywood, Burn."

The emotionally engaged artists, rather than the intellectually detached, best represent the concerns of the people. The American slave spirituals, Lead Belly, Woody Guthrie, and the protest songs of the 1960s continue through to the British and then New York youth rage of punk music, and to rap and hip hop music. We see similar cultural, expressive, social, and political themes and streams in Woody Guthrie's "Do, Re, Mi" and Puff Daddy's "It's All About the Benjamins." This is the retelling of the American Dream in musical tones, with a little bit of edge and distortion.

Billie Holiday's "Strange Fruit," written by Abel Meeropol, was a work that connected all these traditions. Holiday first performed this song in Café Society, a racially tolerant and mixed performance space. In this place in 1939, leftist teachers and progressive intellectuals joined together their concerns and critiques of the injustice of the American system, and especially of the injustice, racism, and violence of lynching. While it has been argued that roots music is not typically "popular music," the impetus, whether the songs feature an acoustic guitar or a raging Jimi Hendrix solo, remains the same: people use music to communicate their anxieties, rage, and need to roam, search, and express.

An examination of the lives of creative individuals who best exemplify and champion the experience and expression of everyday people suggests that their works are produced and powered by the people's uprisings as they confront oppression and injustice. Ultimately, we are looking at the ways that music and culture collide, corroborate, and assign meanings, the ways that music practices in culture ignite, confound, confront the central debates, provide voice, and empower gender and race identity, while also critiquing and celebrating American cultural conditions. This is the construction of cultural codes.

Meaning in the Marketplace:
Black Music as Significant Cultural Form

In his *African Music: A Peoples Art*, Francis Bebey writes that "music is an integral part of African life from the cradle to the grave," and African music "covers the widest possible range of expression including spoken language and all manner of natural sounds." The term *griot* is used throughout West African society to designate a professional musician. Music is at the heart of all the griot's activities, and is further proof of the vital part music plays in African life. According to Bebey, the griot speaks not only the history of a society but also "the wisdom of its philosophers, its corporate ethics and generosity of spirit, its thought-provoking riddles. . . . The virtuoso talents of the griot command universal admiration. This virtuosity is the culmination of long years of study and hard work under the tuition of a teacher." Andre Jolivet, noting that griots are seen as "the inventors of melodies, poems, and rhythms," found that the role of the griot is "essential to . . . ceremonies that are the combination of philosophy, mythology, technique and art." And Bebey writes, "The African musician is an artist who dedicates himself to the service of the community at large."[12]

Black American popular music, in terms of its musical performance function, is closely tied to the roots of all Black music in the diaspora, be it in Europe, the West Indies, New York, or New Orleans. The line of artistic and cultural evolution is very clear: griot, spirituals singer, plantation fiddler, slave preacher, blues singer, singing preacher, poets of the Black Arts movement, and today, rappers. The function or role of rap's performance and delivery style bears family marks resembling every kind of Black music. Note the similarity between Ellington's "It don't mean a thing if it ain't got that swing" and the contemporary rap line "It don't go if it ain't got that flow."

We should not forget Congo Square, the eighteenth-century "public designated" place where enslaved Africans were allowed and encouraged to practice West African performance traditions known as the ring shout. This has come to be known mo' better as the soul train line. African retentions are prevalent in every Black style that has developed in the American public marketplace. The griot is studied as an artist and an important carrier of traditions of marked significance. Contemporary popular artists are modern griots, albeit sometimes misguided.

There is, in fact, a search and a need for meaning in the marketplace, even among youth. The market sells a product that appeals to an inner call and identity of consumers. But this is where the concern and responsibility of the industry stops. It is really the artist's job to provide meaning in the marketplace. Even the slightest recollection of youth urges from the jazz age through to Elvis and the Beatles reveals that morality has not been what has driven youth to the marketplace in search of culture. But there has been a search for something.

The market is not interested in morality but in marketability and materiality. It exists to provide a forum for making saleable commodities and popular artists, and the products are hugely profitable. There have always been artists who struggled happily with this rub and the dilemma of creating work that sustained a core audience while making music that illuminates and moves people beyond. Generally, popular artists grow up and their interests and core audience change. This is why, in order to stay alive, the record industry is always looking for some new, young face to exploit. The public's need for more substantial human-value-based music will, I hope, always outweigh temporary excesses in empty entertainment and fascination with exploiting youth.

The role of artists in the marketplace is to, by conscious construction, allow their gifts to find and speak to a core audience for the purpose of moving people with and to joy and to lift up and even entertain (which, in a traditional sense, is good and meaningful). Ultimately, it is the responsibility of the artist to command the marketplace.

A Journey for Music, Art, and the Value of Self-Activity

Music gives pleasure. Our music gives joy. Our music is about awakening the Spirit. When joy comes to call, no one can ignore the message.

—Marvin Gaye

Carlos Santana, on his 1999 *Supernatural* CD, quotes Gabrielle Roth: "Many of my favorite shamans are rock stars. They probably don't even know they're shamans but they know how to get to ecstasy and back, and they know how to take others with them. They may not have a license but they know how to drive." In his notes, Santana thanks all his musicians with similar gratitude for their "songs which capture our mission to spread hope, peace, love, light and the joy to the heart of the listener." In her 1999 CD *Amen*, in a song entitled "God Is Watching," Paula Cole states, "God is waiting for us to overcome. God is waiting for us to just love one another." Lauryn Hill is another example of a popular priestess. In "Superstar," from the 1998 release *The Miseducation of Lauryn Hill*, she sings, "Now tell me your philosophy on exactly what an artist should be? Should they be someone with prosperity and no concept of reality?"

Artists, through their musing, provide a space for people to be moved, touched, and inspired. Rapper and hip hop producer and now elder cultural statesman Chuck D, in his completely informative and insightful autobiography *Fight the Power: Rap, Race, and Reality*, makes this case very clearly: "Educating through music is what I was meant to do."[13]

The Broader Market Implications of Music Dipped in Purpose

As Jackson Browne states in the documentary film *The History of Rock and Roll*,

> I have always thought it was my responsibility to talk about life as it is for everybody. In my music I use a personal narrative to talk about things that are, in the final analysis, universal, helpful, if I am doing it right, and they are not just about my life but are about your life too. It was put in my mind very early on that you should discover yourself and bring that out, and that's what people would be interested in, what you have inside what you have to say. For me writing songs is like collecting, or harvesting the residue of a life. This is what happens when you later take your experiences reflecting on them and arrange them in some order.

The questions for us primarily have been: What are musicians doing? How is their work a reflection of society? How do these artistic reflections connect, benefit, respond, represent, and provide illumination, hope, a critique, or a search for expression and meaning?

There continue to be musical revolutions, new eruptions of social dissatisfaction expressed in song. Then the industry co-opts that energy, markets it. More musical reactions rise up against this, and a new form develops. Bebop reacted against the jazz status quo; rock was a reaction against a suburban status quo; ska and reggae were a reaction against British and American capitalism status quos; punk reacted against the rock status quo; rap reacted against the soul status quo. Black American vernacular musics, in particular, have carried every generation's angst, identity, youth, and artistic revolutions.

Our interest is always in how music carries ideas about human living. A theological/sociological probe involves looking at the music as an expression of joy and inspiration. Where there is darkness and desolation, music is in dialogue with that "scream" and illuminates, gives meaning and hope, a "soul-ution" to the needs of the human condition. The claim is that Black music traditions in popular culture literally and powerfully changed the world. That expressive spirit resonated in the music of the spirituals to free jazz and beyond. And we are different because of this artistry. Over one hundred years ago, European master artists began to open their mouths publicly and proclaim these artistic movements as genius filled, claiming that these voices were a modern revolution that America should have recognized, appreciated, and celebrated as greatness. Much short of this, America mostly commodified the voices.

Music that grew in connection with these claims of genius is most prevalent from the spirituals to punk. Progressive hip hop, grunge, and contemporary popular music today center on the "dealing activity" and reflect and respond to what I call "feeling, dealing, and healing" with music. In popular music, images of poverty, crime, poor housing, police brutality, job discrimination and unemployment, sexism, and other ideas and issues powerfully symbolize social/cultural/political concerns. The way these ideas are formulated, carried, and disseminated in our culture shapes contemporary identity in art. This shaping is both a spiritual and artistic matter. If we add to this the youth angst that has bubbled to a boil artistically from the 1960s to the present, then that is the stuff of our musics.

We need to look and listen critically and carefully to the music/art of this present generation and how this music provides a voice and critique for today. What is the critique in contemporary forms in all styles?

Rap and hip hop music were not the only work that reflected a tremendous amount of stylistic, cultural, and political change during the late 1970s and 1980s. Black music reflected and submerged itself with the major tenets that were developing in the larger popular American mindset. Some review of these styles is helpful.

- In 1970–1971, the deaths of Jimi Hendrix, Janis Joplin, and Jim Morrison served as tragic symbols for the closing of the first decade of rock and roll. Musicians now asserted that popular music was a major movement of style, art, ideas, and the expression of youth culture, and this blossoms.

- During this period, there was great musical variety, drama, and musical fantasy: "Let's live; it's our times." In the excesses of baby boomers, experimental music blossomed, supported by the industry that during this period actually invested and allowed originality as musicians created their music.

- In the 1970s, disco began to be music to serve something else. John Travolta's hero in *Saturday Night Fever* (1977) exemplifies the clothes, discothèques, and style, all adding to the larger-scale "partnership" of music and big industry commercialization.

- The musicians abandoned their hope for a revolution in values and began to turn inward. The music too began to reflect a somber, conservative mood, becoming introspective. Core mainstream Black music turned softer and retrospective as well, as seen in the O'Jays' "I Love Music" and Stevie Wonder's *Music of My Mind*.

- Rock mingled with classical and jazz music forms. The great examples are Herbie Hancock's Headhunters, Chick Corea's Return to Forever, Joe Zawinul and Weather Report, John McLaughlin and Mahavishnu Orchestra, Tony Williams's Lifetime, and others such as Carlos Santana, Pink Floyd, Yes, and Emerson, Lake, and Palmer.

- 1970s pop folk gave rise to James Taylor, Carole King, Carly Simon, and Joni Mitchell. Then came Elton John, another "blessed British invasion."

- Theater rock and horror emerged, including David Bowie, Alice Cooper, Iggy Pop, Queen, KISS, Parliament Funkadelic, and Earth, Wind & Fire.

- Stadium and corporate rock, as well as music-industry heads, really took over, spoiled it, and changed it all. Artists and Repertoire (A&R) directors, once musicians and songwriters, were replaced with non-musician executives. Some companies even banned the piano from corporate offices, preventing the performances of potential songsters who, before, could make their pitch musically to executives who were musicians themselves.

The questions arises: Does fame, fortune, and the pursuit of cash in music lead to destructive or more progressive music?

Something of Substance

Once I realized that I'm a voice that people listen to, I realized I had to fill my voice with something of substance. Through rap music I've seen people all over the world magnetized to thoughts and ideas. My goal is to be used as a dispatcher of information.

—Chuck D, *Fight the Power: Rap, Race, and Reality*

In the event of my demise when my heart can beat no more, I hope I die for a principle or a belief that I had lived for. I will die before my time because I feel the shadow of death. So much I wanted to accomplish before I reached my death. I have come to grips with the possibility and wiped the last tear from my eyes. I loved all who were positive.

—Tupac, "In the Event of My Demise"

Our times desperately need to be in touch with the practices of the past, which linked together performance values rooted in musical excellence that helped secure our culture against crisis. The soul era stands out as a period in Black artistry where the music communicated a general philosophy of refusal to accept the undesirable and a determination to both illuminate despair and create a better future. "A Change Is Gonna Come" (Otis Redding), "Wake Up Everybody" (Harold Melvin and the Blue Notes), "Higher Ground" (Stevie Wonder), "What's Going On" (Marvin Gaye), "Yes We Can Can" (Pointer Sisters), "Ain't No Stoppin' Us Now" (McFadden & Whitehead), "I Will Survive" (Gloria Gaynor) are songs which suggest the alignment of strong moral and community commitment and great commercial artistry. This has not gone away. The entire wave from the new r&b movement out of Philly with Jill Scott, the Roots, Erykah Badu, MusiqSoul Child, and others show us where hip hop style and old-school talent and sentiment in the marketplace have collided again among a number of new record-industry acts. Cornel West has written, "The future of our artistry may hang on the quality of the response to our contemporary social challenges depending on not just the talents, but moral visions, social analyses, political strategies which highlight personal dignity."[14]

Toni Morrison's beautiful discussion of our great Black music literature sums it up best: "a sustaining force, which healed, nurtured and translated Black experience into above all else, art."[15]

There are still numerous examples of music that move within the popular traditions while managing market and morality. Many of these popular music traditions are greatly steeped in the tradition of telling human stories for the purpose of uplifting by examining the pain, and working ways through to wholeness. Singing and performing are just one strategy employed by creative artists to manage the madness and provide joy and a lifted spirit in the face of the consequences of the everyday.

CHAPTER SIX

Black Music Studies

Through his artistic efforts the Negro is smashing this immemorial ste-
reotype faster than he has ever done through any method he has been
able to use. He is impressing upon the national mind the conviction
that he is an active and important force in American life . . . he is a
contributor to the nation's common cultural store . . . he is helping to
form American civilization.

—James Weldon Johnson, *Black Manhattan*

Connecting Black history studies, Black music studies, and cultural studies to musicianship is important if consideration of cultural codes and an
aesthetic philosophy is going to matter. A brief history of Black studies and
the emergence of schools of thought which attempt to address some of these
hurdles is helpful here. Black cultural studies wrestles, too, with shifting
values and generations of thinkers who bring new paradigms to the study of
Black people and to the discipline as it has been growing for well over one
hundred years. Since W. E. B. Du Bois's classic 1898 paper "The Study of
the Negro Problems,"[1] Black studies has grown into a multidirectional academic discipline, focusing on Black people from around the globe and their
impact on the development of human history. There have arisen forks in
the road and many questions as to what should be the direction of what was
first called Black studies and now might be called Africana studies. Most are
unaware that numerous individuals and movements have turned ideas over
many times, and that there exist different platforms and positions on which

debating teams have stood and are standing. The question of what has mattered, related to Black life and pursuits, is far more complex than the classic bifurcation of a Du Bois versus Booker T., or a Malcolm versus Dr. King. As we define this discipline today, it is necessary to consider not only race, but also class, education, economics, integration, and more.

As Manning Marable explains in his essay "Black Studies, Multiculturalism, and the Future of American Education," we need a discipline of study which rightfully respects and reflects the cultural diversity that makes up the society in which we live, and to which students are being prepared to contribute. He believes that general education requirements would be enriched by including "explorations into the African American experience," and that the "serious study of the African American experience is important not just to Black students but to all students, regardless of their ethnic background or heritage." He also advocates "cultivating an internationalist perspective on education, recognizing that the solutions to the problems in learning in rapidly changing societies are not confined to any single country or culture."[2] Marable argues for the necessary connection between academic excellence and social responsibility, not merely to interpret the world, but to change it.

Marable echoes what Langston Hughes stated over eighty years ago in his great manifesto "The Negro Artist and the Racial Mountain." Hughes wrote, "We younger Negro artists who create now intend to express our individual dark skinned selves without fear or shame." His strong words energized Black artists of his time. The same connection can be seen today as Blacks across the globe—in the United States, Europe, Africa, and elsewhere—rally around hip hop as the aesthetic and stylistic voice of their generation. This cross-global, transcultural dialogue is crucial to the understanding of Africana studies, the connections among Black academics, musicians, and folks.

Classic Black Studies

Classic Black studies begins, as mentioned earlier, with W. E. B. Du Bois's case study of the Negro life: "The Study of the Negro Problems." Du Bois argued that the study of "the Negro" was full of possibilities: it was "rich and a mass of truth worth knowing." As he expressed it, because of America's "central and all absorbing need" to sustain and develop wealth, American society experienced a complex race and class problem. In what Du Bois termed America's "peculiar environment," the Negro people developed unprecedented cultural responses. He suggested that there were four windows through which to study this—historical, statistical, anthropological, and sociological—and he assigned two agencies to oversee this work: the government and the university. After some time teaching in the South and living among the folks, Du Bois went on to publish *The Souls of Black Folks*, where he would emphatically champion Black culture. He declared that America could not reach its potential until Blacks were allowed the social right to democracy. He also noted that Blacks' songs of spiritual striving, sorrow songs, were the "richest example of profound human testimony," of marked significance, "more profound than anything that humanity had yet accomplished." He asked, would America even be America without its Negro people?

As Du Bois posed this political and sociological question, an answer was found in aesthetic and cultural terms. The very Negro people who were burdened socially with this "peculiar environment" transformed their striving largely by their artistic response. While there was certainly intellectual and social progress made, it can be argued that the artistic and cultural expression received the strongest "hearing." For our discussion, the musical note is of great interest.

There are generally six major movements or waves of thinking about Black social/cultural existence in America. These have all come largely from within academic circles and can be seen as descriptive of literary and cultural developments.

1. The Du Bois social/academic studies model (University of Pennsylvania, 1898 study).
2. The Carter G. Woodson corrective history model (Association for the Study of Negro Life and History, 1916).
3. The Harlem Renaissance (1920–1935), with the work of Hughes, Hurston, Bontemps, Still, Savage, and others. While not solely an academic response, its movement tenets impacted education by providing an impetus for scholarly inquiry as seen in Alain Locke and others who called for a literary/cultural academic movement.
4. The civil rights movement (1950s–1960s). This was a second national rise in Black consciousness, exemplified first by individuals and groups such as Jackie Robinson, Althea Gibson, Ralph Ellison, Gwendolyn Brooks.
5. The Black nationalist, Black Arts, Black power, Black studies, and "Black experience" or essentialist/culturalist models (1970s), as seen in, for example, Harold Cruse, Karenga, Asante, and Afrocentricity.
6. The postmodern, interdisciplinary globalists (1990s), and new elites— Gates, West, hooks, Dyson, or what Marable calls the radical, democratic multiculturalists.

Black music studies notes connections between African American and traditional West African music practices. As Eileen Southern asserted in the seminal work *The Music of Black Americans*, "The Black musician has created an entirely new music in a style peculiarly Afro-American that spreads its influence all over the world."[3] Hip hop, for instance, was actually mobilized by a Jamaican DJ who settled in the Bronx in the early 1970s, but who played r&b records in his hometown. Hip hop music revolutionized American popular music culture, then went out again to move Black thought and expression around the world. Popular culture becomes a significant model through which we can study social connections.

Mobilization and Cultural Creation: The Rise of African American Consciousness

Several factors help guide our interpretation of African American historical and cultural development:

1. African Americans came into slavery with a rich African cultural heritage known either by direct experience or by oral and cultural transmission—what Du Bois called "social heredity." Many of these cultural values continue to have a profound effect on the way African American history and culture evolve.
2. Multidisciplinary probes—including methods of social, political, economic, religious, and aesthetic sciences—are necessary to examine African American history and culture.
3. A resistant spirit that includes constant growth, constructions of meaning, and redefinition of existence in a new world characterizes African American history.

Approached in this way, the deep truths about African American culture and history surface and can be interpreted within the many parameters of the Black experience. In short, as Herbert Gutman suggests, Black resistance to total White domination in America produced many personalities, institutions, cultural creations, and an African American identity.[4]

Music is one of the most visible and influential cultural creations of African American existence. Black music is art, a manifestation of the skillful use of the imagination to create objects of human expression. Like all Black creations, this art is closely tied to the hardship of African American experience. We must consider the unique aesthetics of Black musical expression.

African American music is tied to Africa in artistic quality and cultural function. In its initial stages, African American music expressed emotion and frustration as well as hope in a higher power, a God who was always among the people. It was religious music and, as James Cone suggests, it was social and political.[5]

An aesthetic probe into African American music reveals its social and psychological implications. The music is direct expression that is pure, often includes religious affirmation or social protest, and entertains. African American social and religious music can be interpreted as existence art organized around social circumstance. The social element more than any other aesthetic reason provides us with a functional definition. Beauty must initially be found in the sincerity of the song that symbolizes inner expressions and yearnings which are the root of any artistic creation. Black art is concrete expression.

> O freedom, O freedom,
> O freedom over me. And before I'll be a slave,
> I'll be buried in my grave
> And go home to my Lord and be Free.

The African American form of the folk song, the reconstructed European hymns, the field or work songs, the jigs, the spirituals, the blues, and instrumental art pieces with fiddle, banjo, and guitar improvisations are all culturally tied to the African aesthetic/social meaning of art. Music in Africa is a concrete expression of every aspect of community life. The griot/composer/poet, the priest, the mother, the worker, and the children all use the "African song" as a constant form of human expression and sharing. In *The Music of Africa*, J. H. Kwabena Nketia writes:

> The treatment of the song as a form of speech utterance arises not only from stylistic considerations or from consciousness of the analogous features of speech and music; it is also inspired by the importance of the song as an avenue of verbal communication, a medium for creative verbal expression which can reflect personal and social experience. . . . [The songs] may deal with everyday life or with traditions, beliefs and customs of the society.[6]

The African aesthetic base of Black art remains in American art. This point is crucial. Much of African American music, especially the spirituals and the interpersonal blues or folk songs, can be characterized by the simultaneous saturation of religious and social experience in the artistic expression. This gives Black style a depth and sincerity which is, for lack of a better word, "soul." Any discussion of the aesthetic quality and meaning of Black music must consider the art as the expression of both the social context from an African American perspective, and a rich, indelible African heritage. In this situation, African Americans created, in essence, cultural extensions of Africa by restructuring and integrating European religious concepts and new musical sounds to express their experiences.

The discussion of these issues brings to light an understanding of cultural creation and consciousness and attempts to view African American history and culture from a multidisciplinary perspective. Within the matrix of European intentions for world expansion and the resulting American Dream, Blacks began a consistent and determined resistance against White domination. An overview of the growth of an African American cultural consciousness is impossible without social, political, religious, and ethnological considerations.

The degree of African retentions which still exist in African American culture shows how Black response to social conditions necessitated the conscious creation of Black mobilization and other cultural structures. Further study would incorporate the role of the African American family in the struggle to emancipate and elevate enslaved members. Out of this immediate family struggle came the creation of an African American culture defined by religious expression, song, and literature. African Americans were also determined to formulate a public philosophy based on the principles found in a restructured constitution and the God-ordained liberties afforded to all created souls. African American history and culture are fascinating because of their incredible richness and complexity. My interpretations only scratch the surface of the vast amount of information that needs to be considered. A quest for meaning, an analysis of social structure, a search for family values, an encounter with religion, a political and economic probe, an experience of heart and song, a journey into the minds and hearts of an incredibly beautiful and strong people are all necessary to rewrite a story that has been barely told.

From Old School to New Schools
of Thought in Black Music Culture

Today, Black music studies, or Africana studies in music, can be defined as the study of the history and culture of Black people in music. It is a specific discipline that drives questions, analysis, and examination. Its primary themes explore what matters in Black music, in this art form. The discipline asks: How does music function in relation to people existing in their worlds? Identity, power, form, ritual, and purpose are part of the discussion. Even though history is the line which the questions and developments are set upon, the discipline goes beyond historical inquiry. Africana studies revolves around the exploration of the culture of Black people in the diaspora, and the implication of their presence as it relates to the development of the modern world. This is a discussion of sociology, artistry, aesthetics, meaning, and practices. It is an ultimate cultural study.

The Black music programs in many southern colleges were first in focusing on usable models of Black music culture, exploring spirituals, rag, and jazz. Fisk, Hampton, and Tuskegee, for example, began this exploration before established music schools and colleges introduced jazz or popular culture studies into their curricula.

From James M. Trotter's *Music and Some Highly Musical People*, published in 1881, we see an important development of Black music studies.[7] Even though these musicians were largely "classical" artists, the embodiment of Black culture ideas as a study is significant. The printing of race and coon songs, the minstrel traditions, and ragtime, as musicologist Guthrie Ramsey points out, helped elevate Black music to the academy. "Jazz criticism played a crucial role in elevating international perceptions about the values of indigenous American music making during the 1920s and slightly before, writers of various stripes—composers, journalists, music critics, musicians published books and articles in magazines."[8] Of note during this period is pianist/historian/arranger Maud Cuney-Hare, a classically trained pianist and graduate of the New England Conservatory, who wrote the 1936 *Negro Musicians and Their Music*. Of further interest for us, she was engaged to W. E. B. Du Bois and spent some time as editor of the *Crisis*.

Du Bois, William Monroe Trotter (son of James Trotter), and Cuney-Hare were affiliated and community connected in Boston. It is here that music scholarship, and especially Black music scholarship, began to create bridges connecting music, culture, and the community. These bridges were the beginning of the cultural codes that we are developing and exploring in this book.

While jazz band and chart arranging courses among interested Whites emerged early in places like Berklee College of Music, founded in 1945, formal music education in Black popular music outside of spirituals and jazz was largely nonexistent until the 1960s and 1970s. The civil rights movement, Black Power movement, and Black Arts movement all voiced concerns about a lack of Black cultural content in colleges and universities. In the late 1960s and 1970s, courses looking at the blues, r&b, and soul emerged in higher education—for example, at San Francisco State College, Howard University, Fisk, and Indiana University. Debates arose among musicologists, ethnomusicologists, and other scholars of music regarding the study of Black music. Several scholars tried to answer the fundamental question, "What is Black music?" In one way or another, Amiri Baraka in *Blues People*, Addison Gayle in *The Black Aesthetic*, Dominique-Rene De Lerma in *Black Music in Our Culture*, Eileen Southern in *The Music of Black Americans*, Ben Sidran in *Black Talk*, David and Lida Baker in *The Black Composer Speaks*, Nelson George in *The Death of Rhythm and Blues*, Samuel A. Floyd in *The Power of Black Music*, and Guthrie Ramsey in *Race Music* all address this question.

These books examine and cement the importance of the questions surrounding the historical/aesthetic identity and value of Black music. All emphasize that this music means and symbolizes Blackness as a global connection, language, and philosophy of cultural conditions and worldviews in and outside Africa, and throughout the diaspora. Scholars have boldly argued that we cannot do the unthinkable and unbearable—we cannot separate Black music from Black life, Black thought, Black sound, Black participation, Black culture. As Ben Sidran pointed out,

> Black music can be seen as a function, and to some extent, a cause of a peculiarly Black ontology. Thus the investigation of Black music is also the investigation of the Black mind, the Black social orientation and primarily, the Black culture. . . . The first Black solo musician on the scene was the blues singer. . . . These musicians composed their own songs, based for the first time on secular problems of the Black individual.[9]

This is why, in teaching and talking about Black music culture, we cannot separate Black music function and meaning from its connection to Black life.

In the landmark *Black Music in Our Culture*, resulting from a meeting among scholars, composers, and educators at Indiana University in 1969, Dominique-Rene De Lerma focuses on the relationship between Black music and the traditional Black church and educational system; the relationships among jazz history, Black dance, and audiences; and the role of the composer in addressing the Black situation. Wherever Black people landed, De Lerma explains, they responded to their condition and celebrated their living through musical expression.[10] By the time these larger discussions opened up in scholarly circles in education and in the streets (as evidenced in the soul movement reliance on Black tradition, African notions of beauty, community, solidarity, etc.), Black music was understood as popular, sacred, secular, European-based, experimental, avant garde, protest, and vernacular. Music in Cuba, Brazil, Jamaica, Haiti, and South America, wherever Black people landed, could be seen as a response to and celebration of people's living conditions. In this incubator, a great and powerful tradition has sprung, and its "copyation," exploitation, and commodification have spurred debates about how the music is actually used in market culture and what effect this has on and with the folks.

How to Shape the Cultural Study

Black music studies shares with and takes from its cousin discipline of Black literature studies a critical stance and need for its own preservation and advocacy. The overarching goals of a full study of Black music culture could be:

1. A music/culture exploration, establishing a purposeful discourse that adequately contributes to the full study of Black music culture, history, and people, and an analysis of the social, political, and cultural environments that gave rise to various traditions. This discourse/study must link American and global traditions, outlooks, meanings, and Black cultural phenomenology—art, culture, social politics, history—throughout the African diaspora from West Africa, to Cuba, West Indies, Europe, North and South America.

2. A reconceptualization of history, methods, rituals, performance practices, values, and conventions related to the creation of Black culture/music practices over time, keeping in view the artistry, artists, and forms that have been recognized as seminal in establishing traditions, such as Louis Armstrong, Son House, Duke Ellington, Dizzy Gillespie, Thomas Dorsey, Mahalia Jackson, James Brown, Aretha Franklin, William Grant Still, and others, as well as West African griot and the music traditions created by Afro-Cuban, Brazilian, Caribbean, and West Indies artists.

3. Models, paradigms, theories, and forms for intellectual, aesthetic, and philosophical clarity that bring unification within the discipline that is seen as viable, aesthetically and academically credible.

4. A balance between intellectual academic rigor and multiple music performance practices—from blues, gospel, jazz, and urban popular forms—with purpose and relevant connections that reach, reflect, and affect everyday people and their life practices.

5. A respectful balance of focus among interdisciplinary camps, integrating the study of social history and culture with the disciplines of music, theater, dance, and literature. Also, a balance of traditional and new

industry/cultural values that cultivates an appreciation of vernacular, contemporary, and traditional "classical" modes of Black music practice: that is, hip hop and jazz, gospel and spirituals, pop and art songs, blues and symphonic forms.

6. A usable, flexible, and unifying set of themes, such as the functionality of music culture in creating community, ritual, West African retentions, blues modality, rhythmic vitality, centrality of political potency in the music, cultural creation and commodification, race, identity and image representation, music industry business, and politics. Above all, artists should be exposed to the ideas of cultural meanings, community, and activism through their music, communicating ideas for the betterment of society.

Casting a new set of codes to construct a philosophy requires courage and frank conversations among participating artists and educators who are committed to studying our traditions and advocating for new art and societal work. Are there enough of us talking, enough of us willing to listen and to hear? And do our questions dig deep enough to unearth the new inventive talent it will take to create the new sounds, the new experiments? Most importantly, will we take the time to do this? Will we stretch to work with younger artists? Will we patiently engage our slower bosses, our stuck music directors, our "old school," "old religion" pastors, our even-tempoed conductors, our budget-busted departments, our apples and raspberries A&R personnel?

It feels great to dream about a philosophy of what music means in the twenty-first century, but will we work to hear the songs in new ways?

PART III

MAPPING BLACK MUSIC, HISTORY, MEANING, CODES, AND ARTISTRY

Bitches Brews. *Oil on canvas by Tara Banfield*

CHAPTER SEVEN

⧂⧂

African Roots to
Blues, New Orleans, and Ragtime

Art by definition says, this is beautiful, and this is valuable. Black arts expressions depict Black people as beautiful and their story as valuable.

—Nelle Painter, *Creating Black Americans*

[T]he police beating Negroes' heads, that ole club says, Bop, Bop, Be Bop! That's where Bebop came from, beaten right out of some Negroes' heads into their horns.

—Langston Hughes, *Selected Poems*

Black music culture and artistry move rapidly, changing with people and time. There are few modern cultural movements which, when examined, create such a diverse sprouting of ideas, cultural interests, reflective song banners, styles, cultural controversy, colorful personalities, and unforeseen genius. Heroes in Black music are born, made, faithfully delivered and followed with such devotion, it baffles the mind as to the depth of the creative bank. It's an artistic history that never fails to generate a profound feeling of deep appreciation among those who listen and watch. Learning about Black music culture illuminates the depth and richness of human history, providing an understanding of modern music. This is a culture study that enables us to examine how people, through Black music, foster worldviews, establish patterns of lived normalcy, neutralize oppressive systems, and create shared cultural values. This chapter highlights major musical movements, cultural

Some Major Developments in Black American Music

1619	First enslaved Africans arrive at Jamestown.
1651	*Bay Psalm Book*, colonial hymns, work songs, field hollers emerge.
1707	Isaac Watts publishes hymns.
1730	Great Awakening revivals in the colonies and spirituals emerge.
1770–1830	Second Great Awakening; Logan County, Kentucky, participants complain that the "Blacks" were singing their "spiritual songs" loudly.
1774	An Englishman reports on "Negro fiddle jigs."
1788	First Black Church is formed, Savannah Baptist.
1794	African Methodist Episcopal Church is formed.
1801	Richard Allen, Black church bishop, publishes collection of hymns and spiritual songs. Francis Johnson (1792–1844, Philadelphia), first African American to arrange American music, sails to Europe and performs.
1820–1870	Black minstrel shows; Zip Coon and Jim Crow characters popular. American song publishing is born.
1820s	First School of Black Musicians, Philadelphia.
1861–1865	Civil War; 1863 Emancipation Proclamation.
1867	*Slave Songs of the United States* published by William Allen, Charles Ware, and Lucy McKim Garrison.
1867	Founding of Boston, New England, and Cincinnati conservatories.
1870	Fisk Jubilee Singers begin American and European tour.
1877	Thomas Edison invents the phonograph.
1887	Emile Berliner invents the gramophone.
1892–1895	Dvořák directs National Conservatory in New York and establishes first conservatory-educated Black composers: Will Marion Cook, Harry Burleigh.
1897	New Orleans legalizes jazz as entertainment music.
1898	*Clorindy: The Origin of the Cakewalk*, by Will Marion Cook, is first all-Black Broadway musical.
1899	Scott Joplin publishes "Maple Leaf Rag."
1901	Victor Talking Machine Company records Bert Williams, George Walker singing Black songs.
1903	Scott Joplin composes the opera *A Guest of Honor*, then works on his major opera, *Tremonisha*.

1912–1914	James Reese Europe's Clef Club Orchestra, an all-Black orchestra of 100+, performs music by Blacks at Carnegie Hall.
1912	W. C. Handy publishes "Memphis Blues."
1915	Jelly Roll Morton publishes "Jelly Roll Blues," first published jazz arrangement.
1920	Mamie Smith records "Crazy Blues," first major recording by a Black American artist, sets the stage for race records and Black popular music catalogue.
1927	Duke Ellington appears at the Cotton Club, New York; national broadcasts of his orchestra propel him to stardom and he becomes a symbol of American popular music.
1931	*The Afro-American Symphony*, by William Grant Still, is first symphony by a Black composer, based on Black vernacular music and conventions.
1934	Virgil Thomson's *Four Saints in Three Acts* is the first mainstream-produced American opera with an all-Black cast.
1935	*Porgy and Bess*, by George Gershwin, is called the first American folk opera.
1940s	Minton's Playhouse, a club where bebop develops.
1950s	Founding of Atlantic Records; Bill Haley's "Rock around the Clock," Alan Freed Rock Radio Shows, Elvis Presley.
1960s	Bob Dylan, Motown, Beatles, Jimi Hendrix, James Brown.
1970s	Disco.
1979	"Rappers Delight," Sugarhill Gang.
1980s–1990s	MTV, BET, Videomania, Pre-Millennium Revolutionaries, Arrested Development, Me'shell Ndegéocello, Alanis Morissette.
2000–	50 Cent, Black Eyed Peas, Beyoncé, Jay-Z, Justin Timberlake, . . .

conventions, and styles, and it explores biographies of artists whose work and lives have shaped Black musical and cultural codes.

Aesthetic Reflections, African Global Effect

I speak in several instances of the gifting, fluidity, elasticity, and vigor of expression in Black creativity as a unique human phenomenon. The continued evidence of a Black art being used as creative, intellectual power throughout modernity to mark struggle and triumphs is something to note and cherish. This is artistry at its highest manifestation: the interpretation of impulses, what could lie ahead in terms of cultural forecasts, new expressive forms and dynamics that guard against downward spirals and push for progress. As we begin here to map Black music culture, we look deeply into African aesthetic conception and its connective impulses from the Caribbean to the Mississippi Delta to Detroit and beyond. When, for example, we listen to live Cuban music in South Beach, Florida, we are hearing the same great powerful performing code of African music culture, sound, ritual that has grown and developed over time, while holding onto a powerful and common aesthetic. This African aesthetic conception is a global historical occurrence yet permanently a part of several shores and centuries. Examining what Black culture sounds and feels like in the world is monumental. It is like trying to understand why and how the universe spins. It is the powerful continuation of an impenetrable force.

In viewing African art, for example, one notices the power and boldness of spirit in the shapes, forms, and beauty of practical simplicity, yet the pro-foundness in detail and effect, in textures and more. Struck by the awesome beauty of a Guinea-Baga tribe mask, we ask ourselves, "My God, what kind of people can create with their ideas, imagination, their hands, an artifact that tells a history, raises ideas about being, evokes ritual, and holds such expressive power?" Picasso in 1917 wrote, "My greatest artistic emotion was aroused when the sublime beauty of the sculptures created by the anonymous artists of Africa were suddenly revealed to me. These works of religious art, which are both impassioned and rigorously logical, are the most beautiful of all the products of the human imagination."

Collectors speak of the lucid distillation of the human body, the immediacy of the visual language, and the palpable sense of spiritual underpinning. The same cultural codes found in the masks are also deeply imbedded in Black music, and most modern Black art is indebted to African art aesthetics, a point I cannot emphasize enough. For example, when in a traditional bwiti initiation ritual—Kete peoples of Gabon, the mitsogho (tsogho men)—and in the musical performances of bwiti playing the eight-string ngombi harp, the transfer of knowledge is critical. The harp is believed to be associated with the culture's creation, the songs of the harp being the very sound of creation. One statement from the culture is, "Life is given shape through the tentative movement of music." This embodies the aesthetic that is at the heart of Black music. The entire way of life, expression, art, meaning are fused and inextricably bound. This powerful aesthetic is retained and manifested in all kinds of Black practices in art, dance, philosophy, poetry, and music throughout the diaspora.

Still in West Africa today we hear another example of the Black aesthetic in the music of the Tuareg, a nomadic people of mixed origins and faiths who use their music among youth to generate social, political, and cultural consciousness, ideas fired with the needs of preservation and protest, contesting constrictive government forces and oppressive greed-driven politics. Their music asks us to consider their effort to retain an ancient nomadic culture in the midst of a modern, urban, sedentary lifestyle; to retain traditional farming practices, crafts, and herding against the backdrop of a changing culture looking toward land development to supply international markets. Their songs search for the right notes to capture the folks' last living rites and livelihood. Even in the twenty-first century, the Tuareg bands, or orchestras, as they call themselves, of roaming musicians and poets are kidnapped, interrogated, and beaten for their songs. They rap, they "poet," and they create concerts in the desert that unite people. And when we hear this great music, it is like hearing Hendrix, Muddy Waters, and Bob Dylan. As we listen to the ancient musical traditions of the Tuareg, we hear African past and African modernity.

This is another example of the ways that ideas, stretched across generations of Black musicians, connected and contained within the functional aesthetic of Black expression. These modern-day griots use music to maintain a sane view on the world. As one poet writes, "My heart is my soul which I nourish and follow." Through this poetry and music, we realize that Africa still drives a formidable and connective cultural aesthetic and shares in the construction of the people's songs. This is the reassessment of the casting of the codes, a look toward Africa.

African Roots of Black Music Practice

As John Miller Chernoff writes:

> The depth of music's integration into all the various aspects of African social life is an indication that music helps to provide an appropriate framework through which people may relate to each other when they pursue activities they judge to be important or commonplace. Music is essential to life in Africa, because Africans use music to mediate their involvement within a community, and a good music performance reveals their orientation toward this crucial concern. Participation in an African music event characterizes a sensibility with which Africans relate to the world and commit themselves to its affairs.[1]

A full appreciation and understanding of Black music is possible only after first looking at the African cultural and aesthetic root. All Black arts created within the diaspora (including Europe, the West Indies, North and South America) are cultural derivatives of traditional West African practice, philosophy, and worldview. These arts include dance, music, sculpture, poetry, quilting, storytelling, instrument building, and religious practices. The African spiritual worldview and practice are the roots of Black music and African American cultural practices. Africans in most traditional belief systems have held a particular philosophy about life that grows from their understanding of human community in relation to the divine-directed communal spirit. For our purposes, arts, life, and religion are not separate operations; they are equal mirrors, expressions of reality.

All Black music represents West African music culture as evidenced by the immediacy and relevance of African retentions, or those traditions and practices of African culture that still remain in Black music today. "Africanisms" are the root of this unique cultural expression. These can be traced to Nigeria, the Yoruban, Congo, Dahomian, Mali, and other West African countries. Rhythm, scale formations, fluidity of language, rhythmic dynamism, movement, and the philosophy of the meaning of musical expressions all come out of incredibly powerful African worldviews.

Many of these African cultural ways, or worldviews, are ingrained already into our notions of modernity: for example, (1) the idea that musicians share "a community's message of note"; (2) the idea that making music is a spiritual gathering; (3) the idea that a musician's music, performance, and presentation, even though reflective of an individual's understanding of the world, is also universal; (4) the idea that music has to be "in time, in the pocket, or in the groove." These are all African cultural worldviews that affect the way musical reality is perceived. Music is thought to be an organizing principle for reflection, and a way to order reality.

The Western-educated slave Olaudah Equiano states, "We are almost a nation of musicians, dancers and poets."[2] And the narrative of his life, published in 1789, reminds us that there were sophisticated, ordered, cultural systems in Africa, old and dynamic, and that these traditions were greatly, greatly disrupted with the fifteenth-century exploits of an imperialist European conquest for power and greed.

Role, Meanings, Traditions, and Practices of the West African Griot

The griot is an African professional musician who specializes in the art of evoking spirit, who tells the history of the people, the genealogy and wisdom of the ancestors/philosophers. Griots are living archives of the people, the historians of the region. They are trained by an apprenticeship that often passes from father to son, uncle to nephew, and elder to younger. Griots are song traditionalists, preservers of traditions, rituals, and celebrations. They are dedicated to the service of the community at large. As one griot from Mali reported, "I teach the kings of their ancestors so that the lives of the ancients might serve them as an example, for the world is old but the future springs from the past."[3] The West African griot tradition is one of the world's richest musical heritages. In Mali, Senegal, Niger, and Gambia, the griot is an itinerant entertainer and historian. Some traditions preserve more than one hundred songs that function to tell the history. A griot today is still defined as a West African professional who serves as historian, provides the traditional music, the rituals, and is the most virtuosic of singers and players.

Kings trusted griots to tell history because of their training and knowledge; their words and songs are valuable and meaningful. Griots, in their apprenticeship period, sometimes studied on the road for several years. During this time, the student practiced with his teacher's kora—a twenty-one-stringed, plucked harp of tremendous harmonic/modal beauty—and sang the traditional songs as they traveled from village to village. The people provided gifts, money, and materials for the student to build his own kora. The teacher helped the student build the kora, which took about two months, and then invited the elders to hear the student perform the history. Upon approval, the student then became a griot himself.

The griot song "Lmabango" explains, "Oh, music! God created music." The West African griots are artists who dedicate themselves to the service of the community at large. This role is essential to ceremonies and rituals that combine philosophy, history, moral teachings, mythology, technique, and art.

The griot/priest uses music to call upon the spirit to watch over the community. The practice of music to bring unity and community is symbolic of spiritual connection and function. As I explain below, I see this tradition taking a modern form in African American music: one African American derivative of this tradition can be seen in the wandering bluesmen of the nineteenth century: for example, in people like Charley Patton, a singer and preacher who chronicled the 1927 Mississippi floods on 78 rpms. We can also see it in Sun Ra, the Art Ensemble of Chicago, Earth, Wind & Fire, and the Buena Vista Social Club.

African Music as a Root of Philosophy

Music and artistic expression in the traditional West African worldview are used as extensions of the thinking about who "we" are in relation to a divine spirit and each other. Music as a cultural expression is a by-product primarily of this world and community view, and is used to help keep these sensibilities in place. The African saying "The Spirit will descend with a good song" grows from an understanding that, when the song reflects the thinking of the whole community in relation to divine interaction, God's spirit descends among the people.

Traditional African music carries a wide variety of expressions. One can't help but notice the colors, shapes, and textures of African arts in sculpture, instrument making, costume, and daily dress, all of which signify the spectacular resonance of life which reflects an African worldview. All this can be seen, heard, and felt in the vibrancy of African music, especially in rhythmic dynamism.

The horrific African slave system lasted more than four hundred years, and was followed by more than one hundred years of legalized segregation and racial separation. Through the slave trade, a heavy concentration of enslaved Africans came out of West Africa—Dahomey, Togo, Ghana, Nigeria, Senegal, Guinea, Ivory Coast, Cameroon, Gabon, Congo, and Angola. A direct line or route from West Africa leads to South America, the West Indies, Haiti, Cuba, the southern United States, and very notably, New Orleans. Once Europe and the Americas were in contact with Africans—a huge number of peoples, languages, and cultural practices—Western culture was influenced, changed, and reshaped. The very ignorant assertion by historian Arnold Toynbee that "the Black races have not contributed positively to any civilization" and similar remarks by others are now, for the most part, understood as mindless racist theory.

Because music is such an important part of the African worldview, it is not surprising that enslaved peoples brought much of this practice with them to their new homes and environments. It is estimated that more than 10 million Africans survived the middle passage—from estimates that close to 50 million people were brought out of the African continent. With such a mix of customs, music became one major linguistic and spiritual link that could unite African peoples in their new environments.

In traditional West African life, music accompanied every social, political, communal, and spiritual activity. And the principal carrier or tradition bearer of musical cultural/practice in West Africa was the griot, also called the jali. This West African music tradition continued to serve as a life support system, sustaining Blacks through slavery. It is from this group that our notions of the role of artists have been handed down. We are influenced as well by the Western European model of the artist as "cultural hero," promoted by philosophers such as Schopenhauer and Nietzsche and the composer Richard Wagner. The role of the artist and the artist's representation of myth, symbols, histories, moralities, and people stories reveal the importance and power of the musician in contemporary times.

African musical expressions are in many cases synonymous with speech as communication. This gives a variety, a flexibility, to musical rhythms, tones, and pitches, and these expressive pitches are important to African language and speech. We can hear this lyrical expressivity in the languages. When Blacks in the diaspora express themselves in musical ways, it carries with it, too, this emphasis on expressive meanings synonymous with speech. This is one of the most salient points of Black artistic expression. African musicians must also blend musical ability, good memory skills, and technical mastery.[4] Musical practices in West Africa included song, scale, and rhythmic conventions and traditions, with a staggering array of instrumental families and subgroups including xylophones and marimbas (pitched wooden pianos); stringed instruments (zithers, bows, and koras), brass, wind flutes, bells, rattles, whistles, and one of the world's largest assortments of drums. It is interesting to see the speed of amalgamation of so many diverse African musical instruments and practices with those of the West, the outcome of which has revolutionized music-making in modern times. The most enduring and influential forms were manifested in the American slave creations: the spirituals, blues, and jazz, which expanded to become ragtime, gospel, swing, bebop, r&b, rock and roll, soul, pop, and hip hop. These styles of African American practice gave rise to some of the most important creative artists of the Western world.

Many performance and expressive concepts help us to speak about definable characteristics that shape African American music. These African retentions have become staples of African American music, thought, and performance practices. Consider the following elements found in African American music which are based on African roots: the music is communally based; it reflects collective and individual improvisation; it is spirit led; it exhibits rhythmic dynamism; it features the "sound" of the Black voice or uses the horn as an extension of the Black voice; it includes social commentary and employs inexhaustible variations of repetition and metric layering, which includes guttural expression (moans, groans, screams, shrills) as beautiful; it encourages active listener participation and reaction; and the expressions incorporate physical movement as part of the performance practice.

The communal aspect of group participation is key and evident in every example where Black music is performed. (It would not be proper to stand up and say, "Play it," during an orchestra concert.) The communal activity that accompanies music and dance has as much meaning and importance as a medium to exchange information as the music and dance itself. As a result of this basic premise, music helps to provide the "appropriate framework through which people may relate to each other," according to John Miller Chernoff,[5] and this characterizes most Black music-making in the creative diaspora.

The Spirituals: Definitions

The spirituals are a body of religious Black American slave songs, created by plantation Blacks who fused Western European harmonies and forms with West African songs, modalities, and practices, creating an African American church song tradition. The result was Black American slave songs used in religious meetings among slaves. These represent the first collectable body of newly formed African American music, called the spirituals. The early accounts of this practice are given by ministers who recognized Black singing tradition among the slaves in the early 1740s. By 1867, *Slave Songs of the United States* by William Allen, Charles Ware, and Lucy McKim Garrison, had been published, documenting in notated form religious slave songs.

Here is the joining together of two major religious, cultural, philosophical, and musical worldviews and practices: one from Africa and one from Western Europe. This is one way to begin to explain the binding of practices and beliefs behind the unique formation of Black Christianity and its supporting musical and ritual conventions.

In traditional West African belief, the religious values and communal ethos are believed to be integrated in the musical and social exchange. The musical participation embodies one's commitment and beliefs, and that which is a part of the communal exchange, including values, wisdom, and cultural practice. Music is a part of this sensibility. The Black spirituals encompassed the "newly accepted" Christian beliefs and symbols in song text but wrapped them within the African notions of spirituality, functionality, performance practice, and sounds.

Black music practice has an appeal that transcends its culture, and the prevailing issue is the human struggle to survive, as well as the hope to overcome oppression and discrimination. This is the universal message of the spiritual song traditions. The relevance of the spiritual songs and their theological significance and power can be seen among Black believers. The abstract understanding of a European version of Jesus Christ was transformed into a direct and personal identification with the pain, power, and resurrected spirit of the Christ figure. Scholars have called this Black identification with the Jesus event "Black theology." Slaves identified their struggle with the Israelites and their bondage. One of the major concerns of the church, its dilemma, was the justification of the slave system and the "Christianization" of the slaves. By the earliest baptizing (1641), there was an indoctrination of enslaved Africans by colonists with biblical stories and Western Christian concepts. And while this escaped the slaveholders, it is easy to see how the savior figure in Jesus became a saving figure for slavery. Christ's triumph over death became Black triumph over the evils of the slave system. The biblical hero Moses, delivering his people out of bondage, became another powerful example of this forced cultural transfer.

So we have the creation of a body of works by Blacks in the spirituals, which are at once a cry for liberation, a spiritual/cultural expression, and artistic individualism. Therefore the art piece becomes a place of extremely intertwined meanings. Songs such as "Freedom Train," "Oh, Freedom," and "Swing Low, Sweet Chariot" are examples of a mix between religious sentiment and social/political expression. For instance, the words to "Go Down, Moses" read: "Go down, Moses, way down in Egypt land. Tell ol' Pharaoh to let my people go." These songs reinvented and placed a premium on using the song to convey, contextually, the realism of the singer's trials. It is also easy to trace the principal performers from traditional African songsters, griots, and jalis to the slave preacher, blues singer, gospel singer, soul singer, and rapper, and to mark how the traditions and African retentions remained.

As Ray Pratt has observed in his *Rhythm and Resistance*, "The Spirituals suggest music may function in a profoundly utopian way, seeking to transcend the existing order." According to Pratt, "music is that space, that realm of freedom." The spirituals were "impressive creations of an oppressed minority who used the music as a mode of psychological revitalization."[6]

The Spirituals: Process

How were the spirituals created? The spirituals, as musical expressions, are the amalgamation of African scales, rhythmic and style sensibility, and the European hymn traditions of Isaac Watts and others. As slaves were required to participate in the White religious services, they adapted and transformed creatively the song traditions they heard. Slaves were exposed to these traditions through examples seen in the *Bay Psalm Book* of the colonies (1651) and later Watts's hymns (1707) and John Wesley's psalms, hymns, and spiritual songs (1742). The later evangelical songs were livelier, as they were used in religious revival contexts. These later Christian songs had more rhythm, were more "loose" and adaptable. This was a perfect opportunity for African embellishment and appropriation to combine with an African formulation of song expression and performance. Numerous observers began to point out that the slaves were doing something quite different with the religious music. In the 1760s, a Reverend Wright "heard the slaves at worship in their lodge, singing songs and hymns in the evening and again in the morning, long before the break of day. They are exalted singers, and long to get some of Dr. Watts's Psalms and Hymns."

Beyond the religious, individual yearning for meaning and artistic considerations, there also is the all important context of the slave plantation system. As scholar Roger Abrahams has written in *Singing the Master: The Emergence of African-American Culture in the Plantation South*:

> I see the events as being characteristic of a dynamic process taking place on the plantation in which the slaves neither divested themselves of their African cultural heritage nor acculturated to the behaviors and patterns of their white masters. The practices emerged as forms of resistance, not in the sense that they attacked the system but rather in ways in which they maintained alternatives toward time, work and status. In the process new cultural forms emerged . . . an African American culture was developed by slaves in counterpoint to "planter" ideology . . . [and] a good deal of culture building then was taking place in the yard between the Big House and the slave quarters, in contested areas betwixt and between two worlds.[7]

Examples of the new culture building include the spiritual songs and social protest/Black theology that developed in the "Invisible Institution," the underground Black church, that was developed by slaves in resistance to and independently of the "traditional" church. After hours, the slaves would gather together and create their own services. The music they created in spiritual resistance was the Black church music that has been the foundation of most Black American music forms. In the colonies, the independent Black churches emerged more fully in the 1790s; an example of this includes Richard Allen and the AME (African Methodist Episcopal). But most spirituals were essentially slave songs and were developed orally first on the plantation. This formed the first African American "literature forum" that underpinned many Black social, cultural, political, and artistic approaches. The spirituals are the first renderings of an African American philosophy.

The Spirituals: Types

There are generally three kinds of spirituals:

1. The folk spiritual, still sung in many traditional rural churches.
2. The hymn spiritual, a regular part of congregational hymn books.

3. The concert spiritual, represented by choral arrangements and performances by the likes of Paul Robeson, Robert McFerrin, William Warfield, or contemporary opera greats, such as Jessye Norman, Kathleen Battle, or Denise Graves.

The concert spiritual is the most "artistic," notated rendition, sung by trained concert singers and choirs. These notated spirituals began to be collected, preserved, and given international exposure first through the Fisk Jubilee Singers (1870s) and other Black college groups (at Hampton and Tuskegee, for example), which emerged after the Civil War. These groups sang spirituals passed down orally as slave songs, as well as European-styled classical music.

In regards to everyday music-making, slaves for sale were listed in newspapers as "very fine fiddlers and banjo players," and this musical element increased their marketability. Music-making of all kinds was happening, and many shapes of this synthesis of traditions by Black Americans were evident as early as the late seventeenth century. There are also examples early on of Black composers of African descent working in Europe, such as the Chevalier de Saint-Georges (1745–1794), who directed the Parisian orchestra in the late 1700s, and English-born Samuel Coleridge-Taylor (1875–1912), who was called during his lifetime "the greatest living composer since Beethoven."

In both of these cases, we have Black artists combining the tradition of Western art music with the identity, expression, and cultural traditions of Black people. These efforts were first crystallized in our American form with the numerous arrangements and spiritual compositions penned by early African American practitioners like William Wesley Work. This music was "raised" to the concert repertoire again in the early part of the twentieth century with the efforts of traditional Black (trained) concert singers who performed this repertoire of "Negro spirituals" in recitals and liturgical services. Following the successful concretizing and worldwide appearances of the Fisk Jubilee Singers in the 1870s, Black American singers helped to make this work a part of what has become mainstream repertoire. European composer Antonin Dvořák in 1893 praised American slave music as "the most striking and appealing melodies that have yet been found on this side of the water unrecognized by most Americans."

So here emerges the spiritual, a religious song tradition shaped simultaneously by European structures and sonorities and African scales and melodic traditions within Black rhythmic performance traditions. These songs were performed by Blacks to give voice to spiritual meaning and creative expression. Simultaneously the slaves used the spirituals as encoded message pieces which eventually served as resistance songs carrying the message of human freedom and liberation. There are several things to keep in mind in summation of the exploration of the spirituals as Black cultural product.

From about 1690 to 1890, there developed largely from slave singing a repertoire of thousands of religious songs that are known today as Negro spirituals. These songs are the earliest style that emerged from what were called field hollers and work songs. The spirituals contain numerous themes that are conscious and are evidence of literary wit and personal/communal resolve in terms of the songs serving as protests. The themes include:

- Liberation and freedom.
- Divine justice.
- Living in exile.
- Having faith in adversity.
- Death and suffering.
- Jesus as friend and savior.
- Antislavery sentiment.

There is a widespread use of metaphors and double meanings: a train as a way of escape; a chariot as a group of escapees heading north; a cloud, on the other side of which is heaven; Jordan as the North and freedom; and pharaoh as the slave master. All of this is a clear articulation of Black theology and philosophy in song and religious practice. This is a unique form of Black Christianity among Black believers.

Blues: It's a Leading Thing

Amiri Baraka, in *Black Music*, writes of "'the blues,' its 'kinds' and diversity, its identifying parent styles." As Baraka says,

> This phenomenon of jazz is another way of specifying cultural influences. The jazz that is most European, popular or avant, or the jazz that is Blackest, still makes reference to a central body of cultural experience (The Blues). The impulse, the force that pushes you to sing . . . all up in there . . . is one thing, what it produces is another. It (the music) can be expressive of the entire force, or make it the occasion of some special pleading. . . . We simply identify the part of the world in which we are most responsive. It is all in there. The elements that turn our singing into direct reflection of our selves, are heavy and palpable as weather.

The blues comes most directly as a form of secular Black music growing out of the spirituals. The blues is a musical form and style of playing that evolved out of the slave hollers, spirituals, and free-styling, melismatic, improvised melodies, which created songs and folk heroes such as John Henry and Stago Lee. Blues can be thought of as plantation and country songs taken on the road and to the streets. Black men were now free to roam, to search for families and jobs, and they created this music to accompany this new life. They were known as the bluesmen.

At the turn of the twentieth century, bluesmen had jobs as sharecroppers, builders, timber cutters, railroad layers, and transporters of crops. The blues are songs and poetry concerned with common experience. Instrumentally, they are driven by a sole, nonspecialist folk singer on the banjo, guitar, or diddley bow (one string attached to the side of a house or a board). Later, the blues instruments extended to the piano and horns and eventually ensembles. This is common, country, Black folk music.

But the most salient point of the blues is how it sounds and how it functions to give a "deep-down real feeling" about experiences in the world, usually troubling, but always meant to be uplifting, to "play the trouble away." The blues is expressed in slurred, moaning, gutsy singing and playing, using what is sometimes referred to as "blued" or minor tones within a scale. This "singing between the pitches" was a uniquely African embellishment to the European musical scale, theoretically characterized by lowering (flatting) the third, fifth, and seventh pitches of a major scale even against the major chord sonority or sound. But through the courage of the blues singer and the profundity of the form, the blues addresses expressively how Black people are feeling and "dealin' with it." It has been said that blues music or bluesy expression is "Black music language," inner beliefs and feelings the musician is playing, telling the story. Blues is the "mother tongue" of all Black popular music.

Windows for Viewing the Blues Forms

That's what the blues is, it's a leading thing, something in your mind that's keeping you going.

—David Honeyboy Edwards

The blues is the first great Black American music form with its own unique musical language, structure, practice, style, ethos, and philosophy, complete with cultural mythologies and cosmology and a form that provides a vehicle for inventive, individual creative musical expression. It is as well an openly social form that represents the freedom and desire to speak what you want about your experience, which is universally adopted and understood as a form that evokes and contains this as "existential musical meaning." It was the first popular music form that the world could point to and say, "Black people, they created that." This is why it is so fundamentally important in the historical quest for definition and identity in Black American culture. What Cornel West calls the "Black blues rhythm impulse" is the mother tongue of all Black music forms, and highly influential in the shaping of all modern popular American roots forms. It is a music tradition that marks great human achievement, a classical art form.

One way to view this form is to see this through the window of social history, of how it came to be. Blues is the music of post-slavery migrant workers, traveling, carrying stories, putting on minstrel shows, and using these made-up songs to accompany their lives.

The second window is through the recordings of the men and women who created and performed the form. The classic creators who set the patterns and codes so powerfully were artists like Charley Patton, Son House, Robert Johnson, Blind Lemon Jefferson, Lightnin' Hopkins, Bukka White, Ma Rainey, Bessie Smith, Alberta Hunter, and Koko Taylor.

Another essential consideration is the third window, the musical elements which shape and determine blues harmonies, scalar definition, text, structure, and form. The blues is a musical form that is performed in a traditional 12-bar, repeated cycle pattern. That is the accepted principle these old singers set in place. Those 12 bars are outlined and built musically on a 1 (4 musical bars, 1–4), IV7 (4 musical bars, 5–8), and V7 (4 musical bars, 9–12) cycle of sonorities. This is called a 12-bar blues form. The blues melodies are built on "blues scales," where the major scale has been seriously "bent" by African pitch conventions. You hear a consistently lowered or pulled down flat (b3), (b7), and sometimes flat (b5). The story line falls in a poetic structure of AAB text format and rhyme scheme that is unforgettable, distinguishable, and memorable. Everybody "gets it" and accepts the form, tune, story, rhyme, and game of the songster. The performance practice grew with slides and slurs, from phrase to phrase and pitch to pitch in rhythmic and pulsating sway.

The AAB form looks like this:

I got the blues, and I'm feeling bad. (In F major; for example, the first 4 bars on a 1 chord, F dominant 7)

I got the blues, and I'm feeling bad. (2 bars on the 1V chord, Bb dominant 7 and back to the 1 chord for 2 bars)
I say, I got the blues and I'm feeling so bad, 'cause I lost the only girl I ever had. (1 bar on the V chord, C dominant 7, 1 bar on Bb dominant 7, 2 bars on an F dominant 7)

The fourth window through which to view the blues involves hearing this music as representing and signifying an ethos, a feeling, and a philosophy of life that evokes a reflective sentiment of "troubled" existence, the song as a release for "that trouble." That's the ethos, the feeling of what it gives on purpose. The blues has a rare earthy, lamenting feel that is unique with this African-derived poetic song.

The fifth interpretive window is to recognize basically the four different types into which the blues has developed:

- Rural blues—from the rural migrant worker/singers.
- Classic blues—the stylish entertaining ladies such as Ma Rainey, Bessie Smith.
- Jazz blues—a jazz instrumental form developed by musicians and heard in Louis Armstrong and the Count Basie band, among others.
- Urban blues—sometimes called Chicago blues of the 1940s onward that influenced rock and roll. This includes the electric guitar blues of Muddy Waters, B. B. King, and Howlin' Wolf.

The blues is a simple form that allows a rich variety of ideas, forms, sentiments, and styles on which "musical modernity" in all its complexity is based. There is no easy way to explain the blues. It is a music one must hear and experience really to "get it." The most meaningful explanation is that this is a music created solely for the purpose of engaging in song conversations about life's experiences.

Regional Distinctions

The blues grew from four originating regions: the Mississippi Delta (Charley Patton, Son House), southeastern Texas (Blind Lemon Jefferson, Lightnin' Hopkins), the Carolina Piedmont (Blind Gary Davis, Blind Boy Fuller, Sonny Terry), and New Orleans (Lonnie Johnson, Lead Belly, Jelly Roll Morton, Professor Longhair). And there are the places—juke joints, taverns, streets, and parks—where the blues settled and "set in" in the major cities such as Chicago, Memphis, and Kansas City. We can see the transfer in terms of the role of the musician who handles the forms going from the griot or jali, to slave plantation musician and lead singer/shouter or slave preacher, to now the wandering, individual bluesman. Numerous slave musicians were very skilled, generating folk traditions on fiddle and guitar. These mixed with rural, poor White English and Irish ballads and jigs. These musical traditions were eventually taken to the cities. The blues became the foundation or root in many ways of all other forms to grow out of the Black vernacular, from gospel to urban contemporary.

Due to the decentralization of southern Blacks after the Civil War, from the 1860s to the 1920s, the worldview, the daily experience of Blacks now extended beyond the plantation and plantation church experience. We had "roaming Negroes," men in search of jobs, who were, for the first time, solely responsible for providing for a family. This was a new experience. The downside of it, the angst and powerlessness of this new identity provided a new social context. Mixed in was the reality of broken love, sex, tragedy in interpersonal relationships, death, and travel. These expressions inform the blues.

During this time, even in the South, the Black community was divided into several social or work classes, including tenant farmers, migrant laborers, clergy, tradesmen—including shoesmiths, locksmiths, iron men, and storekeepers—as well as professionals such as teachers, dentists, lawyers, and doctors.

Before the migration of so many Blacks to the cities, the largest concentration of Black migrant workers comprised the farmers of the Mississippi Delta region. Here we find an isolated and dense population that sustained older African traditions cultivated during slave life. Again the blues was the dominant musical style and tradition. Many of these traditions are still practiced today. We can find the drum and fife bands, instruments, and remnants of African song traditions.

Musically, the structural and stylistic limitations of the work song and traditional spiritual forms could no longer contain the experiences of the wandering singer-poets. The blues as an expressive form became more elastic and improvisational; it became an elusive, somewhat structured, somewhat free poetic musical form that contained stories of Black experiences from about the 1890s into the first decades of the twentieth century. The form began to evolve and grow, and this expressive styling became the most persuasive music form created in America. Every derivative popular form from country-western to Broadway and the mega-productions of Hollywood in the 1930s and 1940s has developed from and deeply dipped into the blues. Much of what is contained in the blues (form and structure, style, musical syntax) has become the foundation for music written by composers from William Grant Still to the Beatles. The blues is the equivalent of a standard blueprint that an architect might use to construct a new building. The blues is the root approach, the grounding, the quintessential musical note, the phrase, the feel, the form, and the code for Black music.

The philosophy or ethos of the blues is found in its insistence and focus on the life, trials, and successes of the individual on earth; it is a manifestation of the whole concept of human life. The blues gives emotional meaning to the individual, to one's complete personal life and death. It is musical existentialism. Americans didn't have a music that was so personal, so introspective, so much the "real deal." This is a part of its appeal.

The result is the urban blues heard in Chicago which eventually transformed to jazz, r&b, and gospel. These more urban versions of Black vernacular Mississippi Delta blues are the result symbolically of a turbulent ride up the Mississippi River, the result of social hardships, loss of love, and an endless search for new roots, better economics, and a clear identity. To understand the Mississippi in this light is to keep in mind what it represented as a vehicle to escape one version of White hatred only to find newer, sometimes harsher versions in the North. The urban blues is the musical result of the Black awakening to this new social reality. The blues of these Mississippi Delta farmers now looking for work in the cities is the "reporting on" the travels of these displaced worker/singer, urban soothsayers. It was not all gloom and doom, though. There was freedom, and there was the excitement of exploring the Mississippi and the lure of the great cities for work and opportunity in very vibrant towns, such as Memphis, St. Louis, and of course Chicago.

W. C. Handy

Then one night in Tutwiler, Mississippi (1903) . . . life suddenly took me by the shoulder and wakened me with a start. A lean loose jointed Negro had commenced to plucking the guitar. . . . The effect was unforgettable. His song too struck me instantly. The weirdest music I had ever heard.

—*W. C. Handy: Father of the Blues*

William Christopher Handy was born November 16, 1873, in Florence, Alabama. His parents were slaves who inherited property from his grandfather, also born a slave but raised to prominence as a respected minister. Handy, later called the Father of the Blues, is known mostly as the first trained Black composer to notate, publish, and make famous the style and music called the blues. Despite his grandfather's and father's calling to the ministry, Handy was called by the common music he admired as a child. He later became one of the earliest to bring structural, notated organization to the blues form. Handy trained under a strict singing teacher in grade school, and further taught himself the rudiments of music on guitar, piano, and trumpet. His father disapproved of his music, claiming, "I'd rather follow you to the graveyard than to hear you had become a musician."

But Handy left home, traveling with the Mahar Minstrels, and soon became the group's music director, arranging, conducting, and performing. In 1900, he found himself appointed as a professor teaching music at Huntsville A&M College. He served for two years and returned to the road and the more prosperous minstrel shows, directing bands in the South. Handy first heard the blues in Tutwiler, Mississippi, during a stay in the Delta from 1903 to 1908. Before he heard the name, he referred to some of this music as "boogie house music," the music played by the locals as party and entertainment music. Moved one night by the melancholy sounds of a sole "blues singer with guitar," he decided that he would become an "American composer." Soon after, Handy published his "Memphis Blues" in 1912 and "St. Louis Blues" in 1914. His "Yellow Dog," "Beale Street Blues," and "Hesitating Blues" followed with much success. These put into notation the 12-bar form, based on the I, IV, V chord sequence, that became the standard practice among musicians.

Handy's "St. Louis Blues," his best-known work, went on to be recorded by major artists such as Bessie Smith, Louis Armstrong, and countless others. Handy stated, "I came to think that everything worthwhile was to be found in books. But the blues did not come from books. The blues were conceived in aching hearts. . . . I saw the beauty of primitive music . . . it contained the essence." Handy was the first to codify the blues, and he started a publishing company in 1918 in Memphis with businessman and lyricist Harry Pace, which was known as the Pace and Handy Music Company. In 1921, Harry Pace went on to form Black Swan Records, producing the first all-Black-owned recording company. After the Great Depression and closing of Black Swan, Handy continued with Handy Brothers Music Publishing, run by his brother and sons. He also continued composing, directing, and playing with various bands. In 1938, a concert was held at Carnegie Hall to honor his sixty-fifth birthday. In 1941, his autobiography, *W. C. Handy: Father of the Blues*, was published. He had by this time gone blind. In 1943, he fell onto subway tracks and suffered with his injuries for the remainder of his life, dying in 1958. During this same year, a major movie based on his life, *St. Louis Blues*, was released. The film starred some of the biggest names in Black music and showbiz, including Nat King Cole, Mahalia Jackson, Ruby Dee, Eartha Kitt, Pearl Bailey, and Cab Calloway. This was a most fitting celebration of one the century's most important musical figures.

Rural Definitions, Origins, Migrations

Historian Paul Oliver writes,

> The Mississippi Delta is often regarded as the birthplace of the blues. Many blues singers came from this area, where the Black population equaled and in many cases far outnumbered whites. The proximity to Memphis and the relative ease with which record executives could reach the area by rail from Chicago also meant that it was well placed for location recording. Similarly, many Mississippi blues singers were able to migrate to Chicago.[8]

As stated earlier, during the first half of the Reconstruction period (1867–1877), there emerged wandering men who performed and adapted Black song traditions to comment on and express their secular condition. These were the wandering bluesmen who traveled, performed, and took the blues North. The earlier rural blues and work songs were created to accompany the needs of the worker or the migrant looking for a job and home, lost in the city. But these forms could no longer contain the new experiences of Black people as they began to participate more fully in American society. Toward the end of the nineteenth century and approaching the First World War, migrant and out-of-work laborers numbered in the hundreds of thousands and set into motion a new socioeconomic urban life pursuit. All of this is reflected in the music.

The South during this time enacted racist vagrancy laws that prohibited the movement of Black men, instituting jail sentences and prison work camps for men found without having proof of work. This condition is mirrored in the text of the blues as well. In the 1857 infamous Dred Scott decision, Supreme Court Justice Roger B. Taney declared, "Blacks have for more than a century been regarded as beings of an inferior order and altogether unfit to associate with the white race either in social or political relations, and so far inferior that they had no rights which the white man was bound to respect." In 1896, the courts further upheld a doctrine of "separate but equal," mandating segregation in public transportation and facilities. Between 1889 and 1899, with the terrorism of the Ku Klux Klan, lynchings numbered around 189 per year. This precipitated a series of great migrations of Blacks from the

South. Thousands of men and women moved to the North. Of course, they brought their music with them.

In this urban mix, the blues came to be big business. Blues songs were notated and recorded by White rural music collectors and then disseminated through a new industry called race records, the precursor to r&b. As mentioned earlier, W. C. Handy, who had lived in Memphis, heard blues singing as early as 1903 and published his "Memphis Blues" and "St. Louis Blues." By this time, the practices and tradition had moved up the river to the major urban areas.

The so-called classic blues were sung many times by a more lovely and glamorous version of lamenting women, often on the stage and in front of cameras. The first race records (blues records: Okeh, Columbia, Victor, Paramount, Decca), a regular series of commercial recordings of Black popular music, were initiated by Perry Bradford, a songwriter and manager of a traveling singer named Mamie Smith (1883–1946). Okeh Records released her single "Crazy Blues" in 1920, which became a hit. Soon other White recording companies began to record and issue series that were catalogues of Black performers. Mamie Smith is credited as the first commercially successful popular recording artist, and many would soon follow this pattern. Black Swan Records and the Pace Music Company should be mentioned here again, because these were the only completely Black-owned and operated recording companies which produced diverse recordings from blues to concert singers. Their great staff arranger was the celebrated dean of African American classical concert composers, William Grant Still.

Some of the best examples of traditional blues singers from southern regions are Charley Patton (1880s–1934), Son House (1902–1988), John Lee Hooker (1917–2001), Muddy Waters (1915–1983), the great Robert Johnson (1911–1938), and B. B. King (b. 1925). These musicians made an impressive mark on our culture. Black singing and style became performance characteristics that established a unique Black popular projection, image, sass, and flavor. The codes were set. The other half of the equation were women such as Ma Rainey (1886–1935), who introduced the blues in traveling Black minstrel shows as early as 1902; Bessie Smith (1895–1937); Alberta Hunter (1895–1984); and Ethel Waters (1896–1979). They helped to cement blues traditions and style in the modern era of commercialism. The contributions of these women and men greatly enhanced the popular presence of Black artistry and made it a significant achievement in the West. Blues became the most important grounding style of Black music. It defined the culture, reintroduced the parameters for a distinct aesthetic, and set down the codes for Black popular music performance.

Bessie Smith

Once I lived the life of a millionaire, spending my money, I didn't care. I carried my friends out for a good time, buying bootleg liquor, champagne and wine. When I began to fall so low, I didn't have a friend and no place to go. So if I ever get my hands on a dollar again, I'm going to hold onto it till them eagles grin. It's mighty strange without a doubt, nobody knows you when you're down and out. Mmm, I done fell so low, nobody wants me around their door.

—"Nobody Knows You When You're Down and Out," Bessie Smith

If the most pervasive form created by Black musicians and singers to make a mark on the shaping of modern society is the blues, then there is no singular voice in the form better known and more influential than Bessie Smith. The sheer power of her voice and her presentation of the music made her the "Empress of the Blues." Bessie Smith was Black America's first recording star, the equivalent of a pop icon such as a Michael Jackson or Aretha Franklin.

Her 1929 movie short *St. Louis Blues* included music composed and orchestrated by W. C. Handy that had been recorded by Bessie first with Louis Armstrong in 1925. Arguably the first mainstream popular "music video," the film set the stage for gospel, r&b, rock and roll, and urban contemporary singing. Bessie Smith was one of the most influential singer/stylists in the twentieth century; without her, there would be no Mary J. Blige, Macy Gray, Pink, Christina Aguilera, Joss Stone, Whitney Houston, Aretha Franklin, or Janis Joplin.

She was born in Chattanooga, Tennessee, in 1894, one of seven children. Her family was poor and desperately so after the death of her parents. Before his death, her father was a Baptist preacher and ran a mission. Her mother passed when she was eight. Smith began her performing career at age nine— so that her now parentless family could live. To the accompaniment of her brother Andrew on guitar, she danced and sang with her brother in front of the White Elephant, a Chattanooga club. This was 1904. Even at that age, she "could shake the change out of pockets," as someone remarked. In her full powers, her effect on a crowd was described as "mass hypnotism."

In 1912, she and her brother Clarence joined Moses Stokes's traveling show, where she met Ma Rainey, now recognized as the Mother of the Blues. While the exact musical influence of Rainey is a matter of some debate, there is no doubt that she became Smith's mentor and would have passed on the tricks and tips of the trade, including choreography and approaches to singing a varied repertoire of songs—the codes. Black blues singers were now in vogue in what is commonly called the classic blues of the 1920s. In those days, singing and performing were attractive alternatives to sharecropping and domestic work, particularly in the South.

The industry changed in 1920, when Mamie Smith recorded "Crazy Blues," the first commercial blues recording, an American popular music record which sold over 100,000 sides. This created a major stir, in the new industry, which was quick to find singers who could fill the public's need for the new idiom of Black poplar song: the blues or race records. In 1923, Bessie Smith signed an exclusive recording contract with Frank Walker, head of Columbia Records and the new race records division. During the following ten years, she became the foremost recording artist in the world. She recorded "Down-Hearted Blues," which sold 780,000 sides in six months. From 1923 to 1933, she recorded some 156 sides and was earning as much as $2,500 per week. It is reported that during this period she sold an estimated 5–10 million records, touring the United States and Europe, becoming the highest paid entertainer in the world. She purchased her own railroad car so her troupe could travel freely in the South. Her works ranged from "St. Louis Blues," "Mean Old Bed Bug Blues," and "Black Mountain Blues" to jazz and show numbers such as "I Ain't Gonna Play No Second Fiddle."

When the Depression hit in 1929, blues sales dropped, and the interest in recording waned in favor of talkies, but Smith still did shows: the Bessie Smith Revues, Harlem Frolics, Hot Stuff, and Black Bird. She reinvented herself in the 1930s (and continued to do so until her untimely death). She resurfaced with a greater ambition to be mainstream and evolve in her style, themes, and image. During this same time, she performed with some of the leading early jazz musicians, reflecting her broad style. She recorded with Louis Armstrong, Benny Goodman, James P. Johnson, Coleman Hawkins, and Fletcher Henderson. But her decline from such heights was inevitable during the Depression. The advent of talking pictures and the radio, on the one hand, severely set back the recording industry and gave her audiences other sources of entertainment. On the other hand, the Depression reduced the disposable income of her potential customers. Moreover, she was married to a shark of a man who swindled her out of her money and was perhaps the main source of many of her blues songs. After a turmoil-filled relationship, she made her break from her husband and planned a comeback.

She had new costumes, a new image, and a new repertoire after the blues had gone out of vogue. In fact, in 1936–1937, not only her personal but also her professional life seemed on the way to a comeback. There apparently were major recording sessions and joint appearances in the works with the upcoming leaders of the musical world—including Benny Goodman and the

Count Basie Band. In addition to this, a critic of the time observed that the "Empress of the Blues" had gone far beyond such limitations and was "the greatest artist American jazz ever produced," perhaps transcending even the term "jazz."

Tragically, Bessie Smith was killed in an automobile accident in September 1937, near Clarksdale, Mississippi, the home of so many Delta blues artists. It is ironic that she died in the fertile surroundings of the birthplace of the blues. Her funeral was among the largest ever held in Philadelphia. She has become one of the most beloved artists of all times, and a pattern setter for the modern popular singer.

Early Jazz Development in New Orleans

Jazz can be defined as America's first modernized urban entertainment music, and its formative performance roots are found in the city of New Orleans. The city of New Orleans was founded in 1817 and was called, during the nineteenth century, the most cosmopolitan and musical city in the United States. In 1764, New Orleans was ceded to Spain by France, but in 1800, France, through Napoleon's efforts, got it back. Then the United States, in the Louisiana Purchase of 1803, obtained it. It was a major seaport for the United States, and the slave industry transported a large number of slaves through New Orleans.

From its beginnings, New Orleans was heavily French, Spanish, and American. It has been argued that the Spanish influence was already largely touched by the Africanisms of the Moors. But people from all over the world came to New Orleans. New Orleans was made up of Irish, Italians, Germans, Africans, West Indians, and all parts of the slave southern mix, with Catholic, Black Church, and Voodoo influences. The city boasted three opera companies, two symphony orchestras, Western European classical music, and West African and southern music forms. These styles all mixed to create a "gumbo" of traditions that has come to be known as New Orleans music.

The year 1897 is said to be when the New Orleans red-light district, later called Storyville, was open for business. Travelers, sailors, and locals who wanted to dabble in the "entertainment" were witnessing musicians who had been developing a syncretistic dance and instrumental style that came to be known as New Orleans early jazz. The music was performed by trained musicians, or at least by musicians who were sharing ideas with European professionals in a rich environment that was more tolerant of exchanges of all kinds between Whites and Blacks. Keep in mind that many of the styles, sounds, forms, and practices (spirituals, folk songs, minstrel music, ragged piano) among Black musicians from the rural South were similar and had been preserved, shared, and exchanged among Black people. Various "Black ways" of doing music had been established for nearly two centuries already. More exchanges in New Orleans produced a music that apparently allowed a European instrumental and Black fusion to emerge, flourish, and become performing conventions.

The synchronization, the blending of separate cultural elements, and the ability of African performance arts wholly to transform European culture is one of the great human narratives, and it was possible due to the power of West African music practices. The diasporic remains of this blending can be seen from Cuba to Brazil to Chicago to Haiti to Colombia to New York.

Cross-cultural assimilation thrived in New Orleans at Congo Square, a well-known gathering place, where, on Sunday afternoons even in the antebellum South, slaves were allowed to mingle, celebrate rituals, sing, and dance "freely." The square resonated with an African-influenced mix of instruments, songs, and dancing. Some descriptions mention gourds, drums, banjos, and other instruments in what might have been the first jam sessions. The great New Orleans international composer Louis Moreau Gottschalk (1829–1869) penned his famous "Banjo, Dance of the Negro" in 1851. This mirrored the impression he heard musically in Congo Square. This was the pattern for a syncretization of Black music tradition merging with European tradition that set in motion the creation of many forms to follow. Of note as well are Edmond Dede (1827–1901), his son Eugene Arcade Dede (c. 1865), Charles Lucien Lambert Sr. (1828–1896), Lucien-Leon Guillaume Lambert Jr. (1858–1945). These are prominent classically trained composers of color, of African/Caribbean descent, living and producing in New Orleans. These two groups of musicians—Creole European classically trained, and nonclassically trained Blacks—all participated in parades, funerals, feast days, carnivals, Mardi Gras, and more.

So Western European classical music was prevalent. Southern slave traditions of the work songs and spirituals were other present forms of music, along with the Jim Crow tradition of minstrel song. These formed yet another stream. In this tradition of the minstrel show, Daddy Rice, a White singer/performer, saw a Black man named Jim Crow perform. Rice imitated the man's movement and songs and started a one-man show which appropriated Black style—and an industry was born. White appropriation/imitation of Black tradition became the standard for American entertainment forms through rock and roll.

In 1861, Louisiana seceded from the Union but New Orleans was forced to surrender. Union occupation allowed freedom. A burst of happiness, freedom, exuberance, and jubilation created the musical expression which soon came to be known as jazz. But in an 1877 deal known as the Hayes Compromise, the Union troops were withdrawn, southern White rule was reimposed, and sharecropping, the Ku Klux Klan, and lynching became terrorism for Blacks who now lived under race segregation.

In 1894, New Orleans enacted a segregation code downtown, and creoles of color had to move uptown and live in the Black community. This set in play practices and styles of early jazz codified as an approach to popular musicianship that grew out of the mix of all these exchanges. There were many great musicians and mythical folk heroes who forged the styles, such as Buddy Bolden or Jass-bo Brown (who, as some reported, gave us the name jazz), and most certainly the great traveling New Orleans musicians like Jelly Roll Morton (1890–1941) and King Oliver (1885–1938), who, in the early decades of the twentieth century, spread the sound, style, and influence of New Orleans rag, blues, and early jazz as far as Chicago and California. With the infectious syncopation of newly arrived ragtime from the Midwest in the 1890s and the melancholy bent blues notes traditions from deeper South, all this music culminated in one of the most incredible cultural exchanges in modern history. That cultural-art mix in New Orleans is French, Spanish, European, West African, West Indian, and blues, spirituals, band music, European parlor music, languages played and heard by all kinds of aspiring musicians, street singers, and church musicians.

Ragtime

Migrations of all kinds followed the Civil War, and musicians were traveling from region to region. Ragtime, while originating in the Midwest, traveled down to New Orleans to influence further the mix of traditions already in place. Many simultaneous musical styles, great artistry, and cultural developments merged, and it was actually in the music that the synchronization of much of this was accomplished. Ragtime music produced the first image and identity of a consciously artistic Black musician: Scott Joplin (1870–1911). Ragtime became the rage of early twentieth-century popular culture and was the precursor, in a sense, to jazz music, which crystallized in other major cities: Chicago, Memphis, St. Louis, New York, and Kansas City. A midwestern urban musical form, ragtime was largely instrumental and was personified by Joplin, the best-known Black ragtime composer.

Ragging a piece of music means rhythmically breaking up the melody, essentially syncopation, "ragging it." This reflects the Black cultural style that brings to music a rhythmic feel or jump and a blues tonality. Trained Black musicians who settled in the East and North were able to take some music lessons and applied their own ethnic/vernacular feel to European parlor piano music or band music. The result was a notated, written form pulling from the two worlds, and the music phenomenon became ragtime. At first it was principally a piano music, but it later became instituted in band, chamber, and even orchestral music. For Black families newly freed and settled in the North, one of the ways they showed their independence was to purchase a piano. This was an American, largely northern show of middle-class values. But the style emerged also out of necessity. Many Black musicians were hired to provide music for saloons and eateries, and as W. C. Handy noted, these Black players were piano thumpers. These were one-man bands, consequently developing a style of piano playing that was dance orientated, while simultaneously steeped in traditional European melodic and harmonic stability and grounding. The Black pianists were continuing long-standing practices of Black musicianship, playing plantation jigs, blues-like call and response numbers that had been parts of indigenous Black music unnamed and oral. The "two worlds" on piano became rag piano or ragtime.

Scott Joplin

Scott Joplin, a Negro, an extraordinary genius as a composer of ragtime music.

—*St. Louis Dispatch*, 1901

No European music can express this American personality (Ragtime). It is today the one true American music.

—*London Times*, 1913

Scott Joplin was born in 1870 in northeast Texas and settled in the Midwest. By the age of twenty-nine, he was widely recognized as the "King of Ragtime Composers," having created the best-selling American composition of the early twentieth century, "Maple Leaf Rag." Joplin was ragtime's most prolific and influential composer. Here we have a Western-trained Black composer capturing vernacular Black performing traditions in notated music. A well-respected musician, composer, performer, and teacher, Joplin is one great example of artistry in the late nineteenth and early twentieth century. It is extraordinary that a Black man born just after slavery ended could rise so quickly to become the premier composer of American music, gaining reviews, publications, critical acclaim, and commissions in much the same way as European composer-musicians living in their major cultural centers. Given the constant attacks and degradation Black music practice would receive from the media (critic Edward Bachelor Perry said, "The victims of ragtime should be shot like dogs with rabies; an infectious disease . . . like leprosy"), it's ironic that ragtime now stands on the "high art" side of all American popular music.

Like W. C. Handy's maturing in Memphis, cementing the blues in another musical city, Joplin matured as a musician with ragtime in the very musical circles of turn-of-the-century St. Louis. This was a city rich with saloons, opera houses, brothels, and social clubs. Joplin made his way in all these venues. His work is said to be as important as that of any American composer yet, as important as Foster, Gershwin, Bernstein, Sousa, and Ellington. He made ragtime "classical" by perfecting the American hybrids of styles: European parlor piano, marches, dances, plantation slave shouts, spirituals, and Black rural and party minstrel music, heard and performed by Black musicians in the nineteenth century.

Joplin's parents provided a musical home. His mother, Florence, played banjo and sang, and his father, Giles, born into slavery, played violin and taught all his children to play. Robert and William, Joplin's brothers, went on to become musicians in vaudeville circuits. Florence actually purchased a piano for Scott when he was twelve. In a 1959 interview, an elderly neighbor recalled the young Scott as being "serious, ambitious and spoke of his intentions to make something of himself." He studied with several local teachers as a youth, including a German immigrant, Julius Weiss. By age sixteen, Joplin formed a touring quartet and sang, arranged, and played piano in local towns and dance halls. Joplin also taught guitar and mandolin. By eighteen, he left home to travel to Louisiana, Missouri, Illinois, Kentucky, and Ohio, eventually settling in St. Louis. He also spent some time in Sedalia. As a youth, he attended Lincoln High School for Negroes in Sedalia; he later returned to live in Sedalia in 1893, and he attended George Smith College, where he studied music harmony. In Sedalia, he made a huge impression on the town in both the Black and White communities as a musician, playing in bands and playing for polite society and Black dance functions. It should be mentioned that these events were what one might call "upwardly mobile" Black social functions. An important part of Joplin's music and social life was his association with two of the city's Black social clubs: the Black 400 Club and the Maple Leaf Club (from which the title of "Maple Leaf Rag" derived). These two social clubs—which rented floors of buildings to throw parties, dances, and socials—were home to the educated, business, and socially minded Blacks.

In addition to creating a school of students, Joplin encouraged many younger bright stars who went on to do great things with music. These include Arthur Mitchell, Scott Hayden, Brun Campbell, James Scott (a Joplin protégé called the "Little Professor" who, like Joplin, had perfect pitch and composed endlessly), and the piano virtuoso/genius Louis Chauvin.

In 1899, when Joplin's "Maple Leaf Rag" was published by music store owner John Stark—the first time a "publishing deal" had been given to a Black artist—Joplin was paid $50 plus royalties on sales. The piece was a huge success. In 1900, Joplin, now married, moved to St. Louis and again immersed himself in the musical community, composing and teaching. The local conductor of the St. Louis Choral Symphony, the city's leading music institution, called Joplin "a Negro of extraordinary genius. His work is so original, distinctly individual and so melodious withal."[9] This was a first and rare acknowledgement of Black genius at the turn of the twentieth century by the American classical musical establishment. By 1903, after the success of several rags, Joplin produced his own opera traveling company and created the first rag opera, A *Guest of Honor*, named for the historical occasion when Theodore Roosevelt invited Booker T. Washington to the White House.

Two other masterpieces, "The Cascades" and "Chrysanthemum," followed. In 1907, after a failed run of his touring opera, the death of his child, and a split from his wife, he published "Gladiolus Rag." In 1908, he remarried, toured, and wrote a ragtime instruction book. For the next seven years of his life, he immersed himself in the creation of his second opera, *Tremonisha*. But this crowning achievement of his life was not performed until well after his death, when the Atlanta Symphony produced it in 1972. Joplin had tried unsuccessfully to produce it in New York. Suffering with ill health and depression, he died in 1917 at age forty-nine. *Tremonisha* is now recognized as one of the first and great American operas and has been performed, recorded, and filmed. Overall, Joplin's work made a major imprint on American music and introduced a pre-jazz Black form respected throughout the world.

Jelly Roll Morton

I decided I would travel about different little spots. . . . I would often frequent the old honey tanks, where nothing but the blues was played. There were fellows around like Skinny Head Pete, Old Florida Sam.

—Jelly Roll Morton, 1938 interview with Alan Lomax

In the 1938 interview conducted by folklorist Alan Lomax, Jelly Roll Morton, a founding conceptualizer of jazz, tells of being "down on the Gulf Coast in 1904" and says, "I missed going to the St. Louis exposition to get in a piano contest that was won by Alfred Wilson of New Orleans. . . . I was very much disgusted because I thought I should have gone . . . I knew I could have taken Alfred Wilson." He tells his story while sitting and playing music. What we note immediately in terms of patterns—codes—is that there was at the time an established practice concerning music conventions and artistry. While vestiges of both ragtime and blues arrived in New Orleans, players like the famed Jelly Roll Morton saw ragtime as the early technique that was most influential, while blues became the characteristic foundational Black musical flavor. There were also standards of performance, criteria, and judgments—about who was better playing these styles and about methods by which you could "take" a rival musician. All of this provides evidence of Black music as having established codes very early on. We know musicians were traveling to different spots to play; we know them by their names; we know they were grounded in the mother tradition, the blues.

This says a great deal about Black music culture. Since the nineteenth century, it was well established at least in terms of popular music conception. These blues players were, by this time, pianists. The powerful transfer of the old rural farmers who sang on plantations in the 1890s was, by now, a permanent aesthetic fixture among groups of traveling musicians. The codes had been set in place. In Morton, there was the great combination of grand Black traditions: New Orleans early jazz, blues, ragtime, and what he called the Latin-tinge. All of these "mixed down" further and came to be known as jazz.

Jelly Roll Morton, who claimed he was the inventor of jazz, grew up in the city of its birthing, New Orleans. He was born Ferdinand Joseph Lemott Morton, and he began playing piano at an early age. Instead of doing homework and going to school, he could be found playing piano in the Storyville district. In the Lomax interview, Morton tells us he played ragtime, French quadrilles, popular dances, songs, and light classics. Around 1904, he traveled, taking his playing on the road. He worked in Louisiana, Mississippi, Alabama, and Florida. He later expanded his tours to Memphis, St. Louis, Kansas City, and even Los Angeles, carrying these traditions all over the country.

It is clear when listening to the records that Morton had already begun to do what great musicians in these traditions often had to do—beg, borrow, adapt, recreate, and conceptualize. Black musical traditions were fluent now: ragtime, vocal and instrumental blues, minstrel show music, slave cries and hollers, spirituals, music from the Caribbean, and popular songs, clearly creating the map for the practice of early jazz composition. And because Morton began to create his own arrangements of these fused traditions, he has come to be known as an originator of jazz composition. In 1922–1923, he moved to Chicago, the new center of jazz. His first recordings were made there in 1923, with ensemble and sides of solo piano of his own compositions. By 1926–1927, Morton was recording with his own group, the Red Hot Peppers, a seven- or eight-piece band organized for recording purposes and comprising colleagues well versed in the New Orleans style and familiar with Morton's music.

In 1928, Morton moved to New York. There he continued to record pieces, and he remained at heart true to the New Orleans spirit of collective improvisation. This was not as "modern sounding" as his contemporaries—Fletcher Henderson, Sidney Bechet, and Duke Ellington. By 1930, Morton's style, both as arranger and pianist, came to be regarded as "olden and outdated." Later, Morton settled in Washington, D.C., where he managed a jazz club and played on and off.

Folklorist Alan Lomax, later Morton's biographer, in 1938 produced the landmark recording of Morton sitting at the piano, singing, and "telling" stories. In this important oral history, Morton recounted in words and music his early days in New Orleans, recreating the styles of many of his turn-of-the-century contemporaries. His sharing is both oral history and piano performance. Morton is probably jazz's earliest practitioner who "was there and could tell." In this way, he became for notated jazz practice a code setter. And his performances are clear examples of the practice codes: the personally shaped musicality of a performance, the remaking of original blues tunes, values of instrumental exchanges, "battles" as a conventional practice of the trade, and improvisation as the defining mark and representative Black music practice. Jelly Roll Morton is one of the founding artists of American popular music style, commonly known as the jazz art form.

From New Orleans Styles to Modern Jazz Practices

Tracing the blues through to its early transformations, we see a move to the modern, urban instrumental styles of jazz in the late 1890s. This music makes the connection actually from the nineteenth century to the twentieth, and Black music bridges and prepares this cultural modernity. Blues, New Orleans early jazz, ragtime, technology in radio and recordings, and the dance craze known as the cakewalk all created national cultural sensations and sensibilities beyond the one-stop nineteenth-century minstrel show and pointed the way for popular music forms to develop in the twentieth century.

Black music practice includes improvisational forms and styles that are rhythmically varied, and the emotive quality is deep down and inside the singer's story. Blues performers especially are expected to "tell a story," letting their "soul sing out," about freedom, liberation, hurt, triumph. With constrictions all around, the social reality for Blacks tends to create a need for such expressive bursting out. It is helpful to keep in mind the 1896 case of *Plessey v. Ferguson*. Homer Plessey was a racially mixed man who challenged segregation codes by entering a train section reserved for Whites and refusing to move off, since he had purchased a ticket. He was convicted for breaking the segregation laws. Segregation and "separate but equal" practices were legally put into place and upheld by the Supreme Court as the law of the land. Thus "Whites Only/Colored Only" drinking fountains and African American exclusion from voting and public accommodations further cemented racial and social isolation and disenfranchisements of Blacks in southern states.

The blues, ragtime, and other expressions became the musical reaction, music that laments the social conditions of many wandering Black migrants and Black communities. Creoles and vernacular Blacks in New Orleans were now playing together and sharing a common social condition of being "colored" and restricted. Positively, though, in this way, the music was still shared, and thus the spirituals, blues, New Orleans marches, ragtime, and minstrel styles were commonplace to all these musicians, and all mixed together to become what was now known as New Orleans instrumental music, where invention, improvisation, and ornamentation later became jazz.

The faces and sounds of this music during the early twentieth century include Freddie Keppard, Kid Ory, Joe "King" Oliver, Sidney Bechet, and Jelly Roll Morton. All were stars from New Orleans who helped popularize the music as they traveled the musical bridges from the nineteenth to the twentieth century. The most widely known star of early jazz, its principal shaper of instrumentalist/soloist identity, was Louis Armstrong, born in 1901. Armstrong appeared on the Chicago scene from New Orleans in 1922 and went later to New York. Through recordings and appearances, he became jazz's first international star.

Modernity is marked by the partnership between modern technology and music. At the beginning of the twentieth century, jazz and other Black American musical expressions are bubbling up as modernity unfolds. Jazz became the soundtrack of the modern world, as some have suggested. If ragtime "captured the snap and the speed of modern American life," as Irving Berlin said, then jazz would become the music that settled and carried twentieth-century American life into the knowledge of itself.

Early on, ragtime and jazz music in the popular press were reported to be the "Africanizing of American culture." This reflects one of the great American moral/social dilemmas and sets the stage for a stereotyped media portrayal of Black music as crude, and as a factor that lowers White and polite society. The *New York Herald* called ragtime "a national disaster . . . symbolic of the primitive morality and moral limitations of the Negro type." But ragtime brought national dance crazes like the cakewalk, Texas Tommy, turkey trot, bunny hug, and shim sham shimmy. All were born in Black clubs but were embraced also by young White dancers. In 1914, the year that World War I began, ragtime was the music of the day, just as for the next generations the Black popular music of swing, rock and roll, and hip hop would be *the* popular music. Tin Pan Alley, in New York, supplied most published music, and New York played host to most of the nation's recording companies, and a huge number of performance venues.

James Reese Europe (1880–1919), a D.C.-born son of a minister, was musical director for the Vernon and Irene Castle dance duo. He presented softer, milder versions of Black dances, making them polite. He believed in the "musical proficiency of the African race," and his work helped to pave the way for jazz internationally. His band actually was a regiment, the 396th Infantry Hell Fighters, who were war heroes as well. The group mixed Black syncopated songs, ragtime, blues, plantation melodies, and French songs, introducing the new music in Paris during World War I. European musicians thought the Blacks had trick instruments in order to create such "original" sounds. Europe wanted to merge ragtime and jazz and create an original mixture.

Entertainment venues now offered Black musicians real opportunities. Freddie Keppard traveled to Los Angeles, as did Jelly Roll Morton in 1915, and Will Marion Cook from New York traveled to London in 1919. By 1920, jazz had become the popular music of four major cities in the first part of the new century: New Orleans, Chicago, New York, and Kansas City.

The New Age: Chicago and New York

Chicago at the beginning of the twentieth century had stockyards and factory jobs that drew thousands of migrating Blacks out of the South to escape horrible living conditions. This period is known as the Great Migration. From World War I until the 1930s, Chicago papers encouraged hundreds of thousands of southerners to travel to Chicago. Many musicians left the

South to play in Chicago and other cities. In New Orleans, the end of the war brought on the critical closing in 1917 of Storyville, the infamous place of multiple entertainment venues known for drawing musicians for work. New cities, venues, and audiences needed to be found. The music migrations were on. King Joe Oliver, Louis Armstrong's mentor, left New Orleans and settled in Chicago at the Lincoln Gardens, where he made a huge splash bringing the new music styles to the North. Armstrong joined him there in 1922.

When King Oliver moved his band to Chicago in 1917, he hired Lil Hardin, one of the first great women of jazz. She was a classically trained pianist, a valedictorian from Fisk University. Although the mythology was that White musicians notated this music while the Black musicians "played around" in it, remember that these early musicians were, in many cases, well trained, organized, and disciplined professionals. This made an impact on the musical American establishment.

Louis Armstrong formed his Hot Five and Seven, and in 1925–1927, he recorded a series that established jazz as the premier American popular music form known throughout the world. And while James Reese Europe's ensembles can be thought of as bridging the transformation of early New Orleans jazz to modern ensembles, the man who is credited with the modern jazz orchestra is Fletcher Henderson. As he organized his band for playing entertainment venues in New York during the early 1920s, he formed the model of jazz band organization—separate sections of five saxophones, horns, and rhythm section. He is called the father of big band. In this band as well were Coleman Hawkins, who established the saxophone as the serious jazz instrument; and Don Redman, the great arranger.

Here were organized ensembles, a mix of southern and northern styles and musical culture brought together in the leading cosmopolitan city of new-century America. Jazz was the soundtrack to the new modern era. In 1924, Fletcher Henderson took over the Roseland Ballroom in Times Square. Henderson was educated at Atlanta University and, in 1920, had served as the house pianist and arranger for Harry Pace at Black Swan Records, even touring as music director for blues singer Ethel Waters. In 1921, Henderson had been a part of the successful recordings by this first Black-owned recording company, and thus was already an important part of the establishment of this new Black sound in American culture.

During this time, Louis Armstrong, now a major performer, was called in from Chicago to "pep" up Henderson's band. Armstrong brought "swing" to it. His solo phrasing inspired everybody. Armstrong by now was credited with creating a coherent solo, defined by the blues, nurtured in New Orleans music culture, and fused with American pop, Tin Pan Alley, and the sound that large ensembles would later pattern. His became the sound of the now classic big band.

In terms of performance codes, several things are to be noted. The most important musical value here, besides the improvisational tradition baked in New Orleans music culture, is the ensemble aesthetic, or working people who exchange daily and nightly on musical ideas. This created patterns of artistic ritual that defined how great music was made. For this writer, creating a band is the model of how musical ingenuity gets refined in a community of artists. Then those values, sounds, and music get transferred to audiences. From this, like jazz, big band music was born as an American popular music.

In 1926, Louis Armstrong extended his ideas to voice and recorded "Heebie Jeebies"—the "first jazz scat" recording. This influenced everybody's playing style, singing style, and the art of jazz solo and posture. Earl Hines, Armstrong's pianist friend, adapted Armstrong's ideas to piano, becoming the first great piano soloist. This set the stage for the jazz orchestra in the 1920s and 1930s to hire "hot" soloists to spark up the polite social dancing. This includes the Castles, Paul Whiteman, and more—this was the norm of the American White entertainment tradition.

Louis Armstrong was the first great projected image of American artistry in jazz and represented "forward thinking." He was the undisputed great genius of this music. But the American press still had bad things to say about jazz, seeing it as the death of morality and values. However, once White youth and the establishment saw it as something they could participate in and then ultimately gain market control of, that changed. Armstrong's work, along with that of numerous artists performing and recording, coalesced into a Black popular music arts tradition: blues, ragtime, a spiritual impulse and language, the New Orleans band tradition, a unique interdependence of instrumental textures with a blend of European parlor music, Black vernacular, minstrel songs, and the artistic achievement of the solo and improvisational singer as the crowning Black jewel.

W. C. Handy. *Courtesy Institute of Jazz Studies*

Bessie Smith. *Courtesy Institute of Jazz Studies*

King Oliver. *Courtesy Institute of Jazz Studies*

Scott Joplin. *Courtesy Institute of Jazz Studies*

Jelly Roll Morton. *Courtesy Institute of Jazz Studies*

Louis Armstrong. *Courtesy Institute of Jazz Studies*

James Reese Europe. *Courtesy Institute of Jazz Studies*

Lil Hardin Armstrong. *Courtesy Institute of Jazz Studies*

Fletcher Henderson. *Courtesy Institute of Jazz Studies*

Duke Ellington. *Courtesy Institute of Jazz Studies*

Duke Ellington. *Courtesy Institute of Jazz Studies*

Count Basie. *Courtesy Institute of Jazz Studies*

Charlie Parker. *Courtesy Institute of Jazz Studies*

Mary Lou Williams. *Courtesy Institute of Jazz Studies*

Miles Davis. *Photo by Tad Hershorn, used by permission*

Ornette Coleman. *Photo by Tad Hershorn, used by permission*

Sun Ra. *Courtesy Institute of Jazz Studies*

John Coltrane. *Courtesy Institute of Jazz Studies*

Mahalia Jackson. *Courtesy Institute of Jazz Studies*

James Brown. *Courtesy Institute of Jazz Studies*

Jimi Hendrix. *Courtesy Institute of Jazz Studies*

Patrice Rushen. *Courtesy Institute of Jazz Studies*

CHAPTER EIGHT

Jazz: The New Modern Mode of Being

Jazz developed as a Black music and ethnic/cultural expression. It is based on blues, West African reminisces, and field shouts, mixed with European parlor and band melodies, organized for performing dances and entertaining people. Bands provided entertainment and soulful expression for musicians who were sometimes serious, aloof, focused, and always dedicated to making original, innovative blends. But the great artful expression that emerged is modern jazz improvisation: the perfect blend of the skillful use of one's imaginative expression and the logical navigation, negotiation, and composing of musical elements, such as form, melody, harmony, and rhythm. With jazz, there emerged a new identity: the jazz artist. As early as the 1920s—in the midst of some of the most damaging racial propaganda in Hollywood, including *Amos 'n Andy*—Black artistry refuted stereotypes by producing a class of respectable, skilled, educated artists whose work was recognized as genius.

An important phase of jazz as a recognized American form was its acceptance by elitist White musical circles. Internationally renowned conductor Leopold Stokowski, for example, had this to say:

> Jazz has come to stay because it is an expression of the times, of the breathless, energetic, super active times in which we are living; it is useless to fight against it. The Negro musicians of America are playing a great part in this change. They have an open mind, and unbiased outlook. They are not hampered by conventions or traditions, and with their new ideas, their constant experiment, they are causing new blood to flow in the veins of music. They are pathfinders into new realms.[1]

Stokowski echoed the sentiments of composer Antonin Dvořák, who wrote in 1893 that the future music of America would be found in Negro melodies. Leonard Bernstein, arguing in his 1939 Harvard thesis for a new and vital American nationalism, wrote:

> Negro jazz, Negro music, Negro Art, Negro melodic peculiarities, Negro scale variants, Negro poignancy, special Negro flavor, Negro timbre, Negro singing voice, Negro character, Negro species of melodic syncopation, Negro rhythmic patterns, Negro tone color, Negro manner, Negro harmonies and the Negro scale. The greatest single racial influence upon American music as a whole has been the Negro.

Jazz became the musical approach, style, language, and cultural identity associated with the new modernism in music culture, and improvisation became the great benchmark of excellence. The blues was initially vocal-based music and a form, style, and approach to playing. Jazz was first born out of the blues styling as instrumentalists emulated the vocal tradition, making the horns "speak" like a blues singer. While blues singing may well have represented traditional vernacular folk-based style, assimilated Black communities emerged in urban America and their interests dominated jazz.

The sentiment of what was called the "New Negro" was largely reflected in a manifesto by university professor and writer Alain Locke. The New Negro—modern, urban, and self-liberated—created the need for sophisticated forms that expressed these new identities. Segments of Black people felt, too, that vernacular music was "shameful." This stemmed from their own struggles in navigating the map and maze of integration into White society. Despite this, jazz became the next highly stylized instrumental musical form, growing from the vernacular song traditions of the slave hollers, spirituals, blues, and ragtime.

By the end of the nineteenth century, jazz was an urban American music form that had fused with Western European harmonic developments. This cultural amalgamation resulted from the artistic individuality of Black musicians, and the sharing among American gigging musicians. Music historians ask the critical question: "Is jazz Black music?" Yes, it is. It grew directly from Black inquiry, need, and experimentation. But jazz was influenced by and resulted from an open cultural exchange among many communities—Black American, Western European, African, and more. All together, these bake and make this American tradition.

Jazz emerged as the popular voice of the new industrialized, "cultured," and rich America. From the 1920s to the 1950s, this new American style helped to socialize the country in ways that, for the first time, made Black artistry and imagery acceptable. Again, the artistry of figures like Louis Armstrong as an early ambassador projected this American art and human-expressive style internationally. In modern life, "image" is everything. Before the New Negro jazz image, Blacks were portrayed in cartoons as monkeys, hairy dumb creatures, and happy, overweight cooking mammies. Jazz music allowed Black accomplishment and artistry to be exported internationally.

Jazz art became America's popular music, which everybody danced to, loved, and dreamed. Of all the Black musical forms, jazz is the most highly developed from a craft perspective. Yet jazz also maintained most of the aesthetic, artistic standards and staples of the earlier forms, including improvisation, rhythmic dynamism, group interaction, and African-derived expressions of scoops, growls, and blued scale formations. In every way, jazz is an attempt to emulate Black vocal styling. Jazz is also "move and groove" music. It must swing.

Duke Ellington

One of the most respected, popular, and productive musicians to develop during the 1920s–1940s was the composer, pianist, and bandleader Duke Ellington (1899–1974). Born in Washington, D.C., he emerged in Harlem at the time of the Cotton Club (1927), a hot music and entertainment spot in New York that had a national radio broadcast. This helped Ellington gain national status as a music radio star at a time when New York was recognized as a cultural center of the world. Ellington also emerged during the height of the New Negro movement. Ralph Ellison would later write, "Even though few recognized it, such artists as Ellington and Louis Armstrong were the stewards of our vaunted American optimism and guardians against the creeping irrationality which ever plagues our form of society."[2] The music of Duke Ellington and his band represented the highest mark of musical excellence and artistry. His work and dedication to creating and cultivating high Black music forms made him the quintessential griot.

In this way, jazz, as seen through the work of Ellington and many other artists, heightened the image of Blacks as thinkers who were accomplished, respectable, and "cultured." Jazz was also associated with the New Negro movement and the Harlem Renaissance. By the 1920s, writers like James Weldon Johnson and Alain Locke proclaimed Harlem an intense cultural community, promoting Black diversity, and holding the greatest promise for the revival of the arts and for a "crossroads of culture." As Locke wrote, "In Harlem, Negro life is seizing upon its first chances for group expression and self-determination. It is the race capital. The Negro celebrates the attainment of a significant and satisfactory new phase of group development."[3]

Writers, artists, poets, playwrights, choreographers, and composers sought to prove the greatness of the Black race through arts and literature. As a musical and cultural figure, Duke Ellington emerged as a central icon.

Paul Robeson

> The artist must take sides. He must elect to fight for freedom or slavery. I have made my choice. I had no alternative.
>
> —Paul Robeson, *Here I Stand*

Of all the artists from this period, no one better exemplifies the artist-scholar-activist model than Paul Robeson. He was a singer, athlete, scholar, lawyer, and social activist who used his art to advocate for suffering people all over the world. His work and his presence as a Black artist and activist set the pattern for other Black artists, not only to accept the power and challenge of their work for art's sake, but to speak the truth for the causes of people.

Born on April 9, 1898, in Princeton, New Jersey, Robeson was the youngest of five children. His father was a runaway slave who went on to graduate from Lincoln University, and his mother came from a family of Quakers who worked for the abolition of slavery. He came from a family familiar with hardship and with the determination to rise above it. In 1915, Robeson won a four-year academic scholarship to Rutgers University. In spite of open violence and racism expressed by teammates, Robeson won fifteen varsity letters in baseball, basketball, and track, and was twice named to the All American Football team. He was valedictorian of his graduating class in 1919. He chose to use his artistic talents in theater and music to promote African and African American history and culture. He is an early example and one of the greatest of the "race men."

On stage in London, Robeson earned international critical acclaim for his lead role in *Othello*; he won the Donaldson Award for Best Acting Performance in 1944; he performed in Eugene O'Neill's *Emperor Jones* and *All God's Chillun Got Wings* as well as in the musical *Showboat*. He is known for changing the lines of the *Showboat* song "Old Man River" from "I'm tired of livin' and 'feared of dyin' . . . " to a stronger and more dignified "I must keep fightin' until I'm dying . . . " His eleven films included *Body and Soul* (1925), *Jericho* (1937), and *The Proud Valley* (1940).

Robeson used his voice to promote Black artistic traditions, to share the cultures of other countries, and to benefit the social movements of the times in which he lived. He sang for peace and justice in twenty-five languages throughout the United States, Europe, the Soviet Union, and Africa. Robeson became known as a citizen of the world, as comfortable with the people of Moscow and Nairobi as with the people of Harlem. In 1933, he donated the proceeds of *All God's Chillun* to Jewish refugees fleeing Hitler's Germany.

In New York in 1939, he premiered in Earl Robinson's *Ballad for Americans*, celebrating the multiethnic, multiracial face of America. It was greeted with the largest audience response for a radio program since Orson Welles's famous *War of the Worlds* a year earlier. During the 1940s, Robeson continued to perform and speak out against racism in the United States and for peace among nations. In 1945, he headed an organization that challenged President Truman to support an antilynching law. In the late 1940s, when dissent was scarcely tolerated in the United States, Robeson openly questioned why African Americans should fight in the army of a government that tolerated racism.

Like numerous American artists speaking out during this time, he was accused by Senator Joseph McCarthy's House Un-American Activities Committee (HUAC) of being a communist. Robeson saw this claim as an outright attack on the democratic rights of the many people like himself who worked for friendship with other nations and equal rights for all people. After he was condemned by the panel, 80 percent of his concerts were canceled. In 1949, his two outdoor concerts in Peekskill, New York, were attacked by White mobs while state police stood by. In response, Robeson declared, "I'm going to sing wherever the people want me to sing . . . and I won't be frightened by crosses burning in Peekskill or anywhere else."

In 1950, the U.S. government revoked Robeson's passport, leading to an eight-year battle to secure it again. During those years, Robeson studied Chinese, met with Albert Einstein to discuss the prospects of world peace, published his autobiography *Here I Stand*, and sang at Carnegie Hall. In 1960, he made his last concert tour, to New Zealand and Australia. Suffering from ill health, he retired from public life in 1963 and died on January 23, 1976, at age seventy-seven, in Philadelphia. But his towering artistic presence and great model of artistic dignity, using his art to challenge, change, and inspire the world, made him one of the most pervasive American artists of the twentieth century.

Florence Price

Born April 9, 1877, Florence Smith Price was the first Black woman concert composer to reach national recognition. From Little Rock, she was the third child of James H. Smith, the first Black dentist in that city, who was also a published author, inventor, and civil rights advocate. Her mother, Florence Gulliver, was a schoolteacher and business woman as well as a singer and pianist. She taught elementary school, working for the Black-owned International Loan and Trust Company, purchasing a restaurant and selling real estate. This was an incredible feat for a Black woman in the nineteenth century. It's easy to understand the productivity of a child reared in such a home. From an early age, Price was exposed to a progressive Black community that sponsored social, political, educational, and cultural events, drawing national Black figures to Little Rock. She attended the New England Conservatory of Music from 1903 to 1906, graduating with a degree in organ music and a teacher's diploma in piano.

She taught at the Cotton-Plant Arkadelphia Academy until 1907 and Shorter College in Little Rock until 1910, later heading the music department at Clark University (1910–1912). After marrying Thomas Price, an attorney, she stopped teaching and established a private studio in her home. In 1927, the intolerable racial climate of Little Rock caused the family to move to Chicago, where Florence Price established herself as a concert pianist and composer. Major publishers began contracting her works—Theodore Presser, G. Schirmer, and Carl Fischer, to name a few. In 1932, Price won the Wanamaker Music Composition Contest for her Symphony in E.

The premiere of this piece by the Chicago Symphony Orchestra in June 1933 signaled Price as the first African American woman to have a work produced by a major American orchestra. During her career, Price wrote over 300 compositions, including symphonies, concertos, chamber works, art songs, and settings of spirituals for voice and piano. Her best-known spiritual, "My Soul's Been Anchored in De Lord," has been performed by Ellabelle Davis, Marian Anderson, and Leontyne Price. WGN's Radio Symphony Orchestra recorded many of her songs in the 1930s. Her instrumental music reflected the influence of her cultural themes, such as dance music with the southern plantation juba expressed in a classical form. She was one of the few women who characterized the high point of the New Negro movement, particularly in classical/concert music. Florence Price died in Chicago in 1953. She is remembered as a great American classical music composer, and the first great recognized Black American woman composer in the United States.

William Grant Still

In 1930, William Grant Still created the singularly most recognizable and important work by a twentieth-century Black composer, *The Afro-American Symphony*. It is the first symphony based on the American blues form. Long known as the "Dean of American Negro Composers," as well as one of America's foremost composers, Still had the distinction of becoming a legend in his own lifetime. It is important to note that in the early days of the twentieth century, it was extremely rare for a Black man to gain wide acceptance in the European-based field of classical music. The title "Dean" seems appropriate due to the great work and strides Still made to forge a Black voice deep into the identity of classical music.

Still was the first African American in the United States to have a symphony performed by a major orchestra. He was also the first African American to conduct a major symphony orchestra in the United States when, in 1936, he directed the Los Angeles Philharmonic Orchestra at the Hollywood Bowl. He was the first African American to conduct a major symphony orchestra in the Deep South when, in 1955, he directed the New Orleans Philharmonic at Southern University. And he was the first Black to conduct a White radio orchestra in New York City. He was also the first to have an opera produced by a major U.S. company. In 1949, his *Troubled Island* was performed at the City Center of Music and Drama in New York City. He was also the first Black to have an opera televised over a national network. With all these firsts, Still was, clearly, a pioneer. In a larger sense, he pioneered because he was able to interest the greatest conductors of the day in his music, which was truly serious and had a definite American flavor. Still wrote hundreds of compositions—including operas, ballets, symphonies, chamber works, and arrangements of folk themes, especially Negro spirituals, plus instrumental, choral, and solo vocal works.

Born May 11, 1895, in Woodville, Mississippi, to parents who were teachers and musicians, Still was only a few months old when his father died and his mother took him to Little Rock, where she taught English in high school. There his musical education began with violin lessons from a private teacher, and with later inspiration from the Red Seal operatic recordings bought for him by his stepfather. At Wilberforce University, he took courses leading to a B.S. degree but spent most of his time conducting the band, learning to play various instruments, and making his initial attempts to compose and to orchestrate. His subsequent studies at the Oberlin Conservatory of Music were financed at first by a legacy from his father, and later by a scholarship established just for him by the faculty.

At the end of his college years, Still entered the world of popular music, playing in orchestras and orchestrating, working particularly with the violin, cello, and oboe. His employers included W. C. Handy, Donald Voorhees, Sophie Tucker, Paul Whiteman, Willard Robison, and Artie Shaw, and for several years he arranged and conducted the *Deep River Hour* over CBS and WOR. While in Boston, playing oboe in the Shuffle Along Orchestra, Still applied to study at the New England Conservatory with American composer George Chadwick, and he was again rewarded with a scholarship. Still also studied on an individual scholarship with the noted ultra-modern composer Edgard Varese.

Of particular interest was Still's association with W. C. Handy. Still succeeded Fletcher Henderson as music director for Harry Pace's Black Swan Records. He was in the heat and heart of the emerging race records and the Harlem Renaissance, creating music that was steeped in Black vernacular and American popular and classical music traditions.

In the 1920s, Still made his first appearances as a serious composer in New York and began a valued friendship with Howard Hanson of Rochester. Extended Guggenheim and Rosenwald Fellowships were given to him, as well as important commissions from the Columbia Broadcasting System, the New York World's Fair, Paul Whiteman, the League of Composers, the Cleveland Orchestra, the Southern Conference Educational Fund, and the American Accordionists Association. In 1944, with a work called "Festive Overture," he won the Jubilee Prize of the Cincinnati Symphony Orchestra for the best overture to celebrate its Jubilee season. In 1961, he received the prize offered by the U.S. Committee for the United Nations and the Aeolian Music Foundation for his orchestral work *The Peaceful Land*, cited as the best musical composition honoring the United Nations.

After receiving a master's degree in music from Wilberforce in 1936, he earned honorary doctorates from Howard University, Oberlin College, Bates College, the University of Arkansas, Pepperdine University, the New England Conservatory of Music, the Peabody Conservatory, and the University of Southern California. There are few American symphonists who have received such acclaim and made such an imprint on American music traditions. William Grant Still singlehandedly wrote the codes for what it could mean to be a Black American composing artist in the classical music field.

Swing: The New Era of Style

The commercialization and mainstream acceptance of jazz led to a new form—swing, America's popular dance music. Composer Duke Ellington's

1932 hit is aptly titled "It Don't Mean a Thing If It Ain't Got That Swing." Swing became an all-meaningful code for Black music culture as an aesthetic prescription for the music. Black music to be of value must swing. During the Depression, the music helped to lift up America. As President Franklin Delano Roosevelt's New Deal took hold, clubs opened on 52nd Street in New York. NBC featured a weekly Saturday-night three-hour radio broadcast entitled *Let's Dance*. America experienced a cultural upsurge, with music originally created in Black communities and sold as swing. Benny Goodman, a Jewish champion of Black music, became the "King of Swing." The bands of Artie Shaw, Woody Herman, and Glenn Miller were among the best known of the hundreds of territory bands that roamed the United States during the period, playing jazz/swing music and creating a huge industry.

May 11, 1937, is a wonderful moment in music history: the "Battle of the Century," as the Benny Goodman Band and the most famous New York Black Swing band, the Chick Webb Orchestra, "battled it out" at the Savoy Ballroom in Harlem. In some other ways, this was symbolic of the unspoken battle over cultural ownership. Who was the real master of swing, a White musician crowned King of Swing, or the accepted Black leader of the Black dance-hall band in Harlem? In addition to the records and radio programs to which people listened, it was in what Guthrie Ramsey calls the "cultural theaters" that the codes, styles, and conventions that shaped music culture were defined. Here, the band that "swung" the hardest and got the best people

Some Major Events in Black American Jazz History

1938   Jazz concerts are performed at Carnegie Hall for the first time. The Café Society is the first integrated club in New York and is where Billie Holiday first sings "Strange Fruit."

1939   Coleman Hawkins records "Body and Soul." Charlie Parker comes to New York from Kansas City in search of his idol, Art Tatum. Jazz and bebop become symbols for democracy, the freedom to express yourself, and freedom from fascism. Duke Ellington produces *Jump for Joy*, a Black musical suggesting that Black Americans are the nation's creative voice.

1941   A. Philip Randolph, a Black champion of Black workers' rights, threatens to lead a march on Washington if Blacks who are fighting in World War II are not given jobs when they return. President Roosevelt signs the order to desegregate war industry jobs.

1948   President Truman signs the order to desegregate the armed forces.

and dance response won. That night, the two warring swing bands battled and played. And the Chick Webb Orchestra won, a Black band, composed of those who created and then redefined swing on Black musical terms.

Kansas City and Count Basie

In the 1930s and into the 1940s, Kansas City became another great city for defining and shaping Black music. William "Count" Basie (1904–1984), a prodigy of the great piano songwriter and performer Fats Waller, would, like Duke Ellington, become one of the principal stars of the new swing era. Though born in New Jersey, Count Basie came to call Kansas City home. Kansas City had become a major rail town and stopping place, where politics, hustling, bustling, and "adult entertainment" thrived. Many musicians were drawn there for work in the entertainment houses. Kansas City not only produced an important list of major Black artists (Charlie Parker, Mary Lou Williams, and Jimmy Rushing, among others), but it became a place where "jamming jazz" developed, the blues-grounded, big-band swing style known as jazz blues. This was a "riffing" and a kind of groove-oriented playing with the rhythm section. It was the music of Jo Jones, Walter Page, Freddie Green, and Basie.

The mayor of Kansas City at that time was a gangster named Tom Pendergrass. Territory bands, traveling big-band units, went from town to town, and Kansas City was a stop where Pendergrass allowed the music culture to thrive. Walter Page's Blue Devils, the Bennie Moten Band, Andy Kirk and his Twelve Clouds of Joy are examples of Black working bands from which many future players were to emerge, and they spent time in Kansas City. Count Basie took over the Bennie Moten Band and soon became a regular music attraction, with his unique mixture of traditional jazz and a strong emphasis on the blues. Many southerners, first-generation migrants, had settled in Kansas City. Basie's music helped keep the southern blues flavor alive. Soloists like the great jazz saxophonist Lester Young sat in the Basie band. Jimmy Rushing was the great vocalist.

Soon Pete Johnson, Albert Ammonds, and Mead Lux Lewis introduced boogie woogie, another influential piano style of the late 1930s and 1940s. Mary Lou Williams, who began in Kansas City, became known as the first lady of modern jazz. She became the pianist and arranger for the Andy Kirk Band. Charlie Parker came and played with the Jay McShann Band. Black bands prospered and perfected the Black codes for swing.

In Kansas City's "jamming jazz" sessions, musicians jammed on the blues and jazz standards well into the next morning. In this band context, there rose the soloists of the great Black big bands. Duke Ellington's band, for example, contained Rex Stewart, Joe Nanton, Barney Bigard, Paul Gonsalves, Bubber Miley, Ray Nance, Cootie Williams, Harry Carney, Jimmy Blanton, Freddie Guy, Lonnie Johnson, Cat Anderson, Johnny Hodges, and Ben Webster. Billie Holiday emerged as a unique soloist with a completely original style and approach to singing. She helped to create the identity of "the modern lady" as a singer. Other Black bands from this period included those of Cab Calloway, Jimmie Lunceford, Andy Kirk, Billy Eckstine, Lucky Millender, Lionel Hampton, Erskine Hawkins, and Chick Webb.

Bebop

As jazz music developed after the Harlem Renaissance, it began to be "its own self," a music apart from commercial entertainment, and a music seen as "art." Bebop represented a Black sophisticated, liberated, smart, and stylish art with attitude, a social philosophy and dress. As bebop developed, it became difficult to trace what was happening with Black music, and to isolate Black music culture from American music culture. Driven by economics, global relations, technology, and a tremendous number of exchanges, innovations, and experiments by many artists—Black, White, and international—music became an amalgamation of many influences.

As fast as artists created, there were markets demanding the next thing. American music follows the trends of society, but music pacifies society as well. There became, with the post-WWII capitalistic surge, the need for "cultural diversions." During this time, popular culture became firmly cemented as part of the American entertainment industry. Music-making simply became a part of the social matrix.

The jazz art had become the "most sophisticated" or refined of the forms within the Black arts continuum. There are several reasons for this. Because it is instrumental music, it requires a great amount of technical craft and facility. In addition, it is a form associated with accompanying and emulating Black vocal style. Further, it placed a premium on an artist focusing on expression and craft, on interpreting and performing simultaneously and at rapid speeds. It left its vernacular folk form and developed into a hybrid of other cultural perspectives, erupting during a time of great social awareness, as America searched for cultural identity. To probe through this art in even more philosophical ways, jazz forms, as they developed later, could further be described as:

- Focused musical language in connection with human, emotive, expressive ideas.

- Melodic inventiveness.
- Mastery of the instrument and art form.
- Harmonic inventiveness, a freshness as if the listener could hear the artist discovering the music as he or she plays it.
- A mix of wit, pathos, childhood playfulness, and maturity.
- Elegant expression.
- Focused individual interpreting and inventing while commenting on an upheld tradition.
- Lushness.

The jazz musician provides a great example of an artist at the highest level. In hearing the advanced soloist, one has the sense of what it "costs" to speak. In some profound way, improvisation emphasizes why it is dehumanizing to have the liberty of speech somehow taken away. There is this great sense of the importance of "saying something."

This is likened to the Black church experience where a parishioner may shout out to a preacher, "Ahh, you saying something now." The opportunity to speak is not taken for granted, and the solo is the great benchmark of the jazz artist's ability. Black music, especially in jazz, is so very profound in this way because it relies on one's lived experience for its meaning and the quality of its expressiveness. As Charlie Parker often said, "Music is your own experience. If you don't live it, it won't come out of your horn." Popular music attained the heightened sense of an individual's artistic expression from the jazz musician, especially the beboppers, the grandfather of hip hop.

As with the earlier vernacular Black music, jazz is the continued attempt to emulate the sound of the Black voice. Vocalist-musician extraordinaire Sarah Vaughan was the next great style/voice, and continuation of the modern woman in the art form from the bebop era after Ella Fitzgerald and Billie Holiday. She was to bop what Bessie Smith was to blues, what Ella was to swing, and what Billie Holiday was to setting the new image and sound to the first years of the modern age of jazz. Vaughan was the definitive diva and a pianist, too. These women represent the "sound" jazz is attempting to reach. But the bebop approach was a cultural movement within jazz, complete with a new aesthetic, language, and even a dress code. And as Miles Davis put it, "The movement was like reading a textbook to the future of jazz music."

Jazz Transforms to Modern

At the start of World War II, younger Black musicians were left at home to fight discrimination and forge their identities. It was during this time, particularly in the performing venues where they hung out, that bebop emerged. It is of note that this early emergence was not really recorded, due to two factors:

- The shortage of shellac (records were burned and hardened from rubber materials needed to make war products).
- The American Federation of Musicians union struck against the recording industry, due to low wages paid to musicians in clubs and the lack of royalties from records, and especially from "free music" on the radio.

This situation meant that we have relatively few recorded performances of the bebop style of the early 1940s. This continued until the war ended, in 1945.

In the 1940s, "the Street," 52nd Street between 5th and 6th Avenues, featured Art Tatum, Oscar Pettiford, Coleman Hawkins, and more. But uptown Harlem was where the Black musicians lived and hung out and where the new music originated. Musician Teddy Hill managed Minton's Playhouse on 118th Street in Harlem, and this is one of the major spots where bebop was experimented on and worked. Minton's, Monroe's Uptown House—these spots and others gave free food to musicians who came to play their own "nonphony music." Henry Minton was the first Black union member in New York and believed in helping musicians. Charlie Christian, Kenny Clarke, Thelonious Monk, and others created at Minton's the new music called bebop. The Billy Eckstine Band, believed to be the first bebop big band, had critical players, including Miles Davis, Kenny Durham, Bird, Dizzy, Art Blakey, Sonny Stitt, Dexter Gordon, J. J. Johnson, and Sarah Vaughan. And the exchange of ideas among these musicians defined the musical codes that set the pace for modern Black popular music at this time.

Classic bop dominated in 1945–1949, so Charlie Parker, born in 1920, was twenty-five at the start of this movement, and Dizzy Gillespie, born 1917, was twenty-eight. These young artists are the principal definers of the bebop style codes. Bop was a "surprise music," an underground movement made by the younger Black musicians in Harlem. Bop was a musical revolution marked by several shifts in approaches to jazz. Bebop could be heard in scat singing and was really a name for the rhythmic way the musical phrases ended. In swing, there were little or no solos and most of the music was written to highlight arrangers' work for dance. Big-band improvisers based their solos off of sweet melodies, whereas bop solos were based on a working knowledge of the chord changes. The emphasis is on the soloist's inventive fluidity, moving through the changes and turnarounds. Coleman Hawkins, the first great sax jazz soloist, in 1939 recorded a remarkable solo on the standard

"Body and Soul," and it was the great early "pointing the way" example of modern jazz performance improvisation. Many bebop composers took old jazz swing standards and rewrote them with hipper melodies, altering the chord changes. Titles obviously were poetic attempts to be slick, offbeat, hep, and a rethinking of the old guard. The boppers wanted their work to be for musicians and for the music.

All this came out of an atomic bomb attack—the idea of traversing the divide between a younger and older generation, through approach, style, values. The music had broken, harder-edged phrases, dislocated rhythms. There were fractured ballads and the deconstruction of standard tunes reconstructed. Their emphasis was on blues tonality and altering, by extension, the harmonic vocabulary. To the older generation, it all sounded frantic, neurotic, and sped up. These younger musicians were rewriting the musical/cultural codes.

The Great Bebop Genius: Charlie Parker

Bebop, after World War II, was in full swing, especially once the recording ban was lifted. Charlie "Yardbird" Parker—"Bird"—became the first great genius of the new bebop style. He had a new approach to playing because he brought the blues from Kansas City. The glue that held bebop together was the phrasing, and as writer Stanley Crouch noted, Bird brought the "pyrotechnics." Parker's friend Dizzy Gillespie was the great teacher and apostle of the style. Bud Powell and Thelonious Monk became, among others, the great pianists of the style.

Born in 1920, Parker came to New York in 1939 in search of his idol, Art Tatum. By 1942, Parker joined the revolutionary Earl Hines Band, which included Dizzy Gillespie, Sarah Vaughan, and Billy Eckstine. The "jamming on ideas" began here. A younger Miles Davis even sat in when the Band was in St. Louis. It's easy to see how the new thinking, ideas, and bebop approach spread among the musicians.

Parker, after hearing the jazz song "Cherokee," began to discover new melodic improvisations based on chord changes from "the inside." Beboppers changed tempos, melodic and harmonic alterations, and rhythmic extensions, but Parker brought two other things: blues-based riffing from Kansas City and his fluidity of phrasing at rapid tempos. His harmonic invention/revolution was to impose a new melodic conception, building improvisation on acute chord structures he heard extended above the minor and dominant altered 7th chords, giving him a fluidity, dexterity, and choral clarity, specifically in improvisation. The invention in this propelled him and the beboppers way out in front in terms of the old standard of playing around the chord arpeggiation. Musically, they extended the conventional harmonies of jazz with extensive use of 9ths, 11ths, flatted 5ths, 13ths, and stacked polychords. Arpeggiations became a science with the beboppers. You could hear the changes rapidly in their solos, putting the emphasis on the mind and art of the individuals as thinking musicians. This again projected the self-made, free-thinking artist who also happened to be a free-thinking, freely acting Black man in a White-dominated world.

Bebop Beliefs

Beboppers rebelled against the jazz establishment of the 1940s, and especially against swing. In their eyes, Black music had been co-opted by a largely White mechanism (clubs and the recording industry), giving jobs and credit to White musicians. They noted that the art of jazz improvisation, another Black innovation, had to take a back seat to stock arrangements. They saw hypocrisy in fighting fascism in World War II with a segregated army. They were also aware of the pay-scale injustice experienced by Black musicians.

Culturally they decided to wear berets and hip, bright colors. Some wore zoot suits—created by Hal Fox, and featuring padded shoulders, high waists, and long jackets. They turned their backs to the audience and created the language of "hep," to confound the uncool. They picked up the tempos, playing the tunes faster than the standard dance-band tempos, and they made 16th notes and triplets the normative phrasing motif. And they often remade existing tunes, changed the titles, inserted radically invested angular, bebop melodies. They believed they were being released from the "tyranny of popular taste," as a commentator in Ken Burns's documentary *Jazz* points out.

The beboppers believed in inspired, inventive approaches that were revolutionary. Bebop is the first great artist revolution in Black music, and jam sessions like those at Minton's really became the model of the place where new Black music brewed. In 1952, *Downbeat*, the nation's lead jazz periodical, named Dizzy Gillespie and Charlie Parker the best sax and trumpet players. This was monumental. In many ways, it is easy to see that bebop meant "rebels," and that it asserted new models of Black music that forged a generation's identity.

Mary Lou Williams

For any great artistic movement, we cannot talk about ideas and creativity without discussing the relationships between musicians and their mentors.

Maintaining codes is about passing on musical ideas and values, and in this mix there were many great artists, teachers, and personalities who were champions of the music and the culture. There is no greater example of all of this than the person and artistry of Mary Lou Williams, who was thought to be the first lady of modern jazz—and that is not only because she was a woman, but also because she seemed to deserve a regal title. Born in Atlanta in 1910, she moved at a young age to Pittsburgh, a very musical city. A child prodigy, Williams began playing spirituals and ragtime at the age of four. By six, she was entertaining at picnics and dances. In Pittsburgh, she was known as the "little piano girl." As a young woman, she toured the TOBA (Theater Owners Booking Agency) circuit and, in 1928, joined the Synco Jazzers in Oklahoma City.

Andy Kirk and his Twelve Clouds of Joy, a well-known ensemble, relocated to Kansas City in 1929. Through contacts, Williams joined the Clouds, first as an arranger and later as a pianist. In 1931, she became a full-time member of the band, where she stayed until 1942. Williams played such a key role that she was known as "the lady who swings the band." In addition to her duties with the Kirk band, she provided arrangements for Benny Goodman, Earl Hines, and Tommy Dorsey. Her arrangement of "Trumpets No End" became a staple chart of the Ellington band. Due to her gifting and personality, she earned the admiration and respect of the music community. Williams combined the native languages of the blues, boogie woogie, and stride piano. As the 1940s progressed, she became a mentor to the emerging generation of beboppers, becoming close with Thelonious Monk, Bud Powell, and many others. In addition to mentoring musicians, Williams became a champion of women in jazz, recording with several all-women groups. At one point, she also became a visible spokesperson for jazz as a radio figure hosting her own show.

In 1946, the New York Philharmonic performed at Carnegie Hall three movements from her composition *Zodiac Suite*. From 1952 to 1954, Williams performed extensively in Europe. Then, in 1954, she retired from music to pursue religious and charitable interests. She became active musically again throughout the 1960s and 1970s, leading her own groups in New York clubs, composing sacred works for jazz orchestra and voices, and devoting much of her time to teaching. In 1970, as a solo pianist, and providing her own commentary, she recorded *The History of Jazz*. Mary Lou Williams maintained the bebopper's modernist approach for most of her career, but her playing attained a level of complexity and dissonance that rivaled avant-garde jazz pianisms of the time, without losing an underlying blues feeling. The blues coding and the Kansas City imprint defined her aesthetic.

Williams grew toward an even deeper appreciation of her role as shaper of bebop and mentor when she pursued her spiritual musical quest later in life. She had a varied spiritual journey that included preaching at Abyssinian Baptist Church in Harlem. Moving toward the Catholic Church, she conducted her first Catholic Mass, written entirely in jazz music form. She said, "One reason I came out here again is the sound I hear in modern jazz. They're disturbed and crazy. They're neurotic as if the Negro was pulling away from his heritage in music. You have to love when you play. So I've decided to show them, make them hear the soul." She called this, "God's music," the music that heals the soul.

Mary Lou Williams taught at Duke University as an artist-in-residence from 1977 until her death in 1981 at the age of seventy-one. In 1983, Duke University established the Mary Lou Williams Center for Black Culture, which today stands as a campus symbol for Black American creativity.

Miles Davis

Miles Davis, born in 1926, represents the next wave of artistry beyond Duke Ellington and Mary Lou Williams. In many ways, he was the protégé of the beboppers Charlie Parker and Dizzy Gillespie. Through Miles Davis, we are able to grasp another movement in jazz, as the form evolved and moved closer to the American cultural center. Davis was a trumpeter, a conceptualist, and one of the principal players to emerge in New York in the 1940s and to be recognized as a major leader and shaper of jazz culture. But he was surrounded and influenced by the likes of Charlie Parker, Dizzy Gillespie, Thelonious Monk, and schools of players following throughout the 1950s and well into the 1970s, including Cannonball Adderley (1928–1975), John Coltrane (1926–1966), Wayne Shorter (b. 1933), Herbie Hancock (b. 1940), and Tony Williams (1940–1997). Together these voices, along with the media, propelled the artistic emergence of the Black art forms of bebop and several derivative jazz styles.

Miles Davis represents the quintessential or most characteristic example of the art form as culture and as style. While Davis was not always "the originator" of the aesthetic movements and manifestos of bebop, cool school, modal, and fusion, his contributions to and participation in these movements made him a seminal figure. The bebop movement represented a break with the "audience pleasing" commerciality of the swing bands represented by Ellington and Basie. Davis, Parker, and Gillespie were in the forefront of the cool school movement (1949–1955). This represented a break with the fast, complicated, musician-orientated approach of bebop. The cool school approach to playing jazz was less excited and less busy than bebop. It was a smoother, more detached and reflective sound. Davis's *Birth of the Cool* was recorded in 1955. The grouping of instruments included a French horn and tuba, but no piano, giving it a more European, chamber-music sound. Davis not only organized the unique ensemble to record and project this new approach, but he also made for himself a projected "cool" media image which characterized his public persona until his death.

The large orchestrations in Davis's recordings—including *Miles Ahead* (1957), *Porgy and Bess* (1958), and *Sketches of Spain* (1959)—were by arranger Gil Evans. These foreshadowed the "third stream," the mixing of formal European large-range ideas and jazz music with the avant-garde tendencies in concert music seen in the later experiments by Gunther Schuller and the Modern Jazz Quartet.

Modal jazz, yet another stylistic development within jazz, as exemplified on Davis's *Kind of Blue* (1960), was another attempt to move away from the density represented in his orchestral experiments and in mainstream jazz. In Miles's words, "The music had gotten thick. . . . I think a movement in jazz is beginning away from conventional strings of chords, and a return to emphasis on melodic rather than harmonic variation . . . fewer chords but infinite possibilities as to what to do with them."

In his classic quintet period, Davis surrounded himself with younger players, including Herbie Hancock, Wayne Shorter, Ron Carter, and Tony Williams. They formed a refined, sophisticated performing unit. These recordings, during 1963–1968, provided a model for group excellence that became the staple for modern jazz performance. There was a return to making music that was "in tune" with the social movements of the times. Prior to this period, Davis had traveled frequently to Paris, where he visited the home of social activist and author James Baldwin. Davis often spoke of his rising concern for the social plight of Black people in the United States.

Davis's album *Bitches Brew* was a turn away from wearing the "establishment suit" to wearing dashikis and afros, and creating fusion music. Fusion, or rock-jazz, brought a hardened electric edge, forging at once artistic expression with the social rage of the 1960s and the technological experiments of the period. In this way, Miles's experiments looked to incorporate what was going on in popular rock, exemplified in artists like Jimi Hendrix and Sly & the Family Stone. It was a turn toward the impulses of the younger generation, which had become devoted to rock and roll and the protest music of the period.

Davis attracted and inspired a new generation of younger, inventive musicians: Joe Zawinul, Keith Jarrett, John McLaughlin, Carlos Santana, Chick

Corea, and others. The six principle fusion bands to emerge from these experiments with young players were Headhunters (Hancock), Weather Report (Zawinul, Shorter), Mahavishnu Orchestra (McLaughlin), Return to Forever (Corea), Lifetime (Williams), and Santana (Santana). A final stage from about the late 1970s until his death was his emergence and belief in adopting the stylistic and aesthetic resources of popular culture, including pop, urban contemporary, and finally hip hop. His new young model for artistic excellence? Prince.

From Davis's emergence in New York's bebop rage in 1944 until his death in 1991, his creative career spanned nearly fifty years. For many, he represents the emergence of jazz as a cultural style. This refers to the way that he approached jazz, the sound of his horn (the wispy/airy sound of the stemless Harmon mute), the use of "cool" phrasing, relaxed nonspeedy playing, the use of media to project the image of the hipster, dress and attitude. Davis became the most commercially successful jazz artist of his generation. Black musicians becoming millionaires was proof that the art form had reached an important place in the societal configuration of success, marketability, and cultural stability.

After Bop: Jazz Moving into the 1950s

In 1947, Chano Pozo, a Cuban songwriter, dancer, entertainer, and conga player, helped to insert another element into modern jazz: an Afro-Cuban styling which brought the musical culture of jazz back face-to-face with its African identity. After hearing great Cuban bands, Dizzy Gillespie decided to bring conga drums into his band, and Pozo was the player who cemented this. Just as blues brought jazz back to itself with Basie's Kansas City sound, in 1955 the Jazz Messengers—with members like Lee Morgan, Bobbie Timmons, Wayne Shorter—wanted to bring jazz "back home" to its African ethnic heritage. The musicians called this music "hard or soul bop." An example would be tunes like "Dat Dere," "Home Cooking," "Lester Left Town," "Boy, What a Night," and "Grits and Gravy." The idea here was to keep jazz "Black and culturally coded."

Thelonious Monk

Creative movements always unearth innovators, memorable personalities we associate with the spirit, values, and ideas of a time. Thelonious Monk, because of the sheer uniqueness of his performance and compositional approach to playing, is clearly one of the most innovative voices to come out of the post-bop period, remaining a potent force in more progressive jazz until the 1970s. His Five Spot performances, Town Hall concerts, and subsequent albums and European tours provided a rich recording legacy. In Monk's music, the tonal structure from chord to chord is sometimes unpredictable, so one's base as a listener is constantly shifting. Monk was a pianist, a composer of extraordinary originality, with an uncanny individuality that was probably the most distinctive sound in American jazz.

Born in North Carolina in 1917, he moved to New York with his mother and sister. As a teenager, he was a pianist for a traveling evangelist. In 1941, he joined the revolution at Minton's as house pianist. His eccentric dress, speech, and mannerisms raise the question about how we can appreciate and interpret his originality and artistry. He was described as "purely given originality and gift," and the associations as "Monk," withdrawn into his own world, point toward the markings of "otherness." As one of the most outstanding voices in the post-bop period, he was extremely influential for the musicians who would define modern jazz in the late 1950s, 1960s, and beyond.

According to historian Gunther Schuller, Monk propelled the language beyond the traditional chord systems and pushed it like the European avant-garde movements to the edge, toward nontonality—toward music without any fixed tonal center. This artistic freedom helped to institute a social sensibility that helped Black musicians shrug off their dependence on the older, strictly vernacular forms. Many post-boppers were heard to say, "We don't care if you don't listen." This musician-orientated experimentation continued to manifest itself in creative voices throughout the 1960s and 1970s, and with the advent of Black social consciousness during the civil rights era and later.

Ornette Coleman

Ornette Coleman arrived in New York in 1959 and began a movement known as free jazz. "Jazz must be free," said Coleman. He provided the debate about what was now jazz. "The pattern for the tune will be forgotten, and the tune itself will be the pattern." The free jazz movement emphasized distance from commercial jazz movements at the time, particularly cool jazz. Some called it avant-garde jazz or action jazz because of its emphasis on rhythmic energy and vitality. In 1960, Coleman released *Free Jazz*, from which the movement's name emerged. He saw free jazz as the foundation, the center of interest and activity: the melodic line, free rhythmic association and complexity, the invention after the statement of line, the communal, artistic engagement of the ensemble to sustain creative environment, the absence of stacked harmonic dominance, heterophony as primacy. This was the great break back into Black music culture, back to communal expression and invention at the root of the African call, back to free rhythmic complexity and the idea of master drummer, griot, ensemble music-making.

Whereas Charlie Parker got his artistic epiphany from listening to the possibilities of extending structures within and above the harmonic changes, Coleman heard jazz as being completely freed from harmonic constrictions, and he saw the more inventive atmosphere of line development providing an entire world and vocabulary for his new approaches.

In 1959, the Ornette Coleman Group had a several-week engagement at the Five Spot in New York. This was a seminal time in jazz history: Miles Davis recorded *Kind of Blue* in March and April 1959; Coltrane recorded *Giant Steps* in April and May 1959; Ornette Coleman recorded *The Shape of Jazz to Come* in 1960. But sadly, both Billie Holiday and Lester Young died in 1959.

Hard bop and free jazz, the next Black musical movements, were attempts by musicians to reestablish the dominance of the rhythms of Black music, rhythms that had been clearly homogenized in the cool school movement, which was now largely dominated by White jazz players. Hard bop players, in particular, insisted on the heavy reliance of the vernacular sounds of the blues, and even gospel, as in saxophonist Cannonball Adderley's piece "Mercy, Mercy, Mercy," composed by Joe Zawinul. In free jazz, there was also a focus on African identity, ethnic aesthetics and instruments, free improvisation, and collective group improvisation. Other characteristics were the absence of tonality and predetermined chords, loose structural design, suspension of regular beats of time signature, and fragmented melodic textures rather than dependence on melody. While there were many artists who took in various strains of these movements, several individuals and groups stand out: John Coltrane, Ornette Coleman, Anthony Braxton, the Association for the Advancement of Creative Musicians (AACM), Richard Muhal Abrams, the Art Ensemble of Chicago, Cecil Taylor, Albert Ayler, Sun Ra, and later Charles Mingus.

Formed in 1965, the Art Ensemble of Chicago, which emerged full-blown in 1969, was created from and out of support from the AACM. This collective of musicians began to experiment actively, formed a record company, and found a base for concert support and scholarship. The Art Ensemble of Chicago's motto was "Great Black Music—Ancient to Modern." This signaled a real understanding among musicians that a continuum of styles, approaches, and cultural and aesthetic conventions had been upheld in

African American experience and substantiated a cultural forum and identity in creative music.

Sun Ra

> In my music, I speak of unknown things, impossible things, ancient things, potential things. No two songs tell the same story. History is only his-story. You haven't heard my story yet, my story is different from "his" story, not a part of history. My story is endless, it never repeats itself. Why should it? A sunset doesn't repeat itself, nature never repeats itself, why should I?
>
> —Sun Ra

Born May 22, 1914, as Herman Poole Blount, in Birmingham, Alabama, composer, bandleader, mystic, and philosopher Sun Ra was the original modern galactic groove master, complete with forward, free, creative music, electronics, and costumes. He placed himself at the center of creativity and projected his work as a vehicle of interplanetary truths through music. He excelled in his rhetoric about cosmic philosophy as much as his notions about the truth-seeking aspect of art. He also renamed himself Ra (or Le Sonny Ra), after the Ethiopian God of the Sun. His mother had named him Herman after the famous Afro-centric magician Black Herman, who was said to be able to raise people from the dead, and who was an associate of Marcus Garvey and Booker T. Washington.

A precocious youth, Sun Ra was playing piano, sight reading, and transcribing big-band arrangements by ear at age twelve, and he was deeply impressed by Fletcher Henderson, Duke Ellington, and Fats Waller. He was a straight-A student and a voracious reader. In Birmingham, the library of the Mason Lodge was open to Blacks. Its eclectic collection of philosophies made a big imprint on Sun Ra's early thinking. As a teen, he was playing professionally, and in high school, he studied under a well-respected disciplinarian band instructor who had trained many Birmingham musicians. Sun Ra was his high school class valedictorian and was awarded a full scholarship to Alabama A&M University, where he majored in music, studying composition, orchestration, and music theory, but he dropped out after a year. He claimed that he had received a vision in a dream, was taken up to Saturn, and was told by the Saturn beings to speak "only through his music."

After he left college, he became a well-respected, dedicated, and devoted musician. He rearranged his family home into a studio, where he rehearsed with his band and traded philosophy and music lessons. He visited daily the local piano music store, where he copied music and swapped ideas with the music teachers there. After rejecting a World War II draft notice as a conscientious objector, he was assigned to a Civilian Public Service camp, but as he refused that assignment as well, he was arrested and jailed in 1942. After yet another appeal, he was released. The judge declared that Sun Ra was both "a psychopathic personality" and "a well-educated colored intellectual." Sun Ra returned to Birmingham, reforming his band. In 1945, he migrated to Chicago. In this new environment, he was hired to play and write arrangements for his idol, Fletcher Henderson. He also performed briefly with Coleman Hawkins and Stuff Smith. His interest in philosophy continued, as did his interest in Black nationalism. He came to espouse the notion that Egyptian and Black greatness was suppressed by European education and history.

In 1952, he established the Space Trio and attracted established musicians, notably Marshal Allen and John Gilmore. This group created a book club, exchanged ideas and readings, created pamphlets, and formed an independent label, Saturn Records. During this time, they began wearing Egyptian-based costumes and headpieces. They also inserted science fiction themes into their music. Their musical innovations fused bebop with soul, electronic instruments, and vernacular Black music, as well as the spoken word, dance, and visuals.

In 1961, they all left Chicago, traveling to Montreal and landing in New York. Due to the high cost of rent, they lived together and began a regular stint at Slugs Salon in 1966. This became Ra's home for eighteen months straight, every Monday night, and on and off for the next several years. Cannonball Adderley, Jimmy Heath, Charles Mingus, Art Blakey, and numerous musicians began to frequent Slugs. Notable artists such as Dizzy and Monk encouraged Sun Ra. The group's first tour in 1968 included thirty musicians, dancers, singers, and even fire-eaters. The staging and lighting were elaborate. All of this was before George Clinton and Earth, Wind & Fire, who also based their art and philosophy on intergalactic, futuristic Egyptian costumes and popular, semispiritual philosophies.

Regarding the music business and its effect on musicians, Sun Ra commented, "The chaos on this planet is due to the music the musicians are playing that they are forced to play by some who just think of money, who don't realize that music is a spiritual language and represents the people of Earth. When musicians are compelled to play anything, it goes straight to the throne of the creator of the universe, and that is how he sees you, according to your music. Because music is a universal language, and what musicians play is what goes to the creator as your personal ambassador, and your personal nemesis."

Sun Ra's work received impressive reviews and was featured on the cover of *Rolling Stone* in 1969, a major mainstream visibility moment. Following this, he was invited to France, Germany, the United Kingdom, even to Egypt. In 1971, he was invited to serve as an artist-in-residence at the University of California, Berkeley, teaching a course entitled "The Black Man in the Cosmos." In 1978, he appeared on *Saturday Night Live*. During the 1980s, his popularity waned, but there were some appearances over the decade, culminating with a first-time television interview on NBC's *Night Watch*. More European engagements, college residencies, collaboration with famed composer conceptualist John Cage, and a stint at Dartmouth College followed. By the early 1990s, Ra was showing signs of aging and ailing health. After surviving a stroke in 1990, he returned to Birmingham, where he contracted pneumonia and died on May 30, 1993. But Sun Ra remained—like Henderson, Ellington, and Count Basie—one of the last surviving band leaders to conduct an ensemble that lasted almost four decades, an unbelievable feat in modern American pop culture.

John Coltrane and Love Supreme

> The main thing for a musician is to give the listener a picture of the wonderful things he sees in the universe.
>
> —John Coltrane

"I think that the majority of musicians are interested in truth," John Coltrane has said. "They've got to be because saying a music thing is a truth. If you play a music statement, it's a valid statement, that's truth right there. In order to play those kinds of things, you've got to live as much truth as you possibly can." As we consider what it means to be an artist, we must look at the work of John Coltrane, an "explorer," and one of the greatest innovators in modern music. In the history of popular music, few musicians illicit the respect and admiration from musicians, the music industry, and the buying public as John Coltrane does. His superb musicianship, his sense of mission and deep spirituality, his dedication to finding meaning and connections between music and the world all mark his identity as an innovator in "sounding and representations." His philosophy, his demeanor, his spirit, and the resulting music provide a great example of the idea that musicianship is a "priesthood, not a pastime."

The work that most characterizes this is his 1964 album *A Love Supreme*, a project devoted to the exploration of jazz as an inner expression and as a gift from the creator. The album, he said, came to him through inspiration. After a week of composing in isolation, he said that the music came down to him like God came to "Moses on the mountain." The record is divided into four parts: "Acknowledgment," "Resolution," "Pursuance," and "Psalm." In the album notes, he writes, "This album is a humble offering . . . an attempt to say, Thank you, God, through our work."

John William Coltrane was born in Hamlet, North Carolina, in 1926, and he died in 1967, of lung cancer. He was just forty years old. His grandfather was a preacher, and Coltrane was brought up in the Black church. His father died when Coltrane was a boy. After he graduated from high school, the family moved to Philadelphia, where he was awarded scholarships in music composition. He was drafted and fought in World War II. After his return in 1945, he played in r&b bands. In the late 1940s, he became inspired by the new movement of bebop, and he played with Dizzy Gillespie, Miles Davis, Eddie "Cleanhead" Vinson, and Earl Bostic. He played for nearly a year in 1957 with Thelonious Monk at the historic Five Spot Club. Trapped in a cycle of drinking and drugs, including heroin, in 1957 he claimed to have "a spiritual awakening." In 1960, he formed his classic quartet with Elvin Jones, Jimmy Garrison, and McCoy Tyner. He signed with Impulse in 1961.

In 1960, Coltrane also had a huge commercial hit with the movie tune "My Favorite Things." This provided him and jazz broad exposure. Until his tragic death in 1967, he recorded many albums with his "second line-up," the ensemble Alice Coltrane, Pharoah Saunders, and Ali Rashid. Coltrane investigated the music of India, Brazil, and Africa. During all of this, he developed a startling approach to harmonic, chord/scale techniques, one begun by Charlie Parker, that set patterns for the highest level of musicianship, and improvisation.

The true measure of an artist's work is not in popularity or sales. It is in the impressions left behind and the impact that work has on fellow artists. Coltrane's wife, Alice, remarked, "If it's possible through sound to realize truth, that is the essence of his search, and discovery experimentations and exploration. There is a feeling in his music that goes beyond the musical realm. His music represents expression that was meditative, and lasting."

For drummer Jeff Watts, Coltrane had "the cry of the American Church in his tone." As another musician stated, Coltrane's music "testifies like a preacher." Coltrane recognized his church upbringing, his mature adult devotion to search and study, and the fulfillment of his calling as an artist. These define the reasons for his spiritual character. His intensity, "dignified solemnity of purpose," brought legions of musicians to "believe in themselves and their own creative nature," as Keith Shadwick wrote in *Jazz: Legends of*

Style.[4] Branford Marsalis said of Coltrane's *A Love Supreme* that it was "about the expression of the Blues, it is the subtext of the piece, which is not just about sadness but profound understanding in how the music moves beyond complaining but to understanding life."

In this blues-jazz-spiritual way, as some have suggested, Coltrane and jazz performers met the existential challenge with a sarcastic, witty moan, with poem and form that trapped angst and released it artfully. Coltrane's study of religion, blues, and Eastern and African music infused his own music with probing solos. The great Indian musician Ravi Shankar discussed musical statements that matched various states of consciousness. Frequency patterns and vibrations are connected to the psyche and are rooted in universal structures. Coltrane's works suggest Indian philosophy played out musically in drone tones, songs, rhythms, and modality.

Giant Steps, Ohm, Africa, Ascension, Alabama, Dear Lord, Peace, and *A Love Supreme* all reflect Coltrane's commitment to the idea that music is an essentially spiritual and contextually social experience. Coltrane's work suggests that the truth can be found in dedicated sound. His work exemplifies artistry: the significance of the "doing of the music itself," music's ability to transcend market value and connect deeply with human experience, shaping the way people live and think.

CHAPTER NINE

Race Records, Gospel, R&B, and Urban Blues

Rhythm and blues was the urban popular dance/song and celebration of Black communities rejoined with loved ones after World War II. This music was captured on "race records" sold primarily in Black communities. By 1949, this new secular blues tradition would be identified by *Billboard* as r&b. This style and sound grew, becoming the most popular format for Black performers outside of jazz and gospel. While jazz was seen as the carrier of mostly instrumental expression, r&b focused on popular singing and dance traditions, emphasizing love and contemporary life.

Most Black folks heard r&b from jukeboxes in dance halls. Postwar bands were transformed from the larger sounds of the Cab Calloway Orchestra to the slicker, big-beat, commercial love rhyme of someone like Louis Jordan, the pioneering performer of the 1940s. His group, the Timpani Five, had reduced the big band down to a rhythm section, three horns, and Louie on sax and vocals. Jordan had eighty singles on the r&b charts. He set the pattern for modern rhythm and blues and was a trendsetter as a crossover artist. His work had catchy comic lyrics, and it highlighted dance steps, dress, and style. Other groups included the Orioles, Ruth Brown, Solomon Burke, Big Joe Turner, and the Ink Spots.

From r&b came rock and roll, a term coined by White DJ Alan Freed. Rock and roll represented the awakening and attraction of young White America in the 1950s to Black popular dance music. While many Black artists were originally ignored by the mainstream industry, Black music performed by Whites allowed many Black artists to gain for the first time a larger public acceptance. Little Richard, Chuck Berry, and Fats Domino, for example, became huge crossover acts. Alan Freed "discovered" these race records in 1951. His show *The Moondog Coronation Ball*, held in the Cleveland Arena on March 21, drew an audience of 20,000. When Freed moved to New York in 1955, he played this music during prime-time radio programming. This exposure helped rock and roll gain popularity among many young White listeners. In order to make this music acceptable to mainstream American culture, White artists such as Bill Haley and Pat Boone covered older Black r&b artists' pieces. When that happened, America had a new music.

But it was Elvis Presley who became the most recognizable and influential rock star and teen idol. Elvis became the "new" American cultural music phenomenon in 1956 with "Heartbreak Hotel" and "Hound Dog." Jerry Lee Lewis and Buddy Holly followed, also covering Black music and styles. Along with Elvis, Jerry Lee Lewis, Johnny Cash, and Carl Perkins—all part of Sam Phillips's Sun Records—became the catalysts for early rock and roll as an American mainstream, musical/cultural expression. Still, the real fathers and mothers of this music were Black creators who had been evolving out of race records traditions.

The first recognized rock and roll record was Roy Brown's "Good Rocking Tonight" in 1948; then came Jackie Brenston's "Rocket 88" in 1951. Joe Turner cemented it with "Shake, Rattle, and Roll" in 1954. Ray Charles followed in that same year with "I've Got a Woman." The Platters' "The Great Pretender," and Little Richard followed in 1955 and 1956. In 1955, Chuck Berry started the image of hot r&b that became the blueprint for mainstream rock and roll. But if you listen to Muddy Waters, John Lee Hooker, and other blues artists, you can hear the roots of rock and roll way before this.

There also occurred in the mid-1950s a huge reaction against rock and roll. This was an attack against Black popular culture and was really a repeat of past claims against ragtime and jazz. President Dwight Eisenhower stated, "This music represents a change in our standards," and he asked, "What has happened to our concepts of beauty, decency, morality?" The first generation of mainstream rock and rollers fell hard. By the end of the 1950s, Chuck Berry was jailed, Elvis was drafted, Little Richard went into the ministry, Buddy Holly died in a plane crash, Jerry Lee Lewis got in trouble for marrying his fourteen-year-old cousin, and Alan Freed was arrested for a payola scandal. He died shortly thereafter.

Phil Spector, Jerry Leiber, and Mike Stoller were White songwriters who were intensely interested in Black music. In the 2001 documentary film *American Roots Music*, Leiber comments, "Soul, gospel, jazz . . . are shards of this wellspring of Black culture. The whole world is imitating these sounds.

I just find this very interesting." How these traditions are connected is my subject here.

Gospel Music

> The African American worship community—the Black church in its largest expression—has been the nurturing institution for one of the world's greatest music cultures.
>
> —Bernice Johnson Reagon,
> *Pioneering African American Gospel Composers*

The single most important institution that helped to define, shape, and instill cultural codes as well as cement aesthetic and artistic performances standards was and is the African American church. As Amiri Baraka writes in *Black Music*, "to go back in any historical line of ascent in Black music leads us invariably to religion, i.e., spirit worship. This phenomenon is always at the root in Black art, the worship of spirit—or at least the summoning of or by such force." According to Baraka, "The kind of church Black people belonged to usually connected them with the society as a whole, identified them, their aspirations, their culture, because the church was one of the few places complete fullness of expression by the Black man was not constantly censored."

Black church and spiritual music, as well as Black singing traditions anywhere in the Black diaspora—including the Caribbean, West Africa, Cuba, and Brazil—contain most of the essential performative, stylistic, and cultural attributes recognized as the defining characteristics of Black music traditions. Gospel music is known and accepted today as a contemporary musical category and style that continues the commercial and popular manifestations of those historical Black church singing traditions. In the 1960s, it became a part of the great wave of mainstreaming that marked this period as revolutionary in terms of the full cultural/social projection of Black modern identity.

Thomas A. Dorsey (1899–1992) is recognized as a father of gospel music, mainly because of his devotion to making the style known to the masses. But the emergence of gospel followed much the same evolution as all Black music; it began with folks creating home traditions and evolved with musical and commercial developments as masses migrated to urban areas and new cultural forms developed to accommodate that move. One view is that gospel music is the spirituals "gassed up" to incorporate stylistic, musical, and performance conventions already established in the blues, jazz and popular music.

Once these styles were brought into the spiritual singing context and commercialized, gospel as a popular style emerged. In truth, the performers were "evangelizing," taking the message to the community and packaging that message in popular musical forms. One of gospel's most salient distinctions is the textual emphasis placed on "personal testimony." And as the urban experience became sometimes unbearable, Jesus, just as in the slave spirituals, was able to deliver.

Modern gospel also continues "celebratory ritual." The ritual is a part of the music-making experience, so that the "live" church experiences, even the conversions, are a part of the aesthetic, the meaning. Gospel music is only as meaningful as the shared ritual it brings. Some music historians argue that gospel has its own codified musical language, the "gospel style" based on years of good church singing and playing, and is not simply a "jazzed up" spiritual song. This codified musical language is seen in the performance practices of gospel artists who embrace vocal and textual improvisation. This very skilled vocal expression highlights moans, groans, extemporaneous textual illumination, and "musical screaming" heard in few other traditions in the world. At first, some saw this as "devil music," but the masses of Black urban audiences were drawn to gospel because it closely aligned with their contemporary, fast urban environments. As early as 1938, concert promoter John Hammond was organizing Black gospel concerts at Carnegie Hall in New York, where figures such as the great innovator/stylist Sister Rosetta Tharpe mixed up blues and church singing styles. This helped to further cement and codify multiple regional and stylistic approaches mainly among Black musicians and helped fortify Black art as a cultural foundation that again provided a strengthened identity and ideology.

The emergence of twentieth-century Black gospel music culture was an outgrowth of the movement of Black southern migrants, an American holiness movement, the cross-fertilization of Black popular styles, Black education and social interests, and the performance primacy and centrality of Black music in the community. Church musicians developing Black music liturgical traditions, such as the Gospel Pearls; blues musicians playing in the church and the community, including Charley Patton and Son House; and traveling jazz musicians playing and using church forms all facilitated a cross-fertilization of musical languages.

In a sense, all gospel styles revolve centrally around the spirituals, congregational styles and singing structures, call and response forms, slow metered and lined out Protestant hymns, and various styles of Black popular music. The Black church is an invaluable conservatory for interpreting and studying the gospel music tradition. The rituals, the styles of worship, the understanding of committed spirituality, and the evangelical impetus which heightens the meaning and expression of gospel music all provide critical interpretive and performance criteria for understanding.

There are at least four critical developmental stylistic periods:

1. Spirituals and jubilee quartets such as the Fisk Jubilee Singers and Golden Gate Quartet (1870–1920s).
2. Classic gospel, as in the work of Lucie Campbell, William Herbert Brewster, Thomas A. Dorsey, Mahalia Jackson, Roberta Martin, Clara Ward, and others (1880s–1950s).
3. Contemporary gospel, seen in James Cleveland, Edwin Hawkins, Andrae Crouch, and Richard Smallwood (1960s–1970s).
4. Post-contemporary gospel, as in the work of the Winans, the Clarke Sisters, Fred Hammond, Hezekiah Walker, Kirk Franklin, Kim Burrell (1980s–2009+).

Gospel History

The Black mainstream church's institutionalization of gospel music happened in 1930 at the National Baptist Convention in Chicago with Thomas A. Dorsey's "If You See My Savior." After this success, the Convention adopted the gospel tradition as its main musical "devotion device," providing support for conference activities of "praise and worship" as well as Christian affirmation.

It is worth noting that Dorsey, a recognized blues composer and performer, was the pianist and musical director for the well-established blues singer Ma Rainey. This exemplified the inseparable connection between spiritual and secular Black traditions. Dorsey and others fused the more commercial, secular, worldly styles and rhythms and used those to shape the church singing traditions, which were becoming increasingly more urban. In 1932, Dorsey began the publishing company Dorsey House of Music for the sole purpose of selling the work of gospel composers.

Additional support for this emerging mainstream style could be seen in the 1940s radio program *Gospel Train* on WLIB in New York. In 1957, the Clara Ward Singers, a gospel chorale, appeared with major jazz figures at the Newport Jazz Festival. This event again brought another form of Black music to the mainstream masses. The radio shows included national sponsors, and there were even organized "gospel clubs," after-church nightspots where people could go and hear gospel music.

Another voice and a major artistic figure in the popularization of the music was gospel great Mahalia Jackson (1911–1972), known as the queen of gospel music. A protégée of Thomas Dorsey, Jackson catapulted gospel singing to higher visibility by appearing on the nationally syndicated *The Ed Sullivan Show*. She was later seen in her own *Mahalia Jackson Show* in 1954 on CBS. In 1961, Jackson was invited to perform at President Kennedy's inauguration party, and in 1963, a TV show entitled *Gospel Time* emerged. In 1969, James Cleveland, actually a second generation Dorsey, created in California the Gospel Music Workshop of America, which brought together thousands of singers and songwriters to be trained in the gospel tradition.

As the Black student civil rights organizations mobilized, they embraced the gospel tradition. By the mid-1960s, gospel style could be heard in the folk, protest, church singing traditions. Gospel music received yet another boost into a more marketable mainstream when, in 1969, the Edwin Hawkins Singers' "Oh Happy Day" rose in the popular charts as a top-ten single, a first for a "religious" song. This helped establish gospel music as a commercially stable mainstream sound. Soon after, as with every other Black popular music form, rock groups and mainstream artists such as Elton John used gospel harmonies and styling and even incorporated Black gospel choirs as background singers. TV commercials used gospel tracks in the background when absolutely nothing spiritual or religious was being represented.

For our exploration, it is important to note that within Black expressive culture, the artistry is fluid and traverses many and all record-bin categories. "For those of you who thought gospel music has gone too far . . . " is an opening line from Kirk Franklin, the 1990s gospel hip hop star, singer, and impresario. In his work, he samples 1970s bass lines from George Clinton and layers in the hype and noise of hip hop production, to emulate the energy in urban contemporary Black popular culture. He describes this as "a Holy Ghost Party" and as a way to reach a younger disenchanted, searching generation.

Despite its numerous developmental waves, which are also shaped by commercial influences, gospel music remains the most important musical style for preserving Black cultural identity. This is because it squarely sits in the center of Black spiritual life and resides and resonates deeply within and among Black people in ritual. It is the one West African sustaining element that will not be completely commodified.

CHAPTER TEN

Urban Contemporary: Soul, Funk, and Global

Consider creatively Ma Rainey, Louis Armstrong, Cab Calloway, Sister Rosetta Tharpe, Sun Ra, Chuck Berry, Ornette Coleman, Rahsaan Roland Kirk, Ray Charles, James Brown, Tina Turner, George Clinton, Bootsy Collins, Jimi Hendrix, Isaac Hayes, Patti LaBelle, Rick James, Prince, Public Enemy, Grandmaster Flash and the Furious Five, Flava Flav, Busta Rhymes, Missy Elliott, Macy Gray. All that wildly creative, on the edge, frenetic, impassioned, innovative mind toward performance phenomenon—where does this come from? What is the creative, cultural thread that links these artists? From where does this music spring? The source is an old, deep place: an African soul place that was unearthed in our culture due to extraordinary experiences. The West African griots have remained in place, passing on deep cultural traditions, held onto and valued by generation after generation.

It is impossible to speak about the phenomenology of Black creativity in modern popular culture without paying tribute to the music of the 1970s and 1980s, heard as r&b, funk, soul, and urban contemporary. A partial list would include Stevie Wonder, the Jackson Five, Donna Summer, Sister Sledge, Kool & the Gang, LTD, Billy Preston, War, Gladys Knight and the Pips, the Spinners, Patti LaBelle, the Isley Brothers, Al Green, Chic, Barry White, the Four Tops, Smokey Robinson and the Miracles, Marvin Gaye, Diana Ross and the Supremes, the Temptations, Booker T. & the MGs, Otis Redding, the Fifth Dimension, Wilson Pickett, B. B. King, Sly and the Family Stone, Jeffrey Osborne, Earth, Wind & Fire, Natalie Cole, Patti Austin, James Ingram, Tina Turner, Atlantic Starr, Peabo Bryson, Roberta Flack, Donny

Hathaway, the Ohio Players, Aretha Franklin, Lou Rawls, Cheryl Lynn, George Benson, Johnnie Taylor, the Dramatics, the Crusaders, Teddy Pendergrass, Minnie Ripperton, the Chi-Lites, Bob Marley, the Commodores, Rick James, the Pointer Sisters, Curtis Mayfield, Harold Melvin and the Blue Notes, Bill Withers, Rufus and Chaka Khan, Lionel Ritchie, Ashford & Simpson, Cameo, Whitney Houston, the Emotions, the Brothers Johnson, Gil Scott-Heron, Brian Jackson, the Staple Singers, Isaac Hayes, the O'Jays, Luther Vandross, Parliament Funkadelic, Shalamar, the Whispers, the Dazz Band, Gap Band, and more. In all of music production, there has never been a period so rich with artistry. This was simply the most musical time in our modern history, particularly in Black popular music.

Soul Music

Soul music, particularly in 1965–1975, represented cultural and political empowerment, a musical style and category, spirituality and expression, depth and meaning, race pride and civic responsibility. Soul music can be thought of as the Black popular music that accompanied the civil rights years in America. In this turbulent period in American history, this music sought to uphold a social consciousness about race, class, gender, police brutality, human rights, integration, and war protest.

In 1969, *Billboard* instituted soul as the overall category representing Black popular music. As musicologist Portia Maultsby pointed out,

> The soul era was a productive period for Black Americans. Group cohesion, political activism and community self-help programs were responses to the messages of soul singers and leaders of the Black Power movement. The music created by Blacks and for Blacks during this era communicated a general philosophy of refusal to accept the undesirable and a determination to create a better future.

There was a sense that Black music, and therefore Black people, had now arrived and counted in American culture. Soon there was *Soul Train*, a nationally syndicated TV show, which highlighted and projected the positive powerful and influential images of Black artists in the mainstream. *Soul Train* drew the attention of White viewers who traditionally had watched *American Bandstand*, Dick Clark's innovative show of the 1950s. Both shows paved the way for MTV. The three major record labels that dominated production of this music were Motown, Stax, and Philly International. The song titles of this period tell the story of soul:

- A Change Is Gonna Come (Otis Redding, 1965)
- Respect (Aretha Franklin, 1967)
- Say It Loud—I'm Black and I'm Proud (James Brown, 1968)
- Everyday People (Sly & the Family Stone, 1968)
- Choice of Colors (The Impressions, 1969)
- It's Your Thing (The Isley Brothers, 1969)
- To Be Young, Gifted, and Black (Nina Simone, 1970)
- Ball of Confusion (The Temptations, 1970)
- Respect Yourself (The Staple Singers, 1971)
- Love the One You're With (The Isley Brothers, 1971)
- Smiling Faces Sometimes (The Undisputed Truth, 1971)
- What's Going On (Marvin Gaye, 1971)
- Papa Was a Rolling Stone (The Temptations, 1972)
- Slippin' into Darkness (War, 1972)
- Back Stabbers (O'Jays, 1972)
- Love Train (O'Jays, 1973)
- The Revolution Will Not Be Televised (Gil Scott-Heron, 1974)
- Shining Star (Earth, Wind & Fire, 1975)
- Wake Up, Everybody (Harold Melvin and the Blue Notes, 1975)
- Chocolate City (Parliament Funkadelic, 1975)
- Street Life (The Crusaders, with Randy Crawford, 1978)
- Ain't No Stoppin' Us Now (McFadden & Whitehead, 1979)

The song titles suggest themes consistent with the values of the times, and communicated through Black popular culture.

In the work of the great soul artists, much comes together that defines the elements of Black music aesthetic, functionality and meaning: spirituals, blues, gospel, r&b, instrumental facility, training and technique, innovative artistry, international recognition and appreciation, and the power of a relevant social dynamic. While the soul period may have been considered over by the mid-1970s, the themes continued to resonate heavily in Black popular music well into the 1980s and beyond. As a formative aesthetic, soul music is Black music because it is the music created by Black people in Black style. Soul music is Black church music realized on the dance floor and applied to how Black people live and love in society. Soul music is the sound of Black cultural expression. It's the groove, the howl, the sass, the swing, and the feel of the music, too. Like gospel, soul was first baked in the Black church. The codes, the aesthetic, the performance practice really are a secular version of spirit-filled, depth-delivered, purposeful church singing.

James Brown's Functional Funk and Berry Gordy's Motown

> I got something that makes me want to shout. I got something that tells
> me what it's all about. I got soul, and I'm super bad.

> —James Brown, "Super Bad"

A defining style of this period was James Brown's funk style. Titles include
"Papa's Got a Brand New Bag" (1965), "Cold Sweat" (1967), "I Got the
Feeling" (1968), "Licking Stick" (1968), "Say It Loud" (1968), "Mother
Popcorn" (1969), "Funky Drummer" (1970), "Get Up" (1970), "Super Bad"
(1970), "Soul Power" (1971), "Make It Funky" (1971), "Hot Pants" (1971),
"Doing It to Death" (1973), "The Payback" (1973), "Papa Don't Take No
Mess" (1974), "Funky President" (1975), "Get Up Offa That Thang" (1976),
"It's Too Funky in Here" (1979)—a long run of consistent hits. Brown's
music set musical models that defied the era, but he also functioned as the
quintessential soul griot, addressing issues of education, drug abuse, politics,
self-determination, and image.

James Brown owned his own businesses, had radio stations, and was
dedicated to Black people and their lives. He was a griot who even sat down
with and sang in the ear of the president. This period of music production
most succinctly mirrored what Black people were thinking and feeling at the
time. The music was inextricably bound to the way people were living. The
issues, concerns, worldviews, political perspectives, styles, and social customs
were embedded and carried by the music: "get involved," "get into it," "say it
loud," "stay in school," "get down," "get on up," "everybody over there," "get
some," "we got to have soul power," "you got to get down," "I want to get
into it," "stay on the scene," "get it together, right on, right on," "you can't
tell me how to run my life," "you just talking loud and saying nothing," and
"make it funky."

The simultaneous explosion of Black identity and America's acceptance
of this presence could be seen, felt, and heard in volume. The best "American" model of hard work, dreams, and cultural productivity was imaged in
Motown Records and can be seen through the story of Berry Gordy.

Gordy began writing songs in the late 1950s. Encouraged by some success,
he borrowed $800 from his parents and founded Motown Records. That
investment from a Black "bank" allowed him to introduce to the world one
of the most amazing pools of music talent ever. This Motown explosion
stabilized and institutionalized Black music expression in a way never seen
before. In 1988, Berry sold the multimillion-dollar company; its final sale in

1993 was for $301 million. An original $800 investment, and millions and millions of dollars later, we still have our soul affected by this music. How much more powerful is it to learn that Berry Gordy's grandfather was born a slave? After the Civil War, he purchased land and built a farm in Georgia. Berry Gordy's father left Georgia and settled in Detroit, where Berry Gordy purchased a small record store and began writing songs while working in a Ford assembly plant.

Black owned, directed, and operated, Motown was the first label to package Black music as American music. It portrayed "regular American teenage angst" and family values as well as corporate-constructed, "tailor-made" acts whose performers were immaculate, groomed, and well dressed. Motown sought to make music with a "great beat with great stories that anybody can listen to" and that represented "the sound of young America."

Diana Ross and the Supremes, Smokey Robinson and the Miracles, Marvin Gaye, Gladys Knight and the Pips, Stevie Wonder, and the Jackson Five were the living, singing embodiment of what dreams were made of in Motown. The image projected "the old-fashioned American way"—hard work and a rags to riches glory.

Beyond the 1960s and 1970s, Black musical artistry continued to crystallize and be shaped by advances in recording technology and electronic innovations like the synthesizer. New forms grew, such as funk and techno-funk, as seen in Parliament Funkadelic, for example. The newer 1970s funk was driven by an even harder beat, with a bigger dominance of the rhythm section, featuring electric bass, punctuating guitar, drum, synthesizer, and a funky horn section. The music with strong vocal leads revolved around a repetitive driving, syncopated feel, which was created largely to be a social party dance music and gave birth to disco. The music was intended to bring people together to have fun.

The narratives were larger, too. The human experience in this music included humor ("The Bertha Butt Boogie"), fun, fantasy, folly, and foolishness (Funkadelic and *The Mothership Connection*). It is important not to romanticize the era completely, as there were destructive elements, as seen in the lives and deaths of Robert Johnson, Janis Joplin, Jimi Hendrix, and Marvin Gaye. The dangers of drugs and suicide still plagued artists such as Jim Morrison and Kurt Cobain, among others, and remind us of the tremendous battles artists wage. Black popular music, while remaining identifiably Black—with its distinct traditions in sound, performance practice, methods, and delivery—became even more mainstream. Soul eventually morphed into urban contemporary.

The soul sound was created to represent the sonic stylings of certain cities, especially Detroit, Memphis, and Philadelphia. The soul sound and code reflected an aesthetic that was both focused and wide ranging. The musical codes of soul were nurtured in the Black church and worked out in basement parties. Importantly, the music was whistled to and danced to on street corners all over the country. Producers and label owners like Ahmet Ertegun and Jerry Wexler (Atlantic); Norman Whitfield, Berry Gordy, and Holland-Dozier-Holland (Motown); Jim Stewart and Estelle Axton (Stax); and Kenneth Gamble and Leon Huff (Philadelphia International Records) hired great studio groups and house bands—such as Motown's Funk Brothers; Stax's Booker T. and the MGs; and MFSB in Philly. These house bands gave Detroit, Memphis, and Philadelphia distinctive yet related sounds. The creative, far-reaching vision of artists like Stevie Wonder—especially in his masterpiece *Songs in the Key of Life* and *Hotter Than July*—reveals a great deal about how these artists wove social and musical themes and were "in tune" equally with the commerciality of their product.

Jimi Hendrix Defining Rock

Following soul, Jimi Hendrix emerged as the next great towering Black musical figure and innovative genius. His work aligned the cultural coding of soul, blues, r&b, jazz, and pop. The sheer depth, impact, and ferocity of his innovations and expression are undeniable. His untimely death in 1970 was a profound tragedy and great musical loss. Even more than Elvis Presley and the Rolling Stones, Hendrix defined modern rock. He was the pathfinding instrumentalist, writer, singer, performer, and conceptualist who shaped progressive American rock music well past his death.

Hendrix is modeled after the modern consciousness artists of the 1960s, such as Bob Dylan. But Hendrix was a true genius musician and performer who did not emerge full-blown and from nowhere. Hendrix performed under the great models and influences of Little Richard and the Isley Brothers, and he stood in the direct line of Robert Johnson, Muddy Waters, and Buddy Guy. His iconic stature and verbal and lyrical polemic resonated with the social and artistic commitments of the 1960s. Nonetheless, there was his original flair, his stage performance antics, the 1967 Monterey Pop festival "sacrifice" of his guitar, the radical restatement of the national anthem at Woodstock in 1969, his dress and his hair. And there were the "demons" of being carefree, vulnerable, and yet without caution that led to the loss of one of the greatest artists of our culture. Much has been written, books upon books, films and commentary, that speak of Hendrix's revolutionary approach, his creation of a new musical language, his unforgettable sound, and his vocabulary of sustained and artful distortion.

Awestruck, even envious colleagues attest to the "mad technical performance" of this musical wizard who transformed the guitar—a "common pop prop," a singer's accompanying tool—into a partner of virtuosity that came to represent artistic depth, power, prowess, strength, and musical leadership. Hendrix did that for guitarists as John Coltrane deepened the virtuosity, worth, sound, and meaning of the saxophone. There are few original American virtuosos who, like Hendrix, defined a musical movement: Louis Armstrong, Art Tatum, Thelonious Monk, Charlie Christian, Bud Powell, Charlie Parker, Dizzy Gillespie, Sarah Vaughan, Bill Evans, Charles Mingus, Wes Montgomery, and Jaco Pastorius stand out. And, too, there are few whose musical voice is distinctive enough so that it is recognized instantly. The sound of Hendrix's guitar was a lightning rod of musicality, style, and genius that changed the way everyone heard the instrument.

Hendrix was an innovative genius, a code setter, and a definer of musical styles and of the period. He made an unforgettable mark on the social protest and art pop music of the 1960s.

Bob Marley

> Music raises the soul of man higher than the so-called external form of religion. . . . That is why in ancient times the greatest prophets were great musicians.
>
> —Hazrat Inayat Khan, *The Mysticism of Sound and Music*

Without a doubt, Bob Marley is recognized as one of the most important and influential artists in modern music, often referred to as one of the most "transcendent and universally loved" musicians in the last hundred years. His work combines music, Rasta spirituality, national Jamaican politics, Black nationalism, fashion and style, and a philosophy so complete that one writer exclaimed, "There will come a day when music and philosophy will become the religion of humanity if there remains any magic in music."

Marley was a musical icon representing an artistic morality that cut across generations, nations, races, sexes. Simultaneously, he was an international star. His work represented freedom for people all over the world. Marley (1945–1981) was raised in the Parish of St. Ann in north central Jamaica, the same parish as Marcus Garvey, the visionary Jamaican Black nationalist. Marley was born of a British captain, Norval Sinclair Marley, and a Jamaican woman, Cedella Malcolm. When the two married in 1944, Cedella was just seventeen years old, and interracial marriages were rare at the time. Marley's father eventually abandoned the family.

Marley's grandfather, Omeriah Malcolm, was a respected farmer and businessman from the Cromanty people of Ghana. He was a myalman, or healer, and Cedella saw her father in her son. "The finger of the Lord is upon this boy. There is something greater in this man," she said, but her deep feelings about her son were "always too spiritual to talk about or mention . . . even when he was a small boy coming up."

Omeriah's brother was a talented musician who played violin and guitar. Cedella was also a musician and singer. Marley was exposed to church music as his mother took him to the services, but he became completely committed to music when hearing r&b over the radio. According to writer Roger Steffens, "The more the musician is conscious of his mission in life, the greater the service he can render humanity." Marley was conscious of his role as the bringer of the message of Rastafari to the consciousness of the outside world. He believed his work was to call people to God. But in addition to his role as a spiritual leader with his music and messages, Marley was an astute social and political figure.

When he was a child, he and his mother moved to Kingston and settled in the tough area of Trenchtown. He soon began getting together with local musicians and decided he wanted to make a living with music. He was mentored by Joe Higgs, who trained him in jazz and the meaning of musicianship and performing, displaying the ideas of the harmony of the soul, or the connections with a spirit for humanity. The commitment to spiritual ideas is evident in every one of his more than one hundred recorded songs. Marley had many local producers. His "Simmer Down," in 1963, was produced by an independent Jamaican record company. This song rose to number one on Black Jamaican radio stations. Marley then joined with Bunny Livingston and Peter Tosh to form Bob Marley and the Wailers, produced by Coxson Dodd. They listened to Curtis Mayfield, James Brown, the Impressions, and r&b. It is interesting to note that ska, the local Jamaican music, was influenced by American jazz.

In 1966, Marley moved to Delaware to follow his mother, who was now Cedella Booker, having remarried. Marley worked sweeping floors and doing odd jobs in factories. He was greatly influenced and inspired by the civil rights movement. Marley soon returned to Jamaica and sought the spiritual/cultural beliefs of the Rastafari, a Black consciousness movement of the Maroons. These Rasta ideas influenced his music, politics, and focus. Black resistance and spiritual/cultural quests were the root of the Maroons' belief system. They were outcasts from the British occupation during slavery, resisting the British by hiding in the Jamaican mountains and using guerrilla tactics.

Marley's music began to reflect the harshness of his Trenchtown experiences. Produced by Scratch Perry, a local Jamaican, Marley changed his sound and created a new Wailers band—the perfect combination of what became the Soul Rebels. Island Records, owned by Chris Blackwell, signed Marley after that, producing his records for the next ten years. Blackwell's idea was to promote a Black rock band and he pushed them as the Wailers.

Marley became more determined as he spoke and fought against spiritual wickedness in high places. Jamaicans were frustrated with the failure of their politicians to help the poor after the island won independence, and the island was split into warring factions. "Our Belly Filled but We're Hungry," one Marley line goes. Two Jamaican political figures ruled: Michael Manley, a socialist, and U.S.-backed Edward Seaga of the Jamaica Labour Party. Both parties recognized the ability of reggae music to win over people by expressing their wishes and sentiments in songs. Marley's "No More Trouble," "So Much Trouble," and "Rat Race" ("Rasta don't work for no CIA") raised the consciousness of local people. A Smile Magic concert was planned to voice concerns and bring the people of Jamaica together, but Marley and his group were assaulted; Marley himself was shot in his home. Marley left Jamaica and went into exile in London, where he worked on his album *Exodus: 76–78*.

"Is This Love?" reflected this exile, and perhaps his more popular appeal. He returned to Jamaica in 1978 in order to use his fame to hold his *One Love Peace* concert. This unifying concert was meant to help reconcile a divided nation. "It takes a revolution to make a solution," Marley would sing. The concert was a symbolic success as both Manley and Seaga were brought up on stage.

Marley invested his fortune in his own production company, Tuff Gong Records, and began producing his own music. He also called for African unity, and he fed the poor from his home, serving thousands. He was a musical freedom fighter, a prophet, and an avid fan and player of soccer. He developed what he, at first, took to be a soccer injury, but this was soon diagnosed as cancer. On tour in New York in July 1980, he collapsed while jogging in Central Park. He died in May 1981.

Stevie Wonder: Forty Years Straight and Strong

One has to wonder, what would the musical world be like without the artistic genius of Stevland Morris? He is the greatest example of what this book points to: the remarkable genius of Black music. A songwriter of lyrical, melodic, and poetic beauty, insight, depth, and musical versatility, he is incomparable to anyone we have seen in modern music culture. Though he lost his sight at a young age, he sees the world and our times clearly. As Langston Hughes penned the thoughts of Black America in the early part of the twentieth century, Stevie Wonder similarly has scripted the words to the storyline of American life since the 1960s. *Songs in the Key of Life*, *Journey through the Secret Life of Plants*, and *In Square Circle* are gifts of Stevie Wonder's reflective art.

A journey through his works from 1965 to 2005 reveals many things. The announcer who introduced him more than forty years ago as "Stevie Wonder: the twelve-year-old genius" said it all. This introduction was recorded live, and it is followed by Stevie's voice saying, "Yeah, yeah, the jazz soul of little Stevie. . . . I want you to clap your hands, stomp your feet, and do anything that you want to do, yeah." A harmonica solo follows, backed by a big band with a Motown gospel backbeat feel. And this song, in "Fingertips Part 1, 2," introduces another unforgettable sound we have lived with now for forty years. From 1963, he has stated, "Clap your hands just a little bit louder." The codes were set, blues tones and inflections were clear. It's live, it's a Detroit product, full of jazz, soul, and gospel. It's a call and response narrative. It's participatory.

"If you want me to, I'm gonna sing a song," said Wonder. We had here the initiation of a relationship with a public genius and innovator "from the hood," introduced to the world. But in "Uptight," in 1966, we heard a more mature sound, a "Stevie vocal sound" that taught a generation how to sing soul-fully.

This sound would guide us to move closer to the image of the artist as a humanitarian who scripted songs for our culture's changes and challenges. Some of Wonder's inner-reflective tunes made us examine the meaning of being alive, from the perspective of one in love, or one in pain, to one indignant over the inequities that exist in the world, from Soweto to Detroit to Alabama. And through Stevie Wonder's music, there is always a remembrance of Dr. Martin Luther King Jr. Black people do not sing the traditional "Happy Birthday" song to each other; they sing the version of that song that Stevie Wonder created in honor of King, just as Black people remember our heritage when we sing the "National Negro Anthem" by James Weldon Johnson.

Stevie Wonder's ballads, melodic sentimental songs, reach deep down into the love narrative so precious to the living of all Americans. The love ballads include lines like "Hey, love, may I have a word with you. I'd like to tell you just what I've been going through" and "My one true sole desire . . . Don't you know I was made to love, worship, and adore. . . . I was made to live for her, build a world around her" (from "I Was Made to Love Her"). The songs "I Was Made to Love Her," "Until You Come Back to Me," and "For Once in My Life" are among the first Wonder love ballads that moved and shaped one generation's views on romance.

He was born Stevland Judkins Morris on May 13, 1950, in Saginaw, Michigan, moving later to Detroit. Many Detroiters in the 1950s listened to WCHB. There they heard B. B. King, Ruth Brown, Jackie Wilson, and others. Wonder took up an interest in drums and piano, given to him by a neighbor; he sang in church and neighborhood hangouts. By the time Berry Gordy heard him in the Motown Studios, people were calling him a "wonderkid." We next heard the quick maturing due to the help of seasoned artists at Motown: "What a Genius." "Heaven help the Black man if he struggles one more day; heaven help the White man if he turns his back away." "If You Really Love Me" and "Never Dreamed You'd Leave in Summer" were the first clear inklings of genius songwriting capturing the greatest of both American jazz ballad song traditions and gospel-tinged blues r&b traditions.

In "Superwoman," the sound of the Fender Rhodes electric piano from the opening defined the new modern move into the 1970s toward more personal, reflective artistry. In early 1972, in the record *Music of My Mind*, with the vocals, harmonies, and instrumentation, Wonder's true genius fully emerged, heard in the songwriting, electronics, lyrics, arrangements, and productions that defined the next twenty plus years of American popular music. *Music of My Mind* was the end result of a year of Wonder locking himself away in New York, conceptualizing on a Moog music synthesizer. Stevie Wonder, now just twenty-one years old, pressed with a difficult marriage and living in a difficult time in American history, was composing masterpieces. But this period marks another height. He now pushed music, and electronic music technology, to sculpt creative art. In the late 1970s, Stevie Wonder did something that pop artists had rarely done. He signed his new contract with his hometown Motown label with this phrase added: he would maintain "complete creative control of his work."

"Superstition" from the 1972 *Talking Book* album marked not only Wonder's renewed creative individual direction but the staple of funk, the clavinet, and the lead horns of Black urban r&b. On the album cover, Wonder is dressed as a modern griot in a West African man's gown with beads; his hair is braided in African cornrows. He was now poised and positioned to mean Blackness for himself and for all the world. For the first time in modern history, here was an artist who not only composed the songs on the album but produced, arranged, and orchestrated them, and he played all the principal instruments like a refined, seasoned, studio sessions player. And why not? The Motown machine was a natural Black arts training ground, complete with church, family and rituals, technical assistance, road crew, studio experience, and much supportive love. So "You and I" and "You Are the Sunshine of My Life" were now Black wedding standards. His works consummated a generation of revolutionary social-protest workers and generations of married couples.

The next iteration of Stevie Wonder's newer musical mind came in 1973 with *Innervisions* and in 1974 with *Fulfillingness' First Finale*. From those albums came "Too High," "Living for the City," "Higher Ground," and "Boogie On, Reggae Woman." In the latter, Wonder fused gospel, soul, funk, and reggae. The bass line in that song helped to redefine bass lines in popular music. When Wonder asked, "Can I play?" before he soloed on his harmonica, he evoked that call and response talk, that let's rap with our listeners thing that Cab Calloway, James Brown, and Morris Day used before him and that rappers would use decades following. The Black anthem of the time was "Living for the City." Wonder captured how deeply people felt: "To find a job is like a haystack needle . . . 'cause where he lives they don't use colored people." How could Wonder have articulated so clearly the feeling of the urban ethos and experience? This is a fusion, funk, soul, r&b, blues that painted the map for anything rapper Tupac would script later.

Then in 1976, after an almost fatal car crash, Wonder woke from a coma with a new vision that reawakened listeners: *Songs in the Key of Life*. The hits from that album are still hits today: "Sir Duke," "I Wish," "Isn't She Lovely?" "As," "Village Ghettoland," "Pastime Paradise," and "If It's Magic." From "Village Ghettoland" come these lyrics: "Families buying dog food now, starvation roams the streets, babies die before they are born, infected by the grief." By the end of the 1970s came a movie soundtrack, *Journey through the Secret Life of Plants*, featuring the song "Send One Your Love." This is such a poetic, tender piece, it is simply one of the most beautiful ballads ever written: "people say two hearts beating as one is unreal, . . . so blind they are, must be that they cannot believe what they see."

The 1980s brought a musical world citizen, humanist, and political provocateur whose works had defined every period of living since his piercing, pervasive art songs hit us powerfully in 1965. We got in this period "Rocket Love," another love letter to Marley after his death. This period also saw "All I Do," and King's "Happy Birthday" song. In 1985, Wonder released "It's Wrong," about apartheid. This became the banner piece against the worst cultural and political abomination in our midst since Nazism. Also in 1985, he participated in "We Are the World"—a song that gained a global meaning, focused on the pain of people from Africa, but resonating everywhere.

In the 1990s, his urban eyes fixed on the street and cries against police brutality, he gave us "Can't We All Get Along?" Wonder continued King's legacy by marching with one million Black men in 1995 in Washington, D.C. And he worked with Spike Lee on the film *Jungle Fever*, which featured his song "Gotta Have You."

In 2005, some forty years after his first record, still on the downbeat and still on Motown Records, Wonder released *A Time to Love*, with the singles "If Your Love Cannot Be Moved," "A Time to Love," and "So What the Fuss." In this project, Wonder connected across the generations with Prince and with Kim Burrell and India.Arie. In the duet with India.Arie, he passed his Motown torch, singing, "At this point in history, we have a choice to make to either walk the path of love or be crippled by our hate."

The wonderkid has grown up. He has long worked in our lives and continues to inspire the artists of this day, bringing them along to carry the new song as griots do. Stevie Wonder is one of the most important of the music-makers who tower in our minds, and he is the artist who best qualifies and defines Black culture. Stevie Wonder embodies the Black music aesthetic; he represents the culture's very best. It's no wonder.

Patrice Rushen

One of the most important aspects of redefining cultural coding is examining what is meant by the title "musician." Few musicians today are allowed to be successful and creative while also pushing the definition of what it means to be a popular artist. One such musician is composer, pianist, producer, and arranger Patrice Rushen. In refuting the boundaries of a male-dominated industry, she provides, beyond her gifting, a power-defining presence of women in popular culture. When thinking of artists who have had successful and diverse music careers, someone like Richard Wagner comes to mind: a composer, conductor, and impresario-like music promoter. Or we might think of Leonard Bernstein, conducting, composing, performing, while also writing musicals and TV shows, and teaching. Or we might consider Quincy Jones, with movie scores and hit records. Patrice Rushen joins this group. We first came to know Rushen as a young piano wizard in the pop jazz world, but Rushen is a musician who does it all.

At age seventeen, in 1972, while attending the University of Southern California, she performed at the Monterey Jazz Festival. While she was a talented singer, pianist, dancer, and multi-instrumentalist making hit videos, her true love was composition. As a piano student having actually entered the preparatory program at USC at age three, a true modern child prodigy, she later graduated as a composition major.

Rushen has written, played, produced, and conducted for Frank Sinatra, Prince, Janet Jackson, Jean-Luc Ponty, Herbie Hancock, Stevie Wonder, George Benson, Al Jarreau, and Sheena Easton, to name just a few. Rushen won awards and recognition for her soundtrack hit "Forget Me Nots" for *Men in Black*. Other film scoring credits include the hugely popular *Waiting to Exhale, Hollywood Shuffle,* and the HBO movie *Ruby Bridges.* She also wrote the theme music for *The Steve Harvey Show.* Rushen served as composer-in-residence with the Detroit Symphony and was highlighted on National Public Radio, which aired her premiere performance of a new piano concerto with the Grand Rapids Symphony. As an industry leader, she has served as music director for the *NAACP Image Awards, Peoples Choice Awards,* HBO's *Comic Relief,* and CBS's *The Midnight Hour.* She was the music director for the *2004 Grammy Awards Show,* directing Arturo Sandoval, Justin Timberlake, Beyoncé, Prince, Sly Stone, and Outkast.

Rushen has established herself as one of the most versatile performing artists, composers, and producers today, as well as one of the leading women in the industry. Having been nominated for Grammys and being a musical orchestra director for the Emmys, as well as a musical director for Janet Jackson's World Tour, she has covered every kind of music, as she has said, "From Bach to Boyz II Men." In turn, her music has been reshuffled and covered and sampled by Mobb Deep, Faith Evans, Will Smith, MusiqSoul Child, and Kirk Franklin. And she served as the Thelonious Monk Institute's first artistic director. As an educator, she has lectured across the country at universities and colleges, and she has performed for the Yamaha Corporation as a piano clinician.

As in the music of the American composers before her, her works reveal the multiple influences of popular song, classical training, and jazz. When asked how she does so many things, she eloquently and honestly states, "When I went into music, nobody told me it had to be one kind of music that made me a musician. So, since I never knew the difference, I will continue to make music in the many ways I have learned how."

Prince

Prince Rogers Nelson, for many the reigning symbol of the Black pop star musician, became the first graduate of Minneapolis Public Schools to be inducted, in 2004, into the Rock and Roll Hall of Fame. Prince's music continues to be associated with the cultural/social milieu of urban life, and Prince himself is a product of working-class America. Popular, controversial, and eclectic, he has produced consistently a body of distinctive music over twenty years and counting, an extremely difficult feat in pop culture today.

Prince is an example of an extraordinary musician and popular performer, and is thus fitting for the close of this section. He is a walking encyclopedia of post-1950s Black popular music styles. His work traverses all traditions: gospel, funk, soul, r&b, pop, blues, and hip hop. He continues to push popular music to its edge and beyond, allowing us, his audience, to see ourselves and our world through his music. His instrumentation has varied over the years: from the standard r&b sound with bass, guitar, drums and piano, vocal and horns to his 1980s synthesizer sounds. His music has an interesting blend of sexuality, spirituality, and commercial artistry. Some would say it's all mixed up. A great guitar player, he also plays piano with a style that reflects bebop as well as gospel, and he has an arresting vocal range that is unmatched. In the number of hit records, he is surpassed only by James Brown and Stevie Wonder. He also bears one of the ultimate marks of artistry: the ability to evolve while keeping one's signature sound.

CHAPTER ELEVEN

Hip Hop: Connecting the Dots

Many wonder how hip hop music and culture connect with the tradition of Black music practice that has been discussed so far. Hip hop or rap music, as it first was titled, began commercially in 1979 with the release of Sugarhill Gang's *Rappers Delight* and the now famous line, "I said a hip, hop, the hippie, the hipidipit, hiphop hopit, you don't stop." While *Rappers Delight* was the first rap record of marked success, rap music/culture was a movement that emerged in the consciousness of communities long before this record was released. Through the sharing of experiences across the African diaspora, from Jamaica to the Bronx, there emerged a new Black artistic impulse. This expressive form grew from neighborhood parties in the early 1970s, where DJs would spin records and talk with the audience between songs. DJs would also challenge each other with "capping" on their opponents, thereby creating a contemporary urban debate session, couched in slang word battles, rhyme schemes, and humorous ways of telling a story.

In rap, young street poets expressed themselves artistically by claiming to project the most authentic Black style and music. The street corner and the neighborhood party, just as in the past, became the Black performance stage on which community artists reflected their identity and projected their image. The DJ performers had to have "skills" to keep the party going. What made one better than another was his or her ability "to mix it up" between breaks, while changing the record.

The roots of hip hop can be seen in comic narratives, r&b, and gospel—all the way back to the slave preacher and the West African griot. In fact, musicologists and historians have identified African spoken word traditions as some of the world's great early performance practices. We can trace the love of word play and rhymes up to the present, from Muhammad Ali and Gil Scott-Heron, the last poets of the civil rights and Black Arts movements, to little Black girls rhyming to their jump-rope games on urban sidewalks. In one sense, rapping in the Black community is nothing new. But rap music is a unique form that grew from a Jamaican DJ tradition. In 1971, an enterprising and gifted recent Jamaican immigrant named Kool Herc, and nicknamed Hercules because of his really loud sound system, began spinning records for parties, and he did something that had not been done before. Kool Herc's innovations were twofold. First, instead of using the disco tunes that were current, he played funky r&b from the 1960s, like the James Brown songs he favored from his days in Jamaica, working as a DJ. Second, in many of those records, there was "the break"—the place in the record where the singing stopped, and just the drum beat was left. Kool Herc used the break to "rap" to the crowd. And he used two turntables, playing the same record back and forth to prolong the break. The two together would drive the audience into a frenzy, and the break became a marked moment in music history.

Enter the B-boys, a dance crew who specialized in steps, moves, and flips that became known as "break dancing." As break dancing and rapping grew in popularity, there were needs for DJs, dancers, and emcees. Other early rappers introduced new techniques, such as the innovation of high school DJ Joseph Sandler, nicknamed Grandmaster Flash. He was an electronic whiz-kid. Flash created a special switch-box/mixer that allowed him to cue up a record in his headphones so that he could accurately switch between multiple records and select specific breaks. He turned this into great skill long before CDs and digital technology were common. With this, a ritual was born—a ritual with the multiple roles of the DJ, the emcee, and the dancers. This ritual flowered into a self-contained culture that included visual art, clothes, and a very rich vocabulary in addition to the music, hip hop.

By the early 1980s, hip hop had become the next big youth entertainment movement, following the folk, rock, and social protest songs of the 1960s and 1970s. And, as usual, this new music, along with its language and visual symbols, was quickly absorbed into the international marketplace. Today, the number one youth music in most parts of the world is hip hop. But what's interesting about the rise of rappers as central cultural figures is the attention that has been paid to what they are saying, not simply to their skills as party-meisters. With all the hype, it's easy to forget a very important aspect of the hip hop movement: the community of activism. The groups of DJs, rappers, and dancers were "gang size," literally, the size of a gang. In some cases, they were actual gangs.

But many hip hop groups used their messages to promote collective activism. Groups like Afrika Bambaataa and his Zulu Nation created manifestos that strove for "unity in our community," and wove themes into their works such as knowledge, wisdom, freedom, peace, unity, love, and respect. Grandmaster Flash's 1982 hit, aptly titled "The Message," describes the despair that afflicts people living in poverty in America's cities: "It's like a jungle sometimes, it makes me wonder / How I keep from going under." This important element of rap, that it contains a social message within popular form, is often overlooked. Coming right out of the civil rights and war protest eras, hip hop has roots powerfully planted in social consciousness.

Still, since its beginnings, rap has seen the same kind of commodification—watering down and homogenization—that blues music experienced in the 1920s, and r&b experienced in the 1940s. The formula, or process, is very similar. Recall that blues began as a music of poor, rural people. It was recorded. Small New York club bands of Black musicians began to play it. Then along came F. Scott Fitzgerald and others who wrote about it. The jazz age was born as a commercial product, or series of products. Irving Berlin, Paul Whiteman, and Benny Goodman became the kings of ragtime, jazz, and swing. What began as an authentic Black music and art conception became big, big business, dominated really by Whites. Likewise, r&b race records of the 1940s began as urban street-corner music. But the music was recorded and played by DJs. Rock and roll was born. Elvis and others became superstars. Big business overpowered the more authentic roots of the musical form.

As we consider rap music, we see a form that began as Black neighborhood party music. It was recorded and became a national craze. Enter Eminem, and by the late 1990s, we have yet another American music idol.

One of the power tricks that is played in cultural criticism involves reducing the relevance of a particular movement, thing, or person by claiming in print that the form has no history, shows no craft or invention, lacks refinement, and carries no intellectual weight. Many kinds of popular music have experienced such critical dismissals. Jazz was first dismissed as "jungle music" that would destroy the values of young Americans. There was similar outrage over r&b and rock and roll. Hip hop has also been plagued, wrongly, with the same type of dismissals. In fact, there are many musical/performance style aspects in hip hop that should be noted and considered as we seek to understand Black music and culture:

- The rapper/trickster poet is the front-line artist, and this is the speaking role.

- Gestural timing, prosody, the rhythm, and rhyme are key.
- The rap has a message, a coded play on language, or "signifying."
- The message connects to self-renewal, life affirmation, and the post-modern secular or spiritual empowerment of urban Black youth.

Hip hop also looks to past musical traditions for its message. Hip hop covers, samples, quotes, and speaks with other older texts and musical grooves. Hip hop narratives are mostly urban stories of poetic reaction to the decimation of the Black community. Themes include poverty, crime, jail culture, drug/gang culture, police brutality, jobs and unemployment, sexism, urban identity after the civil rights era, the Black male urban image, male/female relationships, and community uplift and empowerment. The narratives provide a critique of America and seek to hold people accountable.

Below, I summarize different periods of hip hop music from 1979 to 2005 and beyond. Note that this is a "sound sampling" and not an exhaustive nor complete overview, but it provides space for some reflection on hip hop's variations.

Early Rapping and DJing

Kool Herc, Sugarhill Gang, Grandmaster Flash, and Afrika Bambaataa were all DJs whose music grew out of the Jamaican tradition of rapping over the beat breaks of old James Brown and other 1960s–1970s r&b records. This music grew into a cultural expression among disgruntled urban youth in the 1980s at the height of Reaganism. Hip hop at this time featured four elements: music, rapping, graffiti, and dance. This was the start of hearing words, a narrative, that drew in the audience. This drawing in was known as "the rap effect," with the most persuasive and important aspect of this music up front, the message direct, rapped straight at the issues and at the listener.

Mainstream Hip Hop: Late 1980s

Run DMC, the Beastie Boys, and Will Smith were among the dominant artists of hip hop's mainstream period. Rap and hip hop were now categories in the record bins and a major force in the national music scene. With examples like DJ Jazzy Jeff and the Fresh Prince's "Parents Just Don't Understand," hip hop was now accepted as popular commercial music. Musicians and producers were not just sampling other music. They were conceptualizing rhythms, harmonies, riffs, turnarounds, and hooks, aided by some of the hottest production technology in the business.

Musical initiative became an equal creative partner to "the rap" in hip hop music. These artists had now morphed from being a part of an underground movement to being mainstream celebrities. Will Smith and the Hammer will definitely go down in history as two of the biggest rapper-entertainers in American musical culture. They were rappers first. Hammer's "2 Legit 2 Quit," well, that says it all, doesn't it! Hip hop had legitimized itself, using its own rhetorical form. The music had created its own rules, and it challenged the rest of the music business to keep up.

Gangsta/Thug: Hard Core Rap

NWA (Niggaz with Attitude), Tupac Shakur, Biggie Smalls, Snoop Dogg, 50 Cent, Eminem, and Master P. represent another variety of rap and hip hop that emerged in the late 1980s and continues today. This music caused and continues to cause controversy. "Gangsta rap" seemed to glorify violence. "You are now about to witness the strength of street knowledge," was the epochal manifesto in NWA's 1988 "Straight Outta Compton." In Chuck D's words, Rap was now a kind of "CNN for the urban community."

A rude, crude, direct, and alarming music/speech had become, for the first time in American mainstream history, a commercially available way to engage the public. Gangsta rap was quickly commodified. No longer "keeping it real," it became a poison. In addition to setting a performance standard, it also set a standard for the use of abusive language and degrading imagery. Parental Advisory stickers were placed on CDs but these do little to stop the damage. And I think it's fair to blame the industry that profits from these records. At the same time, we have to keep gangsta rap in perspective. Its narratives clearly demonstrate the poignancy and relevance of the community activist nature of popular music in America. For this reason, we can't dismiss this part of the hip hop phenomenon.

"Express Yourself" by NWA is an example of the delicate balance between the music as expression and as mindless product for consumers: "it gets funky when you got a subject and a predicate, add it on a dope beat and it will make you think." The powerful style cannot be ignored. Nor can the connection to the r&b tradition, the centrality of the idea of self-expression. The concept of authenticity and originality is a big part of art, and the concept of the power of reality giving voice to the concerns of the community is important. There is much to salvage.

Urban Hip Hop and R&B: 1990s and Beyond

In the 1990s, a new movement grew within hip hop, one that promoted a positive social/political response to the damage caused by gangsta rap. This movement within rap history includes Public Enemy, Chuck D, Queen Latifah, Eric B and Rakim, KRS-One, En Vogue, Salt-N-Pepa, and Arrested Development. As the latter rap, "Take me to another place, take me to another land. Make me forget all that hurts me, let me understand your plan." What happens when you take the hottest r&b female singing group, En Vogue, and couple them with the number one female hip hop group, Salt-N-Pepa? Well, you've created the greatest sexual liberation banner song since Aretha Franklin's "Respect." But here we have the women proclaiming respect for men. It is a big tune and huge cultural statement!

Coolio's 1995 "Gangsta's Paradise" is another example of socially conscious hip hop. Coolio's work was the soundtrack feature of the movie *Dangerous Minds*. Hip hop continued to clean up its act, and it became more legitimate. In 2001, MTV produced *Carmen: A Hip Hop Opera*, adapted from the great masterpiece by Bizet. All of these cultural stuffings and crisscrossings now defined the music. D'Angelo's "Brown Sugar," in 1995, and Erykah Badu's *Baduizm*, in 1997, were examples of the emergence of the mix between hip hop and urban contemporary r&b. Rock artists, including the Beastie Boys, weren't far behind in partnering with hip hop. The music is all meshed together: r&b artists don't just want to sing—they're "flowing," using hip hop styles, the two inextricably bound.

Hip hop further expanded in 1992 when Miles Davis, one the greatest jazz masters of all time, embraced hip hop in his album *Doo Bop*. Likewise, in 2003, Roy Hargrove, one of the leading young lions of jazz, released the hip hop/jazz CD *Hard Groove*. Hip hop artistry has made a mark on jazz culture, as the two styles blend to redefine the Black music tradition.

Kanye West views and comments on the world within hip hop through his songs "Addiction," "Gold Diggers," and "Diamonds." He raps about the travesty of blood diamonds. "Over here we die from drugs . . . over there they die from what we buy from drugs."

With the impact of the positive messages in Talib Kweli's "Get By" and the Black Eyed Peas' "Where Is the Love?" and with the emergence of gospel and Christian rap, we can see that hip hop has diversified, grown up, and become an industry player in the music world, as well as a force of social change. In a Minnesota Public Radio interview, hip hop mogul Russell Simmons touches on this aspect of the music:

Rap is about disenfranchised poor people. And these people have become lead-ers in mainstream American culture, and relevant to all those voiceless people. And 80 percent of those who buy this music are not Black. And that's what makes it so relevant, because people who are driving in their cars in Beverly Hills are understanding the plight of people in Compton. People who live in trailer parks are connecting to the same energy and know that they have the same issues and poverty conditions of people who are living in the urban area, in the projects. Now the connection is made between all young people in America and they are listening and understanding the plight of the poor, and that is a big deal that will change America to be more sensitive to the suffering people in our country.

As Simmons explains,

Jay Z has a scholarship fund, he's registering voters. Hip Hop Summit regis-tered 11,000 voters. . . . Hip Hop Summit people came out with paper and pen in hand to empower their community. They are doing a lot of good. The Hip Hop community is responsible and powerful. . . . They are thinking about higher elevation and consciousness. It's the truth if you listen to it. Hip Hop poetry is truth because people connect to truth. Truth always sells. Hip Hop is the most honest, with most integrity of any commercial art form being dis-tributed today.

There's no doubt about it. Despite all the talk, criticism, and commercial hype, hip hop music is a huge global force from New York to Tokyo, from Brazil to Africa. There are estimates that, at its height, it made $5 billion a year—from the music, the advertising, the clothes, and the merchandise. This is one sure way to measure its cultural force and power in the West. And hip hop culture has become one of America's leading exports, changing the way businesses across the planet are selling their products.

Again, entertainment and cash flow can never be the determining factor for the value and worth of music and art. No art that is based on materialism can survive. But hip hop today is big business. It's gained street like-ability and branding in the marketplace, and it has become an incredible power in contemporary culture. Considering hip hop's pervasive presence, there's no way to escape its meaning and impact in the world today. As Queen Latifah states in her *Black Reign* album, "Cause hip-hop is for real . . . I'm dealing with the truth, cause all over the world, it's aggravated youth."

As Albert Murray states, "Artists use their work to recall human living, and this provides us with the most adequate frame of reference for coming to terms with contemporary experience." Some days, I still cling to my old "trained" musician's ways and feel that too much of hip hop is derivative and is not true art. But hip hop culture is powering so many of our contemporary music impulses that to miss this is to be walking around with one's head in the sand. Hip hop culture, love it or hate it, is a pervasive force that has significantly marked our society.

Jazz Urbane

Jazz urbane is a new musical movement developing in the early years of the twenty-first century. We see jazz urbane in the Jazz at Lincoln Center project, a monumental accomplishment led by Wynton Marsalis and others. The project seeks to ensure the legacy of jazz as a publicly performed art form. Jazz urbane gives hope and promise to the possibility of new breakthrough creative and aesthetic visions.

Let's think back to Ornette Coleman's free jazz and the prophetic line "The Shape of Things to Come" that pointed to Oliver Lake, Steve Coleman, Gregg Osby, *Jazzmatazz*, Roy Hargrove, Christian McBride, Geri Allen, and Regina Carter. Branford Marsalis's *Buckshot LeFonque* from 1997 also suggested all this mixing and merging, bringing together everything from hip hop, rap, synth-driven techno effects, blistering tempoed swing, with edge, rock, acid jazz, and more. All this is largely driven by urban jazz musicians who are positioned to shift jazz back to the public, back to its audience.

Even as the traditional music industry collapsed in the early 2000s, we have seen the continued rise and visibility of thriving independent label efforts. The results have brought forth creative fusions as evidenced in hip hop jazz groups such as Soul-Live, the sounds of neo-soul in Erykah Badu and Mint Condition, and the label Hidden Beach's work with Jill Scott. Newer jazz faces such as Esperanza Spalding, Gonzalo Rubalcaba, Jason Moran, Christian Scott, Stefon Harris, Robert Glasper, Daniel Bernard Roumain, and others suggest that a modern hip jazz aesthetic is at work today. This all-encompassing movement is a new jazz urbane.

Due to the accessibility and ease of Internet music sharing, the rise of more independent companies, the inextricable bonding of mass and electronic media with musical identity and image promotions, there are actually more sophisticated music movements today outside of mainstream hip hop and youth pop culture than in years past. And yet, hip hop's phrase conception and its "feel" have mightily shaped this new music. The artistry that is emerging helps to define and push a new aesthetic as it critiques and challenges the everyday practice ears of the industry and the jazz status quo, just as jazz has always done.

Jazz urbane is jazz music culture seen in contemporary urban progressive artistic environments, where the audiences are drawn to music performed by creative musicians. This musical movement is an outgrowth of artists' ideas in conjunction with independent labels, clubs, lofts, galleries, festivals, and foundation initiatives, all working together to counter the smooth jazz radio marketing and advertising and the traditional pop culture, while staying committed to creative jazz artistry.

PART IV

CODA: CLOSING THEMES

Model A. *Oil pastel on paper by Emily Russell*

CHAPTER TWELVE

Core Values and
the Black Aesthetic Code

When considering "what in our backgrounds is worth preserving," Ralph Ellison spoke to the value of folklore, "which offers the first drawings of any group's character" and impresses on us "those rites, manners, customs . . . which insure the good life, or destroy it." Ellison says that folklore "projects this wisdom in symbols which express the group's will to survive; it embodies those values by which the group lives and dies." These symbols thus represent in art "the group's attempt to humanize the world."[1] The deep meanings and centrality that Ellison finds in folklore have embodiment as well in Black music.

In all its flowering over the centuries, Black music is not an ancillary happening or fragmented cultural strand. This is not a musical movement off to the entertaining side or separated from thinking. It has been at the critical center, a root foundation, of modern sound and living culture. This contribution to shaping modern music is no small thing, because Black music was *the* game changer in modern musical sound. Blues and jazz could only have come from Black people, and this contribution alone is seminal. So what is a Black aesthetic code? We have to return to the question of what it is, and why it is important to define it.

Aesthetics is generally a philosophical concern about the ways in which we perceive, reflect, and know our experiences, what we feel about them, and how we express ourselves artistically. Aesthetics also helps us understand how creativity accompanies and shapes our lives. How do we know and sense artistically, and what is the value, benefit, and effect of this knowing? How do we evaluate and measure this meaning? As philosopher Maxine Greene has written, a new way of "seeing, hearing, feeling, moving . . . signifies the nurture of a special kind of reflectiveness and expressiveness, a reaching out for meanings . . . to seek a greater coherence in the world."[2]

This book has suggested that a Black aesthetic is a philosophy, an upholding of artistic and cultural codes as well as an artistic description for the "what is" of Black musical art primarily. It is my belief that this art accompanies and is tied to how artists view their work and their world. A Black music aesthetic helps us interpret artists' work and better define the work's impact on the world. In addition, this aesthetic provides criteria that validate and enable an examination of Black music. What would happen if such discussions among artists and society stopped? What would happen to the art, the people, the culture, society? In this book, I have offered a critique of and challenge to the media and industries that have diminished the cultivation of art by commodifying and homogenizing originality and creativity. I have also extended a challenge to artists, educators, and communities to be artistically conscious in upholding an aesthetic stance despite this misguided mega-commodified cultural space in which we participate.

I argue also for an identity where the making of art is tied primarily to creative expression, not molded to suit the needs of the popular marketplace. I suggest, as in the Du Bois appeal, that educational institutions should commit to and partner with this effort to ennoble and better prepare our society to retool.

This book journeys through a larger examination of the extraordinary historical development of Black music culture and the Black artists who modeled and maintained the codes. The music culture was grounded in traditional West African practice and art. That art has rhythmic, harmonic, performance, and philosophical functions, tendencies, and conventions, guided by the cultural practice that defines music as an appropriate framework. From numerous West African traditions came yet another cultural retention in the performing Black world, the relevance and role of the griot.

The griot is that master musician, poet, spiritual leader, historian, and jokester who is also a cultural leader. The griot's roles extended from ritual engagement to trendsetter, style creator, and value transmitter. Through this work, core values were maintained and shared, including the communal, participatory, spiritual, and social. This is the essential cultural code, the transfer of core values and beliefs. Traced and observed, they provide a substantive empirical grounding and reckoning. In these core values and beliefs, we find the relevance of a culturally sustained and defined Black aesthetic. These codes are the most tangible definitions, criteria, we have for a contemporary Black aesthetic. In most places where Africans have lived and practice music, from slavery to the present, such codes have been retained.

For the most part, cultural codes are not written, although many scholars have committed time to interpreting and tracking them. Cultural codes are transmitted by creative practices in performance and oral traditions, and are practiced as the normal work that artists do, expect, and live by. The culture reckons and responds. When we do not protect these codes, when we commodify them or homogenize them, we risk losing them. This is exactly what has begun to take place for arts culture in modern times.

To define an aesthetic, then, for Black music and art perspectives by Black artists, we need to examine codes that critically and consciously attach to and grow out of Black artistic expression. In this examination, we discuss, as ideas, the codes that embody the spirit of this work. These codes are consciously interpreted, are worked out toward expressive excellence, and are heard, performed, and experienced in the overriding sound, character, look, feel, and approach to art. Again, they are tied to the creative, social, and cultural belief systems representing the convictions of and connections to Black folks. None of this is new. What's of note is the invitation to continue to insist on the maintenance, review, and relevant retooling of contemporary cultural expressions to uphold and apply these cultural frameworks against a menacing marketplace where this type of examination is largely devalued.

Historically, Black music studies have begun with the "classic" vernacular music and its various root systems, from spirituals to blues, gospel, and jazz, moving forward to include the contributions of "art music," embracing performers such as Leontyne Price and Natalie Hinderas, and composers such as William Grant Still and Margaret Bonds. As we have noted, the academic/ educational approaches and curriculum studies tied to this examination came out of examples like those found in W. E. B. Du Bois's work. All this strongly suggests, then, that somehow when you look into and listen to the center of Black culture, the codes would be representative of ideas, expressions of social critique, rituals of joy, aspirations, struggles, practices, songs, sounds, and the lived experiences in our culture.

These "expressions of experience," as I call them, are conscious attempts to provide maps for people to move humanely forward with a song worth singing. The sum and meaning of that expressive work, idea, style, sound, and music must be read as the result of the art's purpose. Any meaningful creative act in modern culture should be crafted to respond to the conditions of living, thinking, creating, and being, over the emptiness of marketability alone. Lastly, this book posits that our contemporary fight is to beat away the conditions that shrink and commodify our music.

Clarity, Change, Challenge, and Charge

It remains for the Negro intellectual to create his own philosophy and bring the facts of the cultural history in focus with the cultural practices of the present. In advanced societies, it is not race politicians or the rights leaders who create the new ideas and the new images of life and man. That role belongs to the artists and intellectuals of each generation.

—Harold Cruse, *The Crisis of the Negro Intellectual*

In our society, there are traditions of music, movements of music eras, great artistry, and a huge following of people of all sorts who have been moved by music-making in the Black tradition. Our journey here attempts to tie this emergence to important questions of historical and cultural education. When viewing great music movements, one sees the development in all its social complexities. But societies are made up of communities of people. Most of us who make music and teach in a music college find ourselves locked in tussles between the worlds of the "beat on the street" and the "meaning of what matters in the mind." Musical artists sometimes bridge these worlds. What matters to musicians who come from communities, and seek to express those communities, is crucial because their work reflects the impulses, tastes, desires, and worldviews of everyday folks. We must keep in mind that Du Bois's great call was that this music, this study, this life of Black folks in America and throughout the world was of great importance to the full development of the human race.

When we study Black music/culture, we can't help being taken by the way in which the music transformed people's thinking about human meaning and being. We see how people lived in different ways as the music went through them and brought whole communities to different ways of knowing the world. The music changed perceptions and altered possibly the way living could be done. Musicians themselves become an elevated type of human personality, because their expressions give them a hold and a take on what the value of expression really means. These expressions communicate sounds, feelings, and ideas that bring inspiration, happiness, and connection. Sometimes, music solves the dilemma of broken identity.

That is a very powerful concept because human personality is broken or shaped by the projection and perception of sustained and concrete identity. When we study this music, these artists, and the evolution of modern culture—when we see all this activity occurring through the creative arts—there is no denying the critical impressions and importance this music and its creators' culture have had on shaping modernity. The words "innovation," "invention," "original voice," "composer," "idea," "craft," "lyricism," "movement," "control," "finesse," "style," and "genius" are attached to what Black artists have accomplished through music.

Once we look at the music or other artistic creations of a people, our understanding of and esteem for that people are raised. This is significant when we consider the attacks and affronts to Black dignity that have been issued from the society they have contributed to so greatly. With this music that is so eventful and inextricably bound with the rise of the best in human capacity, one has to ask, have not these people, those who poured out this art, shown one of the great examples of leadership in the world?

You may ask, as I often do, why have not those accomplishments, models, and values been held up as a shining light to continue to elevate these people and this great nation? Who now controls the projections of images, ideas, and art, and why now has society allowed its best voices to be subjected to a repackaging for ill effect? Once you hear the art of Louis Armstrong, William Grant Still, Florence Price, Charlie Parker, Monk, Son House, a gospel choir, Count Basie, Billie Holiday, Sarah Vaughan, Bessie Smith, Nat King Cole, Sam Cooke, and Luther Vandross, how can you not be awestruck? After listening to the Black artists who created the music that defined America, the work of artists such as Frank Sinatra and Doris Day registers differently. We see that their greatness is connected to a soil tilled and fertilized by Black people. These Black music movements reveal a unique style that this is something never heard in music before. So you ask about the sources. You examine the creators, and you see the work that Black music has done in the world, the way it has shaped society, and you are moved by the enormous contribution of this art flowering.

This book has been a map to measure the directions Black music has taken. Viewed fully, this music leaves a huge impression on mind, heart, and soul. The codes have been written and remain in place as new ones are added. Black music always matters. The music moves me immeasurably, as it has moved, still moves, and will move millions of others. I hope it moves you as well.

The voice of this book shifts among that of a musician, a preacher of sorts, an educator, a music/cultural critic, and a common citizen consumer. I have meant to be philosophical in my inquiry, while also speaking from my own ethnic and cultural identity. At that same time, I have attempted to speak about universals in art wherever possible. This book—this journey—brings me, as an artist, to certain dimensions of clarity.

We ought to be concerned how history will judge the overall creative work we do today. This is critical. Is our work suggestive of new worlds of expression? Does our work point toward paths that are forward thinking and progressive? Have we embraced each other's humanity and used our art for good? Black artistic culture will always evoke that great, deep-spirited, connective thing. The palpable and reflective/spiritual depth of humanity in all this music is its most important attribute, representative of a great people and their tireless work, faith, and creativity.

In terms of modern cultural expression, we have hit a wonderful moment in some regards. The question rages: Where must we go now? Will it be, as Martin Luther King asked, "to chaos or community"? Our concern is how Black identity and artistic voices and culture have been mangled and maligned at the service of popular music commodification. We must consider how, in this process of remake, an industry must retool the expression and repackage the broken identities already sold in public spaces and places. Hip hop and Black popular aesthetics now are a large part of the world popular aesthetic. So how do we recover what the griots gave us for meaning and shaping, and how do we refute what the market pimped and sold the world?

Our new codes must be focused on all that music/art can do to inspire forward thinking. It seems that if we could teach and create art forms that inspire, lift, and illuminate the creative gifting that impacts lives, that would be true creative artistry. I believe our aesthetic and philosophical discussions and constructions are wide enough to fit with art and ideas purposed in this way. Our next generation of artists will produce the codes and the creative work that will matter and make a lasting impact in the world.

Appendix:
Recommended Music and Songs

The recordings listed here are a sampling of the works that embody and reflect ideas of a Black popular music aesthetic, and that help frame and accompany arguments in this book. The list is inclusive of mainly African American and mainstream American popular music culture through which threads can be drawn from spirituals, folk, and jazz to contemporary urban. From this sampling, the conclusion should be noted that this music is reflective of an ideology of sound, song performance, and meanings which constitute a known body of artistic work.

Spirituals

"How Long"
"Go Down Moses"
"Didn't My Lord Deliver Daniel"
"Steal Away"
"Over My Head I Hear Music in the Air" / "Up above My Head" (Kirk Franklin recording)
"Run Mary Run"

Blues, Gospel, Jazz

"Backwater Blues" Bessie Smith (1927)
"You Gonna Need Somebody When You Die" Charley Patton (1929)

"Kind Hearted Woman Blues" Robert Johnson (1937)
"Stones in My Passway" Robert Johnson (1937)
"Strange Fruit" Billie Holiday (1939)
"Rock Me" Sister Rosetta Tharpe (1941)
"Stand By Me" Sister Rosetta Tharpe (1941)
"Mama and Papa Blues" Lightnin' Hopkins (1959–1964)

1950s–1960s Jazz

"Come Sunday" Duke Ellington (1958)
The Shape of Jazz to Come, Ornette Coleman (1959)
Free Jazz, Ornette Coleman (1960)
"Body and Soul" Thelonious Monk (1963)
"Just a Gigolo" Thelonious Monk (1963)
A Love Supreme, John Coltrane (1965)

Civil Rights/Folk/Rock

1940s
"Do, Re, Mi" Woody Guthrie (1940)
"This Land Is Your Land" Woody Guthrie (1944)

1960s–1970s
"The Times They Are a-Changin'" Bob Dylan (1964)
"(I Can't Get No) Satisfaction" The Rolling Stones (1965)
"Get Off of My Cloud" The Rolling Stones (1965)
"All You Need Is Love" The Beatles (1967)
"Revolution" The Beatles (1968)
"With a Little Help from My Friends" Joe Cocker (1969)
"I Had a Dream" John Sebastian (1970)
"Drugstore Truck Drivin' Man" Joan Baez, featuring Jeffrey Shurtleff (1970)

Soul Music

"A Change Is Gonna Come" Otis Redding (1965)
"Papa's Got a Brand New Bag" James Brown (1965)
"Cold Sweat" James Brown (1967)
"Respect" Aretha Franklin (1967)
"Say It Loud—I'm Black and I'm Proud" James Brown (1968)

"I Got the Feelin'" James Brown (1968)
"Licking Stick" James Brown (1968)
"Everyday People" Sly & the Family Stone (1968)
"Mother Popcorn" James Brown (1969)
"Choice of Colors" The Impressions (1969)
"It's Your Thing" The Isley Brothers (1969)
"Friendship Train" Gladys Knight and the Pips (1969)
"Ball of Confusion" The Temptations (1970)
"To Be Young, Gifted, and Black" Nina Simone (1970)
"Funky Drummer" James Brown (1970)
"Get Up" James Brown (1970)
"Super Bad" James Brown (1970)
"Soul Power" James Brown (1971)
"Make It Funky" James Brown (1971)
"Hot Pants" James Brown (1971)
"Respect Yourself" The Staple Singers (1971)
"Love the One You're With" The Isley Brothers (1971)
"Smiling Faces Sometimes" The Undisputed Truth (1971)
"What's Going On" Marvin Gaye (1971)
"Let's Stay Together" Al Green (1971)
"Papa Was a Rolling Stone" The Temptations (1972)
"Slippin' into Darkness" War (1972)
"Back Stabbers" O'Jays (1972)
"Work to Do" The Isley Brothers (1972)
"Love and Happiness" Al Green (1972)
"Love Train" O'Jays (1973)
"Ghetto Child" The Spinners (1973)
"Doing It to Death" James Brown (1973)
"The Payback" James Brown (1974)
"Papa Don't Take No Mess" James Brown (1974)
"The Revolution Will Not Be Televised" Gil Scott-Heron (1974)
"Shining Star" Earth, Wind & Fire (1975)
"Wake Up, Everybody" Harold Melvin and the Blue Notes (1975)
"Chocolate City" Parliament Funkadelic (1975)
"Funky President" James Brown (1975)
"Get Up Offa That Thang" James Brown (1976)
"Street Life" The Crusaders, with Randy Crawford (1979)
"Ain't No Stoppin' Us Now" McFadden and Whitehead (1979)
"It's Too Funky in Here" James Brown (1979)

Pop, Rock, Soul

1970s
Band of Gypsys, Jimi Hendrix (1970)
"Bridge over Troubled Water" Simon and Garfunkel (1970)
"War" Edwin Starr (1970)
"Imagine" John Lennon (1971)
"You've Got a Friend" Carole King (1971)
"Higher Ground" Stevie Wonder (1973)
"Yes We Can Can" Pointer Sisters (1973)
"Mister Magic" Grover Washington Jr. (1974)
"Fight the Power" The Isley Brothers (1975)
"Message in Our Music" O'Jays (1976)
"One Love" Bob Marley (1977)
"I Will Survive" Gloria Gaynor (1978)

1980s
"Celebration" Kool & the Gang (1980)
"1999" Prince (1982)
"The Message" Grandmaster Flash (1982)
"Sunday Bloody Sunday" U2 (1983)
"Born in the USA" Bruce Springsteen (1984)
"When Doves Cry" Prince (1984)
"Let's Go Crazy" Prince (1984)
"We Are the World" USA for Africa (1985)
"Greatest Love of All" Whitney Houston (1986)
"Sign o' the Times" Prince (1987)
"Man in the Mirror" Michael Jackson (1988)
"Love Will Save the Day" Whitney Houston (1988)

1990s Hip Hop, Grunge, Contemporary Global

"Lithium" Nirvana (1991)
"Power of Love" Luther Vandross (1991)
Death Certificate, Ice Cube (1991)
"Fishin' 4 Religion" Speech and Arrested Development (1992)
"Tears in Heaven" Eric Clapton (1992)
Jazzmatazz Volume 1, Guru (1993)
"Listen 2 Me" Queen Latifah (1993)
"Why We Sing" Kirk Franklin (1993)

"Ironic" Alanis Morissette (1995)
"Brown Sugar" D'Angelo (1995)
The Score, Fugees (1996)
"On and On" Erykah Badu (1997)
"Together Again" Janet Jackson (1997)
Buena Vista Social Club (1997)
The Miseducation of Lauryn Hill, Lauryn Hill (1998)
"Superstar" Lauryn Hill (1998)
"To Zion" Lauryn Hill (1998)
"I Believe in Love" Paula Cole (1999)
"God Is Watching" Paula Cole (1999)
"Put Your Lights On" Santana (1999)
"Brand New Day" Sting (1999)
"Paper and Ink" Tracy Chapman (2000)

Albums 2001–

Acoustic Soul, India.Arie (2001)
Heavier Things, John Mayer (2003)
Hard Groove, RH Factor/Roy Hargrove (2003)
Elephunk, Black Eyed Peas (2004)
Get Lifted, John Legend (2004)
Late Registration, Kanye West (2005)
Livin' the Luxury Brown, Mint Condition (2005)
Hip Hop Is Dead, Nas (2006)
Anthem, Christian Scott (2007)
Growing Pains, Mary J. Blige (2007)
Evolver, John Legend (2008)
I Am . . . Sasha Fierce, Beyoncé (2008)

Notes

Chapter 1

1. Toni Morrison, quoted in Paul Gilroy, "Living Memory: A Meeting with Toni Morrison," *Small Acts: Thoughts on the Politics of Black Cultures* (London: Serpent's Tail, 1993), 181.

2. George Lewis, "Improvised Music after 1950: Afrological and Eurological Perspectives," *Center for Black Music Research Journal* (Spring 2002).

Chapter 2

1. Bakari Kitwana, *The Hip Hop Generation: Young Blacks and the Crisis in African American Culture* (New York: Basic Civitas, 2002).

2. Harold Cruse, *The Crisis of the Negro Intellectual: A Historical Analysis of the Failure of Black Leadership* (New York: Quill, 1984).

3. Paul Gilroy, *The Black Atlantic: Modernity and Double Consciousness* (Cambridge, Mass.: Harvard University Press, 1993).

4. Cornel West, address presented at Berklee College of Music, February 1, 2007.

5. Greg Dimitriadis, *Traditions of Studying Urban Youth Culture* (New York: Peter Lang, 2007).

6. Leonhard Emmerling, *Basquiat* (Köln: Taschen, 2002).

7. J. Kinnard, "Who Are Our National Poets?" *Knickerbocker Magazine*, October 26, 1845.

8. Antonin Dvořák, *New York Herald*, May 23, 1893.

9. Ernst-Alexandre Ansermet, "Sur un orchestre negre," *Revue Romand*, 1919; "Bechet and Jazz Visit Europe," trans. Walter Schapp, 1938.

10. William Banfield, *Musical Landscapes in Color: Conversations with Black American Composers* (Lanham, Md.: Scarecrow, 2001).

11. Gerald Early, quoted in Ken Burns's documentary *Jazz*, Episode One: "Gumbo: Beginnings to 1917" (2001).

12. Alfonso W. Hawkins Jr., *The Jazz Trope: A Theory of African American Literary and Vernacular Culture* (Lanham, Md.: Scarecrow, 2008).

13. Samuel A. Floyd Jr., *The Power of Black Music: Interpreting Its History from Africa to the United States* (New York: Oxford University Press, 1995).

Chapter 3

1. James H. Cone, *The Spirituals and the Blues* (New York: Seabury, 1972).

2. Hoyt W. Fuller, "Toward a Black Aesthetic," in *The Black Aesthetic*, ed. Addison Gayle (New York: Anchor, 1971).

3. Amiri Baraka, *Black Music* (New York: Quill, 1967).

Chapter 4

1. Cornel West, "Foreword," in *Hip Hop and Philosophy: Rhyme 2 Reason*, ed. Derrick Darby and Tommie Shelby (Chicago: Open Court, 2005).

2. Richard Shusterman, "Rap Aesthetics: Violence and the Art of Keeping It Real," in Darby and Shelby, *Hip Hop and Philosophy*.

Chapter 5

1. Paul Tillich, *A Theology of Culture* (New York: Oxford University Press, 1959).

2. Michael Eric Dyson, from a speech delivered June 25, 2000, at the Mt. Olive Baptist Church, Ft. Lauderdale, Florida.

3. Anthony Pinn, *Why Lord? Suffering and Evil in Black Theology* (New York: Continuum, 1995).

4. Tricia Rose, *Black Noise* (Hanover, N.H.: Wesleyan University Press, 1994).

5. Albert Murray, *The Hero and the Blues* (New York: Vintage, 1995).

6. Bernice Johnson Reagon, in William Banfield, *Black Notes: Essays of a Musician Writing in a Post-Album Age* (Lanham, Md.: Scarecrow, 2004).

7. Neil Postman, *Amusing Ourselves to Death* (New York: Penguin, 1985).

8. Susanne K. Langer, *Philosophy on a New Key: A Study in the Symbolism of Reason, Rite, and Art* (Cambridge, Mass.: Harvard University Press), 235.

9. John Miller Chernoff, *African Rhythms and African Sensibility: Aesthetics and Social Action in African Musical Idioms* (Chicago: University of Chicago Press, 1979).

10. Bruce Springsteen, quoted in David Szatmary, *Rockin' in Time: A Social History of Rock and Roll* (Englewood Cliffs, N.J.: Prentice Hall, 2007), 381.

11. Johnny Cash, quoted in Ray Pratt, *Rhythm and Resistance* (Washington, D.C.: Smithsonian Institution, 1990), 75.

12. Francis Bebey, *African Music: A Peoples Art* (Brooklyn, N.Y.: Lawrence Hill, 1969).

13. Chuck D, *Fight the Power: Rap, Race, and Reality* (New York: Dell, 1997).

14. Cornel West, *Prophetic Fragments* (Grand Rapids, Mich.: Eerdmans, 1988), 187.

15. Toni Morrison, quoted in Paul Gilroy, "Living Memory: A Meeting with Toni Morrison," *Small Acts: Thoughts on the Politics of Black Cultures* (London: Serpent's Tail, 1993), 175–82.

Chapter 6

1. W. E. B. Du Bois, "The Study of the Negro Problems," *Annals of the American Academy of Political and Social Science* (January 1898).

2. Manning Marable, "Black Studies, Multiculturalism, and the Future of American Education," in *A Turbulent Voyage: Readings in African American Studies* (San Diego: Collegiate, 1997).

3. Eileen Southern, *The Music of Black Americans* (New York: Norton, 1971).

4. Herbert Gutman, *The Black Family in Slavery and Freedom 1750–1925* (New York: Vintage, 1976).

5. James Cone, *The Spirituals and the Blues* (New York: Seabury, 1972).

6. J. H. Kwabena Nketia, *The Music of Africa* (New York: Norton, 1974).

7. James M. Trotter, *Music and Some Highly Musical People: Remarkable Musicians of the Colored Race* (New York: Lee and Shepard, 1881).

8. Guthrie Ramsey, "Cosmopolitan or Provincial? Ideology in Black Music History, 1867–1990," *Black Music Research Journal* 16, no. 1 (1996).

9. Ben Sidran, *Black Talk* (New York: Da Capo, 1971).

10. Dominique-Rene De Lerma, *Black Music in Our Culture* (Kent, Ohio: Kent State University Press, 1970).

Chapter 7

1. John Miller Chernoff, *African Rhythms and African Sensibility Aesthetics and Social Action in African Musical Idioms* (Chicago: University of Chicago Press, 1979).

2. Olaudah Equiano, *The Interesting Narrative of the Life of Olaudah Equiano* (Norton: New York, 1789, 2001).

3. Jali Kunda, *The Griots of West Africa and Beyond* (Roslyn, N.J.: Ellipsis Artists, 1996).

4. Fredrick Kaufman and John Guckin, *The African Roots of Jazz* (Sherman Oaks, Calif.: Alfred, 1979).

5. Chernoff, *African Rhythms and African Sensibility*.

6. Ray Pratt, *Rhythm and Resistance* (Washington, D.C.: Smithsonian Institution, 1990).

7. Roger Abrahams, *Singing the Master: The Emergence of African-American Culture in the Plantation South* (New York: Penguin, 1992).

8. Paul Oliver, *Gospel, Blues, and Jazz* (New York: Norton, 1980).

9. Edward A. Berlin, *King of Ragtime: Scott Joplin and His Era* (New York: Oxford University Press, 1994).

Chapter 8

1. Leopold Stokowski, quoted in J. A. Rodgers, "Who Is the New Negro, and Why?" (1925), reprinted in *The New Negro: Readings on Race, Representation, and African American Culture*, ed. Henry Louis Gates Jr. and Gene Andrew Jarrett (Princeton, N.J.: Princeton University Press, 2007).

2. Ralph Ellison, "Homage to Duke Ellington," *Washington, D.C., Sunday Star*, April 27, 1969.

3. Alain Locke, "The New Negro," in *The New Negro: Voices of the Harlem Renaissance*, ed. Alain Locke (1925).

4. Keith Shadwick, *Jazz: Legends of Style* (London: Quintet, 1998).

Chapter 12

1. Ralph Ellison, "The Art of Fiction," *Paris Review* no. 8 (Spring 1955).

2. Maxine Greene, *Variations on a Blue Guitar* (New York: Teachers College Press, 2001).

Index

⚮

About the Author

Dr. William (Bill) Banfield is a composer, jazz guitarist, author, and educator. He is professor of Africana Studies/Music and Society in the Liberal Arts Department and director of the Africana Studies Center and Programming at Berklee College of Music. His work focuses on the aesthetic history of Black music culture and the power of music to hold, transfer, and sustain cultural value. His other books include *Musical Landscapes in Color: Conversations with Black American Composers* (2003) and *Black Notes: Essays of a Musician Writing in a Post-Album Age* (2004), both published by Scarecrow Press. He also serves as the editor of the African American Cultural Theory and Heritage series published by Scarecrow Press.

About the Cover Image

The artwork on the cover is a painting by contemporary artist Emily Russell, titled "Ozzy Plays the Guitar." What struck me about this image, in relation to the book's message, is the ways in which artistic expressions are interpreted, calling upon "codes" that are infused with various kinds of identities, histories, values, and meanings.

Albeit a problematic image, Ozzy here is simply a sock monkey made to hold a guitar. For some, he may evoke the image of Robert Johnson. For others he's evocative of a play on Black face minstrelsy. How we "read" this work of art is based on the same principles of how we hear and see music in its varied values from the artists who render them.

What grabs me about Ozzy is the look in his eye: He asks us to decode what he means, and he delights in "playing" with that musical-image idea. This book raises questions about the study of Black music, suggesting that no art can survive without an understanding of and dedication to what values are envisioned from its creators. . . . I believe this kind of exploration keeps us grounded in a rich musical past, answers the dilemmas we face today about what we value, and such a view guides our discussions as we create and make choices about where we are headed. Art [music] is a critical part of our social consciousness, and culture is about how we live in the world. This book is about creative Black artistry and its effect and impact on shaping modern culture and society, and the questions that are wrapped up in discovering these meanings. I deliberately chose this image of Ozzy as a means to provoke those very questions, to ask the reader to decode not just the image, but to examine the culture that informs it.